DUEL FOR THE NORTHLAND

DUEL FOR THE NORTHLAND

Kurt Singer

Coachwhip Publications
Greenville, Ohio

To Hilda who shared it all

Duel for the Northland, by Kurt Singer
© 2023 Coachwhip Publications edition

First published 1943
Kurt Singer, 1911-2005
CoachwhipBooks.com

ISBN 1-61646-568-9
ISBN-13 978-1-61646-568-1

CONTENTS

Introduction: My Most Sensational Interview   7

Part I. Europe's Master Spies
1. The Antagonists   11
2. Pflugk-Hartung: The Master Builder   23
3. Jan Valtin's Boss   43
4. Nazi Puppet-Masters   55

Part II. Something Rotten in the State of Denmark
5. Pflugk-Hartung at Work   73
6. Round-Up of Enemy Agents   89

Part III. Norway Resists
7. What Quisling Told Me   99
8. How Norway's Gold Was Saved   119
9. Sabotage and Counterespionage in Norway   131

Part IV. Intermezzo in Iceland and Greenland
10. Germany's Secret Service in Iceland and Greenland   149

Part V. Spies and Saboteurs in Sweden
11. The Wollweber League   165
12. Sweden—International Spy Center   181
13. Axel Wenner-Gren—Agent of Death   201

PART VI. DOMINIUM MARIS BALTICI
14. Spies and Saboteurs in the Russo-Finnish Struggle   213
15. Sweden in the Pincers   241
16. Labor Traitors   261
17. Agents in Arms   271

EPILOGUE   285

INTRODUCTION
My Most Sensational Interview

This is a book on political, military, naval and economic espionage. It exposes the secret weapons of the big powers in their fight for the domination of the Baltic, the Arctic and the Atlantic.

It happened that one day in 1938, my home became the most observed and the best guarded place in Sweden. I was then living quietly in the outskirts of Stockholm between Lake Mälarn and the Baltic Sea when a telegram notified me that nobody less than the assistant and chief cartographer of the Nazi general and geopolitical expert Karl Haushofer would arrive in Stockholm and I was asked to help him secure asylum in Sweden.

Soon afterwards a young, blue-eyed, extremely good-looking German entered my home, and he it was who brought me into the center of world-espionage.

Ernst Guhl, General Haushofer's assistant, had fled from Germany to Denmark. The Nazi Government had asked for his extradition from Denmark and now Guhl was in my home in Sweden, nervous, excited, hoping to escape the long reach of the Nazi arm abroad.

Guhl had been an expert on Scandinavia for General Haushofer, he had even drawn the maps which General Haushofer published in his books, and he had drawn blueprints which had been presented to Hitler.

From 1933 to 1938 Guhl traveled through Scandinavia, mostly on orders from General Haushofer, and on one of his trips he had met a British-Danish girl, whom he wanted to marry. The Nazis became suspicious, accused her and later even him of being British agents, and thus it came about that Guhl had to escape.

This was Guhl's story and I told him very frankly on the day of his arrival it might be true or not; to prove it, he must be willing to supply me with a complete account of everything he knew about the Scandinavian division of the Nazi Foreign Office and of the Haushofer brains trust.

Ernst Guhl proceeded to give me a complete account of his knowledge; he gave the most alarming details about coming invasion plans; he gave complete lists of the personnel of agents working inside and outside Germany against the Scandinavian countries. He signed his revelations and I submitted them to the Swedish authorities. Within a short time my home turned into bedlam. Wires and cables came in batches. German, Russian, British agents flocked around.

I published a very sensational interview with Guhl in Stockholm's *Social Demokraten*, the newspaper closest to the Prime Minister Per Albin Hansson, and the story went over the whole world.

The reaction was tremendous. Then, one midnight the newspaper telephoned me to say that Guhl was a fake. It appeared that General Haushofer had sent a wire from Munich declaring that he had never seen Guhl in his life. A Finnish statesman had also wired; he asserted that he had never seen Guhl and had therefore never told him that he wanted a Finnish-Nazi alliance, a statement made in my interview.

In the early morning hours Guhl and I drove to Stockholm to present the night editor an original letter, signed by General Haushofer, which mentioned that Guhl was his assistant. We showed the editor Haushofer's own books which contained maps signed with Guhl's name. The next day the front page of the Swedish Government paper gave in facsimile the proof that German generals could lie.

The Guhl-Haushofer incident catapulted me into the middle of the espionage battles for Scandinavia whose course I attempt to relate.

Guhl is now a farmer in South America. I am in debt to him for excellent information about the Scandinavian espionage division of the Nazis, but most of the information on espionage contained in this book has been obtained from the minutes of court proceedings, from police records, and from the investigations of democratic organizations in Scandinavia. Especially I wish to thank Joachim Joesten and the publication *News Background* in New York for their cooperation, and the official Scandinavian sources that continue the fight against Hitler have been most helpful in providing factual material and advice.

Kurt Singer

PART ONE
Europe's Master Spies
1. The Antagonists

The year was 1938. In the course of a lecture tour through Scandinavia, I had come to Denmark. At the conclusion of my lecture before the Copenhagen Peace Society, dozens of men and women from the audience had overwhelmed me with questions. The Munich Pact had just been concluded; and I had stated that if the pacifists neglected to arm themselves, pacifism would disappear from the face of the earth for several decades. It was an incendiary statement to make before a society dedicated to peace, and one of the ladies of the Society was particularly annoyed with me.

I had a long and fruitless discussion with her. I soon forgot what it was we discussed, but I remembered afterwards that this pacifist lady was very attractive and must have been a stunning beauty in her youth. I also remembered her name—Elsa Andersen. A year later I learned the strange and somewhat sinister story of her life.

In 1919 Elsa Andersen was one of the most beautiful and popular debutantes in Copenhagen society.

At a dance given by the Danish Aviation Association she met a handsome young German, a captain of the former Luftwaffe. He was gay, adventurous, and in those days slender. He danced with her, told her of his heroic exploits in the war, and told her also of his private sorrow. He had been engaged to a charming Fräulein of excellent family.

Then came the defeat of Germany and the complete ban upon German aviation by the Allies. He had no job, no career, and in the bargain he learned that he had no fiancée. Her family insisted on a son-in-law who had better prospects. The young man blamed it all on the new German Government, the Weimar Republic.

He now held in Denmark a modest position as instructor in civil aviation. He saw much of Elsa Andersen, and their engagement was soon to be announced. But then a series of accidents commenced. A Danish plane crashed, then another and another. There was no possibility of replacing them for months. A Junkers plane was needed immediately. The young captain offered to sell his own plane; he could go to Germany at once to fetch it, he said.

He turned up the next day at the airport of Niederschoeneweide near Berlin, where some German warplanes were stored, kept hidden from the Allied Control Commission. He told his comrades he wanted to take his old crate up for a spin. He did, but he did not return. Instead, plane and captain landed a few hours later in Copenhagen.

However, the Danish Government was not buying planes that rightfully belonged to the Allies. Moreover, it declared that the German captain was no more than a common thief. He took the hint, and before criminal prosecution could be initiated he fled to Sweden.

In Sweden he met and married rich Karin von Kantzow. It was with ten thousand marks of her money that he later bought his way into Adolf Hitler's inner councils, and received in return the honor of leading the Hitler Storm Troops in the inglorious Beerhall Putsch of November 1923.

This man, as you have guessed, was the present Chief of the Luftwaffe, Reichsmarshall Hermann Goering. And Elsa Andersen, the pacifist lady whom I met at the Copenhagen peace meeting, became one of his best agents in

Denmark. At the time I met her she was speaking passionately to the Danes of pacifism and disarmament in order to promote the plans of her former lover.

For many years after 1919 disappointed Elsa Andersen had heard no more of Goering. When he came to power in Germany, she refrained from writing to him. As a Dane and a Democrat, she disapproved of the Nazi terror—until she came face to face with temptation. That brings us to 1934.

In 1934 Elsa Andersen was a lonely, despondent divorcee. Her life, since the abrupt cutting off of her first romance, had been filled with many distractions but never with happiness. She had lived alone in a magnificent apartment opposite the King's palace, had made pilgrimages to every Bayreuth festival, had been present every time Arturo Toscanini or Bruno Walter conducted in Salzburg, had occupied her loge in the Copenhagen Opera on every opening night. She lost most of her wealth in the depression; afterwards she lived in cheap Danish resorts or *en pension* on the Italian Riviera. Now she was back in Copenhagen in her modest apartment.

One day a magnificent limousine drove up to her house and a tall gray-haired man, apparently nearing his sixties, rang her doorbell. His high forehead, his piercing gray eyes, his quiet fatherly manner, suggested the distinguished jurist or the university professor. He introduced himself to Madame Andersen as Dr. Erich Ring, and begged leave to present to her an envelope from German Field Marshal Goering.

The envelope contained two thousand Danish crowns and a roundtrip ticket for railway and sleeping car to Berlin. Elsa asked for a day or two in which to consider the invitation. Then she went to the Danish Chief of Police, Andreas Hansen, to ask his advice. (We shall, by the way, meet numerous Hansens in this book; the name is as common as Jones in Scandinavia.) Somewhat to her surprise, Police Chief Andreas Hansen assured her that the Government had no objections to her proposed visit—none at all. On the contrary, to refuse the invitation might be regarded as something of a diplomatic snub.

So Elsa spent a week at Goering's fabulous estate of Karinhall. She passed hours among the pictures the Marshal had stolen from German art galleries. She studied the busts of Goering's heroes—Frederick the Great, Napoleon and Mussolini. Goering, now a widower, had not yet married his second wife, Emmy Sonnemann. "What woman," Elsa later exclaimed on the witness-stand, "would not have done what I did? Herr Goering is always a perfect gentleman."

Before the week was up Goering, with his extraordinary gift for combining business with pleasure, had also found a job for Elsa. Elsa was a loyal Dane and no Nazi. But upon being assured that her work would in no wise injure her own country, she accepted the position of secretary to the estimable Dr. Ring.

Her friends in Copenhagen had no reason to be surprised when she presently announced that she was tired of the bustle of the city and longed for the fresh breeze from the sea. But they might have wondered had they seen the twenty-room villa this secretary rented for herself in the fashionable suburb of Charlottenlund, near the seashore.

Elsa herself occupied only two or three rooms. But the rest of the house gradually became populated. At any time of the day or night one or two Germans from Hamburg might slip quietly into the house. They made themselves at home, playing cards or swapping stories, and taking turns at gazing toward The Sound and noting the ships that passed through this bottleneck of the Baltic Sea.

Elsa, though she was in the habit of taking orders and asking no questions, soon realized that her uninvited guests were Gestapo men. One of them, a certain Paul Kraus, was apparently their leader. Readers of Jan Valtin's book, *Out of the Night,* will recognize the name; it is the same man who procured Valtin's release from the concentration camp and gave him a secret assignment for the Nazis. In short, Elsa Andersen had become the front for the central bureau of the German Secret Service in Denmark.

The Nazis felt quite sure of themselves in Denmark. Elsa Andersen's villa was as busy as a beehive. Agents came and went continually. The chief of all these agents was Dr. Erich Ring. Inspector Paul Kraus of Hamburg gave orders to his German Gestapo men, and a Dane who spoke extraordinarily good German directed the activities of the Danish agents. This man was Carlis Hansen (not to be confused with the Danish Chief of Police, Andreas Hansen, whom I have already introduced). Carlis Hansen was the leader of the Danish storm troopers and one of the key men in the German espionage system in Denmark.

Carlis Hansen enters this story on a certain day in May 1934. The place is Room 18 of the German War Ministry on the Luetzow Ufer. Three men were conferring. One of them was General Nikolaus von Falkenhorst, wearing full uniform, even to the red-striped trousers. The second, dressed in the brown uniform of a Storm Troop officer, was a certain Dr. Werner Best, author of the *Boxheimer Documents* which discuss in minutest detail the technique of the German Terror. Because of these documents Best has been credited with being the real brains of the Gestapo, rather than Himmler. The third man was also wearing a Storm Troop uniform, but a closer look would have shown that it bore the insignia, Dansk Nasjonalsocialistisk Arbejder Parti. This man was the brawny, blue-eyed Carlis Hansen.

Carlis Hansen's birthplace was on the Schleswig border of Denmark, and he spoke German as his second mother tongue. He was an ambitious political gangster in Copenhagen, ready to do any unsavory job on a dark street to oblige a Nazi-inclined employer. He was in Berlin more or less as. emissary for his boss, Dr. Fritz Clausen, now the Quisling of Denmark. Clausen was outraged because the Germans had recognized and financed two other Nazi groups besides his own. Hansen was here to secure recognition of the Clausen gang as the sole official Nazi group in Denmark, together with the generous subsidies such recognition would entail.

Von Falkenhorst, a general of the old Prussian tradition, believed that a soldier's business was soldiering and had no liking for this sort of underhanded work. But he had his orders.

Whatever the Prussian general might have thought of Carlis Hansen, the other man in the room admired him. As a specialist in terror, Dr. Best respected the young man's zest for any reckless deed. Best said frankly that Hansen was his man, and the young man returned to Denmark charged with duties he knew to be dangerous, but with a thousand Danish crowns in his pocket—a first installment of promised rewards. It was more money than he had ever had before.

From 1934 to 1943 Carlis Hansen had a hand in every act of political gangsterism, every political murder, kidnapping or robbery, that the Nazis attempted in Denmark.

One day in 1934 Carlis Hansen came to Elsa Andersen's Charlottenlund Villa to hold a council of war with Dr. Ring and Inspector Kraus. The subject of their discussion was an order they had just received from Berlin.

The head of the entire German espionage system, Admiral Wilhelm Canaris, had learned that Soviet Russia was maintaining a secret office of the OGPU in Denmark, and that the West European Bureau of the Comintern (The Communist International) had its headquarters in the Danish capital. The heads of these offices were respectively: Ernst Friedrich Wollweber, former German Communist Deputy to the Reichstag, and Otto Kuusinen, who later became "premier" of the short-lived Finnish Communist Republic.

Canaris ordered that Wollweber and Kuusinen be kidnapped and taken to Germany, where "methods" would be found to extract from them all they knew about Russian espionage in Western Europe. Therefore, they must be taken alive. Moreover, if they were killed, or left injured in the streets, the German agents who were guilty might be arrested and the German Secret Service in Denmark would face the danger of exposure.

Consequently, Dr. Erich Ring's orders were to kidnap and transport the two men alive and unharmed to Germany *"ohne jedes Aufsehen"*—without the slightest public disturbance. The Germans, of course, knew they must not expose themselves to the possibility of arrest.

Ring, Kraus and Hansen knew that Wollweber and Kuusinen were living in a comfortable apartment in fashionable Charlottenlund. Why were proletarian secret agents living in such an expensive and aristocratic suburb? For the best reason on earth: that is where they would be least likely to be sought.

The three Nazi agents planned their job carefully. . . . Late one night two men were walking down a dark and unfrequented street in Charlottenlund, not far from Elsa Andersen's villa. The two were the Russian agents, Wollweber and Kuusinen. Suddenly two automobiles drew up to the curb and eight men sprang out. They fell upon the two OGPU agents and tried to drag them into cars. Six brawny sailors rushed up out of the darkness and began flinging broad Danish oaths and hamlike fists at the attackers. A savage brawl ensued, with the forces of Russian and German espionage pitted against one another in the streets of Copenhagen. A waitress who worked in a small corner café screamed at the struggling men, "I'll call the police." The leader of the kidnappers looked up for a moment and shouted back, "Ask for Police Chief Andreas Hansen."

Andreas Hansen was an intimate friend of Dr. Erich Ring and Carlis Hansen. The Chief of Police had stayed on duty that night at Police Headquarters in order to aid his German friends in case anything went wrong.

The scrimmage went on for a few moments, until a police emergency squad arrived. The head of the squad, Inspector Kaj Yttesen, greeted the leader of the thugs with the words, "Good evening, Carlis." Then he proceeded to arrest the two victims of the assault. After the police left with their prisoners, the others got into their cars and sped away into the darkness.

Police Inspector Kaj Yttesen was a member of the Danish National Socialist Party, and a subordinate of Carlis Hansen. The farcical arrest of the intended victims instead of the kidnappers had been arranged beforehand—in case of an "emergency."

The arrested Russian agents were taken before Andreas Hansen, the Danish Chief of Police, and put through a long examination—long enough to allow Paul Kraus and his Gestapo agents to cross the Danish border to the safety of German soil.

The German plan had proved a total fiasco. The Russian Secret Service had known of the kidnapping attempt for weeks. Warned, Wollweber had made his preparations—which accounted for the appearance of the six Danish sailors on that dark and unfrequented street. Later, it was testified in Court that the man who had warned him was a certain Richard Krebs, alias Jan Valtin, whom the Nazis had thought to employ to lure Wollweber into the trap.

The German Secret Service had taken no chances, however; it had not informed its accomplices in the Danish police force of the real names of the two Russian agents. When the arrested pedestrians reached the police station they identified themselves as Willy Schmidt and Kuhlman Vogel, and presented papers in perfect order to prove their statements. The second of the pair was in fact Kuhlman Vogel, a harmless refugee from Nazi oppression who for days had been doubling for Kuusinen, the latter having left Denmark to conduct his dangerous work in another country. Thick-set Willy Schmidt alias Ernst Friedrich Wollweber was duly deported to Russia at his request. For under Danish law, foreign agents who spy only on one another, and not against Denmark, are, when arrested, subject only to deportation to a country of their choice. Thereupon Wollweber mysteriously vanished, and was never seen at any of his usual haunts in Denmark. Yet shortly afterwards a thick-set, swarthy sailor landed at a Danish fishing port and jumped the ship, and soon the underground work of the Comintern was as active as ever.

Another man who mysteriously disappeared at this time was Dr. Erich Ring. But a tall, impeccably dressed, professorial journalist named Horst von Pflugk-Hartung presently took up his duties in Copenhagen as correspondent for the *Berliner Boersen Zeitung*. Dr. Erich Ring was only the alias Pflugk-Hartung employed whenever he was on a difficult mission.

A few days afterward *Pravda,* the official organ of the Russian Communist Party, published the entire story of the case of Carlis Hansen, the Danish Nazi. The Danish Communist Press reprinted this story, and the case of the Danish Crown versus Carlis Hansen came to trial.

The trial was conducted behind closed doors, but certain details leaked out. It became public knowledge that Carlis Hansen had worked in Germany for the Scandinavian division of Weltdienst, one of the most important

German propaganda agencies. Carlis Hansen's wife poisoned herself after a search of the Hansen household revealed incriminating documents, including a correspondence with Inspector Kaj Yttesen, who had helped her husband escape to Germany.

The trial failed to prove the complicity of Police Chief Andreas Hansen, and neither Elsa Andersen nor her employer, Horst von Pflugk-Hartung, were accused. Their share in the kidnapping and espionage work did not come to light until some years after 1934.

But the case of Carlis Hansen marked the beginning of the duel between the German and the Russian Secret Service, which narrowed to a struggle between two master spies, Pflugk-Hartung and Wollweber. It marked also the opening of the modern phase of the ancient conflict for *Dominium Maris Baltici*, the dominion of the Baltic Sea. The Baltic, which the Nazis have termed their "mare nostrum," once more became a theater of military operations.

General von Schlieffen had once submitted to Kaiser Wilhelm a plan calling for the occupation of Norway and Denmark as bases for an attack upon England. The Kaiser had rejected this plan; Hitler accepted it. From 1934 on he took steps to make it feasible.

I found the strands of the spy network fearfully and efficiently interwoven. They led from Denmark to Iceland and Greenland to Norway, Sweden and Finland, and deep into Russia. The forgotten lands of the Arctic had been brought into the geopolitical field of force of the great powers.

In this area Teuton and Slav have clashed since the thirteenth century, when the Teutonic Knights overran and settled Lithuania, Latvia and parts of Russia. From time to time through the centuries Sweden, Norway, Lithuania, Poland, Denmark, Germany and Russia have in turn wrested the power or the balance of power in that corner of the seven seas. Today and for the past ten years it has been the scene of a struggle between Nazi Germany and Communist Russia. It is a battle to the death in which the other nations have served as the battlefield.

In command of the secret armies in this conflict on the espionage front are: a tall, impeccably dressed, professorial "journalist," and a thick-set, swarthy, blustering "sailor." These men, respectively Horst von Pflugk-Hartung, the German master spy, and Ernst Friedrich Wollweber, the master mind of the OGPU, are the supreme figures in this duel.

2. Pflugk-Hartung: The Master Builder

"The Germans are without the tradition of liberty . . . They lack the pride of the civilian when confronted with a uniform."
                                                CARL VON OSSIETZKY

During World War I two German lieutenant-commanders made the acquaintance in Spain of the master spy, Mata Hari. They were the present Admiral Wilhelm Canaris, who is chief of all German espionage, and his friend, Horst von Pflugk-Hartung.

These men, and Pflugk-Hartung in particular, will some day occupy the same place in the history of Scandinavia as did Mata Hari in the history of France. For it is Pflugk-Hartung, the disciple of Mata Hari, who prepared Denmark for invasion; prepared it so thoroughly that he was able to deliver the country to the German army without a struggle. This same Pflugk-Hartung is known today throughout Europe as the master among German spies.

One of the traits that has made Pflugk-Hartung a master spy is his "nose" for traitors. In 1931, Pflugk-Hartung wrote a report on what friends and foes Germany had in Scandinavia. The report was intended for the espionage division of the Nazi Party. In it he noted that in Oslo he had made the acquaintance of a potentially invaluable ally, a man who was very friendly to Germany and who would gladly cooperate with Hitler's Party and with the German Reichswehr. He added that this man was a chronic alcoholic, and that one could induce him to do anything while he was under the influence of drink. The man was a Minister in the country, had a reputation as a diplomat, needed money but not too much, was, in sum, the very man to further Nazi interests in Norway. His name was Vidkun Quisling.

Admiral Canaris presented this report to his chief, Adolf Hitler, and to the Foreign Division of the Nazi Party —and thus a traitor was marked out by destiny. One must pay tribute to Pflugk-Hartung's acumen in discovering this traitor ten years before the time was ripe to employ him.

Adventurers and men in desperate straits for money are not the only persons suited to the profession of espionage. In general, such men are the hack spies, the trigger men and small fry who do the menial work of spying. These, too, are the men who get caught. But many of the great spies are pure patriots; they really believe in their work and are willing to risk everything to do their bit that the Fatherland may rule the world. Pflugk-Hartung was such a man.

I met him once in Copenhagen. Had I not been dead certain of my facts I would never have believed that this engaging and dignified person, with his thoughtful, professorial manner, could have anything at all to do with espionage. But that is probably one secret of his extraordinary success.

His was a family that had given to the kings of Prussia a long line of General Staff officers. His father was the most famous German historian under Kaiser Wilhelm II, and official historian of the Hohenzollerns. Every child read Pflugk-Hartung's history books in elementary school; I myself learned history from them in the schools of the democratic German Republic, for the Weimar Republic was laggard in freeing itself of the debris of Kaiserism.

The son of the famous historian found all doors open to him. His parents determined as a matter of course that he would become an officer in the military. At fifteen he was sent to cadet school, and by the time he was eighteen he was reckoned one of the most promising of young German naval officers. Throughout Germany he was known as a first-rate rider and duelist. A handsome young Teuton, though none too blond, he had a compelling way with women.

As with all young officers, World War I represented to Pflugk-Hartung his great chance, for a career. He served first on German battleships and soon distinguished himself by his keen observation and grasp of military problems. Several exceptional reports on the harbors, fortifications and positions of the Allies in the Mediterranean resulted in his being called to Berlin. Colonel Walter Nicolai, the chief of German espionage, interviewed him and asked whether he would like to work for the Naval Intelligence Service. Pflugk-Hartung accepted at once; he was promoted and sent off to Spain.

The archives dealing with Pflugk-Hartung's activities in World War I were never found after the war. A Republic court later determined that Colonel Nicolai had destroyed them on the eve of the German defeat.

On November 9, 1918 Horst von Pflugk-Hartung, monarchist to the marrow of his bones, found himself facing a world that for him was now barren. The war was lost, the Kaiser had fled, workers, peasants and soldiers were milling in the streets in vast demonstrations, and had seized the power of government, first in Berlin, Hamburg, Kiel, Wilhelmshaven and Munich, then throughout Germany. The Allies were demanding demobilization; the ancient glory of the Prussian Army had fallen at last.

Pflugk-Hartung refused to capitulate. He refused to deliver up his arms. He banded together with hundreds of other German naval officers who still commanded the remnants of their sailors who had remained loyal to the Kaiser. They formed one of the most notorious organizations of the German White Terror.

In January 1919, in the midst of the chaos released by the German Revolution, hot-headed Captain Hermann Ehrhardt, the reckless murderer Manfred von Killinger, and cold-blooded, calculating Horst von Pflugk-Hartung, entered the Eden Hotel in Berlin with fifty armed men at their back. They declared that the hotel, one of the most elegant in Berlin, was being confiscated by the Schützen Cavallerie Garde and anyone who opposed them would be shot.

The Eden Hotel, which in the past had entertained princes and visiting statesmen, now became the hangout of the terrorists in Berlin. The people of Berlin were still eating kohlrabi and ersatz marmalade, but in the Eden Hotel there was meat, butter and above all genuine French cognac and champagne. Perhaps these eatables were not the prime attraction to patriotic terrorists; nevertheless, the group waxed in number at an astounding pace. German soldiers, returning louse-ridden and filthy from the mud of the trenches, luxuriated in the thickly-carpeted suites of the Eden Hotel.

Horst von Pflugk-Hartung, who still had his father's money to spend, suddenly blossomed into a gentleman with a five room suite, a personal adjutant and a bodyguard of three marines.

The terrorist group was dedicated to preserving order in Prussia and restoring the monarchy. Pflugk-Hartung declared, "I would rather die than break my oath of loyalty to the Kaiser." It sounded well, and was in the bombastic tradition of the Prussian chauvinist.

Pflugk-Hartung's methods of restoring order were simple. He addressed his rapidly growing corps of unemployed officers, sergeants and corporals and directed that the enemies of the monarchy must be "laid out stiff"—in other words, murdered. These enemies of the monarchy were Democrats, Social-Democrats, Spartakists, Communists, and Jews—in short, all who might possibly be opposed to Prussian militarism.

It was later established in court that this group of terrorists arrested without authority and administered beatings to several hundred persons, chiefly workers, and that they murdered or "shot while trying to escape" several dozen defenseless persons.

Over in fashionable Eden Hotel Captain Horst von Pflugk-Hartung was busy with other Junker officers reorganizing shattered fragments of the old Kaiser's army into the skeleton of a new Wehrmacht. These "Free Corps" strongly monarchist in sentiment and hating republicanism, the culture-bed of future Nazism, were nominally parts of the German national army, just as were the red Volks-Marine-Division and other armed units of the left. The government paid them both, but it could not command either and dared not try to demobilize them. But the timid republican Government was more frightened of communist revolutionaries than of Junker militarism. They called in the old officers to crush the people's army and accepted the offer of Pflugk-Hartung and his friends to get rid of the Spartakists and the red Volks-Marine-Division.

One method Pflugk-Hartung used might have been invented by Himmler himself. They stationed some officers, fully armed, in the office of the Volks-Marine-Division in the center of Berlin where the marines came twice a month to get their pay. On payday, as each marine entered, singly or in groups of two or three, he was assailed from behind.

His skull was split by the blow of a revolver butt, or he was pumped full of lead by an officer's automatic. The corpses were thrown into the next room, and the officers took their station again behind doors to await the next arrivals. All morning long the murders continued.

The Volks-Marine-Division and other left units saw it was to be war and prepared barricades in Berlin's East Side, where the population was for them. The Free Corps, with the old Army officers in command, Pflugk-Hartung among them, attacked with artillery, airplanes and flame-throwers. The back of the people's revolution for which Karl Liebknecht and Rosa Luxemburg had sounded the tocsin, was broken.

January 15, 1919 was a chill wintry day in Berlin, and cold days meant intense suffering to the people of Berlin, for there was a shortage of coal. "You can get warm by beating up Spartakists and Jews," Pflugk-Hartung declared to his troops as he gave them the order to arrest two Communists.

Ten heavily-armed, hard-bitten marines drove out to the Berlin West Side. They broke down the door of the apartment of Karl Liebknecht and Rosa Luxemburg, the famous German Socialists who alone had been opposing the Kaiser and the war since 1914. Liebknecht was the only German Reichstag Deputy who had dared to vote against war credits from 1914 continuously to 1918.

These two arch-enemies of Prussian militarism were taken to the Eden Hotel and there led before the chief of the terrorists. No one knows what happened in that hotel room; no one knows what the two Socialists said to Pflugk-Hartung. Our only information comes from the records of the Berlin police: Karl Liebknecht and Rosa Luxemburg were frightfully beaten at the direction of Pflugk-Hartung.

Afterwards Pflugk-Hartung, Lieutenant Kurt Vogel, a Lieutenant Liebmann and an ex-sergeant Runge packed the two anti-war leaders into a stolen automobile and drove toward the Moabit Prison. The car had a flat tire and stopped near the War Ministry on the Luetzow Ufer. Pflugk-Hartung shouted at the two Socialists to leave the car. He then drew his revolver and shot Germany's greatest anti-militarist, Karl Liebknecht, through the head. While Sergeant Vogel shot Rosa Luxemburg, Pflugk-Hartung sent a second and a third bullet into the body of Liebknecht. Thus the two revolutionists who had overthrown Kaiserism were killed, and peace and order were ostensibly restored. The bodies were thrown into the Landwehr Canal, the same dirty body of water that Admiral Canaris can now see every day from his office window. During that period in Berlin the Canal's evil reputation gave rise to a macabre but significant popular song:

> *A corpse is floating in Landwehr Canal*
> *Ship her home to me,*
> *Handle her carefully.* . . .

The news of the murder of the two revolutionary leaders caused a wave of sorrow and confusion among the people. That same day the leader of the red revolution in Hamburg and Wilhelmshaven gave the order that the murderers must pay with their lives. This leader was Ernst Friedrich Wollweber, who from that moment on became Pflugk-Hartung's sworn enemy.

The funeral rites for Luxemburg and Liebknecht in Hamburg drew tens of thousands of people out into the streets. The Hamburg Communists took a mass oath never to forget "Karl and Rosa," as they called their revolutionary leaders, and not to rest until the murder had been avenged. Wollweber then delivered an address.

With tears in his eyes Wollweber vowed that he would avenge the conscienceless murder of his two leaders no matter what the cost. He has not yet accomplished his revenge, but that day in January 1919 marked the beginning of a war to the death between two men which was to involve the whole of the European Continent.

Pflugk-Hartung did not deny that he had committed murder. He offered the defense that from 1914 to 1918 it had been his duty to murder for his Fatherland; that he had always recognized it as his duty to destroy the enemies of his Fatherland, and that Liebknecht and Luxemburg were enemies of Germany.

Germany's young democratic Government brought Pflugk-Hartung and his accomplices to trial. Unfortunately, the new democracy had decided to permit the Imperial Prussian Judges, who were appointed for life, to remain in office. The official before whom Pflugk-Hartung was tried was Dr. Jorns, later Judge of the Supreme Court in Leipzig. Dr. Jorns was an intimate friend of the spy and diplomat, Franz von Papen, and an early member of the Nazi Party. Jorns and Pflugk-Hartung's father had been schoolfellows and fast friends. Under these circumstances, the verdict this "democratic" court would pronounce was inevitable. The verdict demonstrated clearly that the Prussian war spirit still thrived in this new democracy.

Dr. Jorns declared that Pflugk-Hartung had had the natural desire of an officer to restore peace and order to Germany. Spartakists were foes of the country; the two victims were the leaders of the Spartakus League, which later developed into the Communist Party; they had attempted to resist the law as incorporated in the Free Corps and had been shot while trying to escape.

Thus Pflugk-Hartung's monarchist friends saved him from punishment. But everyone in Germany knew he was a murderer. He was a marked man; no one would give him employment, no one would have anything to do with him. The charming, handsome officer had become a social outcast. His family supplied him with money, but an inactive life was impossible for a man like him; he was bursting with energy and could find no outlet for it.

Even the former officers of the Imperial Army let him down. Afraid for their own futures, they refused to be compromised by associating with him. Pflugk-Hartung decided to emigrate. He thought of coming to the United States, then of buying a ranch in South America. But he did not have enough money. He secured a temporary position in the "Black Reichswehr," but when the Government took action against this illegal organization he found himself again out of a job. At last he left Germany and went into voluntary exile.

His accomplices in the murder had left Germany long before—in a manner not exactly legal. For the murderers of Liebknecht and Luxemburg had simply been spirited out of prison. Pflugk-Hartung, who had been released, had forged a discharge order for Lieutenant Kurt Vogel and Lieutenant Liebmann. Together with them he fled to Holland, where Pflugk-Hartung was at once given audience by Kaiser Wilhelm at Doorn.

Pflugk-Hartung's flight to Holland was prompted by his fear of a retrial. A waiter of the Eden Hotel had testified in defense of Lieutenant Vogel that Pflugk-Hartung when he ordered the murder car to be brought had said: "I'll see to it that these swine never reach the prison alive."

And so, in 1929, he went to Sweden, where he met frequently with Goering. The Nazi leader had also gone into exile after the failure of the Munich putsch, and had spent much of his time at Swedish psychiatric sanatoriums.

In Sweden Pflugk-Hartung suddenly appeared to be in funds again. The explanation was that he was on the Nazi payroll. For even this early the Nazi Party had set up its own private system of espionage; the Nazi leaders employed their followers in Germany and all over the world to spy out military and diplomatic information. Hitler's espionage genius, Admiral Canaris, sold this information to pro-fascist news agencies and intelligence services, and to the German Reichswehr. Thus the Party espionage system paid for itself and was able to support such expensive agents as Pflugk-Hartung.

For years the social democratic press in Sweden demanded his expulsion from the country—for no Socialist had forgotten that this man was the murderer of Liebknecht and Luxemburg—but Sweden clung to its traditional democratic principles and refused to deny the right of asylum to a political refugee.

When the Swedish authorities inquired where he obtained the money to live in Saltsjöbaden, Stockholm's most fashionable resort, Pflugk-Hartung blandly explained that he wrote for German newspapers. Indeed, to preserve appearances, he did actually make brief contributions to German military journals, veterans' magazines and similar publications. The authorities were doubtful of this explanation, but since he associated with the best families in the country and had become quite a social lion in Swedish society, they hesitated to touch him.

He had all the qualities that made for social success. Highly cultured, he spoke Swedish very well and with a charming German accent; he danced splendidly, and the iron-gray hair of his temples lent him an interesting and distinguished appearance. Moreover, he did not, like other German officers, tediously recount his heroic accomplishments in the war; on the contrary, he preferred to discuss world problems and broad political perspectives. He was, he stressed, a conservative; he could not deny the traditions of his past and of his family and did not like this modern liberalism. Nevertheless, he said, he could understand that this was the way of modern youth. His Swedish friends were astounded at his political knowledge, but attributed it to his father's teachings; one and all they were convinced that politically he was wholly innocuous.

He was often seen in the company of Swedish officers and Swedish socialists. He loved discussions and willingly gave lectures. Honest and patriotic Swedes were convinced that here was an exceptionally intelligent man who deserved help, and who would go far in his adopted country. His social success was so overpowering that much later, after it had been conclusively proved that he was an espionage agent, the conservative Swedish evening newspaper, *Nya Dagligt Allehanda,* commented that it was inconceivable that a man so charming, of such distinguished family and with such an excellent background, should practice the dirty trade of espionage.

Pflugk-Hartung might never have left Sweden had not one of the fateful accidents of history played him into the hands of the Swedish police.

For years the Swedish Coast Guard had been waging an intensive campaign against rum-runners from Esthonia and Finland who landed liquor on the Swedish coast from small motorboats and sailboats. In semi-dry Sweden this trade was enormously profitable.

It was one o'clock in the morning; the scene was the coast of southern Sweden; a schooner was observed sailing suspiciously close to shore—for even the bright nights of this land of the midnight sun do not deter the entrepreneurs of quick profits. Boxes were unloaded from the schooner into a motorboat and landed along the coast between Malmoe and Ystad.

The Swedish police were on the alert. As soon as the entire cargo, consisting of several hundred boxes, was transported to shore where men had begun loading it into big camouflaged trucks, the Coast Guard and police pounced on the smugglers and arrested them all.

All this was in the normal order of events; it would not be the first time the Swedish Coast Guard had made a big haul. The police and Coast Guard men commenced cheerfully hammering at the cartons to break them open. The prisoners turned white and began to scream incomprehensible warnings. And then the police themselves paled with fright when they saw the contents of the boxes they had been handling so recklessly.

This was 1930; peace was still a reality and there seemed little prospect that it would be disturbed for many years. The surprise of the police was therefore all the greater when they found that these boxes contained machine guns, automatic revolvers of German army manufacture, the most modern rifles, and large supplies of ammunition.

The Swedish police ordered a nationwide investigation. The results were sensational.

The fascist leader of Sweden at this time was an army officer named Colonel Munck. Munck had been seen in the company of Pflugk-Hartung and was in no position to deny that he knew the charming Prussian officer, although none of the arrested arms-smugglers had any idea who their employer was or who was destined to receive the contraband goods. Colonel Munck, it was learned, wanted the weapons for his storm troops; he hoped that by arming them he could win power in peaceful Sweden through a well-timed coup. His movement had been financed by a Swedish banker named A. W. Hoegman, and by several lesser known Swedish army officers. Munck had learned that Pflugk-Hartung was working as a secret agent for the German Reichswehr, and had made contact with him. The result of their meeting was that Pflugk-Hartung sent a report on the "Muncksa Corps" to the Military Intelligence Office in Berlin.

The Reichswehr approved his suggestion that Munck's outfit be given assistance. With the help of the official Reichswehr and the Black Reichswehr, the arms-smuggling was organized. With their usual Prussian precision, the Germans included in the boxes the official inspection and packing certificates of the German Army, and these were found by the Swedish police.

Pflugk-Hartung was warned; consequently, he was not surprised when two days later three officers of the Swedish police in Saltsjöbaden paid a call at his home and invited him to visit the Kungsholm Police Headquarters.

Pflugk-Hartung played the part of the German officer, the man of honor who would not tell a lie. Yes, he admitted, he had served as go-between in the purchase of arms. Why not? It was legal business. He insisted that he knew nothing of the smuggling.

When asked whether he was a follower of Hitler, he replied indignantly:

"I am an officer of the old Imperial Army; I am and shall always be a monarchist." Nazism, he asserted, was a movement of plebeians, beggars and desperate political gangsters. So violent was his tone that both the authorities and the press were convinced.

He was given no punishment, but he was deported from Sweden. And so his wanderings continued. The villa in Saltsjöbaden was vacated and Pflugk-Hartung, now in his mid-forties, left Sweden early in 1931 and emigrated to Norway.

His stay there was very brief. The Labor Party, learning of his arrival, threatened to make the admission of this murderer to the country a political issue and stated that it would try to bring about the fall of the government if "Liebknecht's murderer" were not expelled at once.

Throughout his stay in Oslo, Pflugk-Hartung's life was in danger. Stones were thrown at him as he passed through the streets and he daily received threatening letters. Finally he saved the Norwegian Government much embarrassment by clearing out voluntarily. The few weeks he spent in Oslo were, however, not entirely unprofitable. Since the Labor Party, the Party of the Norwegian New Deal, had attacked him so violently, it was only natural that he should seek out the enemies of this Party. The chief enemy was Vidkun Quisling.

He paid a visit to Vidkun Quisling in his private home on the edge of the city, and a compact of friendship and self-interest was formed at once. The two men were heart and soul in agreement that the Labor Party, those "reds," "New Dealers" and "Communists" (the Norwegian Labor Party was a liberal party with moderate Socialist leanings), must be exterminated. Pflugk-Hartung had found his future traitor.

He had found more. Quisling could be developed into a splendid spy. Pflugk-Hartung gave him to understand that he could use—and pay for—any and all information on Norway, especially on the activities of the Labor Party, diplomatic moves of the British or Russians, trade agreements, and so on. Even to Quisling, of course, he dissimulated. "You see, I am a newspaper man," he said to the Norwegian. "I have no connection with any intelligence service. But my newspapers pay fairly, and they'll pay you fairly." Quisling understood and thus he became a collaborator of Germany's future spy.

Norwegians frequently wondered during the following years where Quisling got his money, for he had scarcely any followers in his own country. When it was suggested that he was receiving money from Germany, Quisling indignantly denied it.

He was telling the truth. For all the money he received came from a gentleman named Horst von Pflugk-Hartung, who lived in Denmark. After all, it was not Quisling's concern where Pflugk-Hartung's money originated.

Pflugk-Hartung's new headquarters was a magnificently appointed mansion in Copenhagen, near the Strandvejen and the ocean. But no one in Denmark seemed to find it curious that a newspaper correspondent could afford such luxury.

The Danish Labor Party, which had been warned by its fellow Parties in Sweden and Norway, tried to have him deported. Labor papers openly called him a spy. Pflugk-Hartung made a gentlemanly reply to these charges. He added in a conciliatory tone that he did not intend to remain in Denmark very long. In this manner he gained time.

Two important events helped him to fortify his position. He made the acquaintance of Police Chief Andreas Hansen, and on January 30, 1933 Adolf Hitler took supreme power in Germany.

For many years Pflugk-Hartung supplied Andreas Hansen with remarkably detailed information on the activities of Russian agents in Scandinavia, on German underground activities along the Dano-German frontier, and on other matters of vital importance to Denmark. The German nobly refused any pay for this information; he asked only that he be permitted to remain in Denmark. After Hitler took power, of course, there was no question of deporting him. Goebbels' Reich Chamber of Culture appointed him official German correspondent in Copenhagen; thereafter little Denmark did not dare expel him. Protected by the shadow of Hitler's might, he spun his intrigues.

Police Chief Andreas Hansen did not know that Pflugk-Hartung's marvelous information on Russian spies came from the Anti-Comintern Department of the Gestapo, the German Foreign Office, and the Secret Service. All he knew was that Pflugk-Hartung had helped him to arrest dozens of foreign agents in Denmark, and that in consequence his own prestige increased by leaps and bounds. Within a few months Andreas Hansen gained the reputation of being one of the cleverest and most efficient police chiefs in Europe. But his methods did not escape the notice of his superiors.

In 1938—by which time Pflugk-Hartung had organized his espionage service in Denmark into a tight system—the late Premier of Denmark, Thorvald Stauning, called Andreas Hansen to his office. Stauning, a man whose long beard was legendary in Denmark, was a Horatio Alger character and a rare statesman. His father had been a locomotive polisher; he himself had worked his way up from a worker in a tobacco factory to Premier.

Stauning bluntly accused Hansen of aiding and abetting Pflugk-Hartung, who had been proved a spy. He informed the Police Chief that certain Britons had protested to King Christian himself that Pflugk-Hartung was being permitted to build the greatest network of spies in all Europe, with Denmark as its headquarters.

Hansen had a ready reply.

"Your Excellency," he declared, "it is better to know a spy and keep an eye on him than to deport him and have another take his place whom one does not know. Your Excellency may rest assured that Pflugk-Hartung will not be permitted to work against the interests of Denmark."

Stauning was not satisfied; he expressed doubt that Pflugk-Hartung could be controlled so easily. To this Hansen suggested that they put the matter up to the Foreign Office and accept its decision. Stauning incautiously agreed to this, and the matter was promptly buried. For by 1938 the Danish Foreign Office no longer dared to take any action against Germany. The officials in the Foreign Office knew very well that "Denmark could be taken by telephone" if Germany desired. Neither Stauning nor Foreign Minister Munch suspected that the man on the Danish end of the telephone line would be none other than Pflugk-Hartung, when the time came for invasion.

It was about this time that I met Pflugk-Hartung in the Foreign Correspondents Club. He was introduced to me by a Danish reporter.

"I've heard of you," he said in an unpleasantly aggressive manner. "I understand that you have published the biography of a German traitor."

"I've heard of you, too," I replied. "If you mean Carl von Ossietzky, who became tubercular in a concentration camp, I can only say that anyone who fights Prussian militarism is not a traitor but a true friend of unhappy Germany."

Pflugk-Hartung observed that I had done a great deal of damage to Germany's prestige by leading the Ossietzky campaign and the campaign to get him the Nobel Prize. I could no longer resist the temptation to provoke him, and said smilingly:

"I've heard that you are not a Nazi, although you work for German newspapers. Tell me then, why are you so angry with me?"

With an effort Pflugk-Hartung controlled his rising temper. He offered me a cigarette; we sat down in the comfortable armchairs of the club, and he began lecturing me as though I were a schoolboy.

"I know it's senseless to discuss this matter," he began. "In history it is deeds that are decisive, words never. I say this in spite of the fact that I personally do nothing but play around with words writing articles. Hitler acted while all his opponents talked. As an old Prussian officer I am, of course, not a Nazi. You'll grant me that under the Empire everyone, including the opposition, was a good deal happier. But I am a German, while you are an internationalist who dreams of international democracy —a chimera. After Napoleon's defeat they attempted to form international leagues, and failed. The League of Nations today is nothing but a corpse. One does not befoul one's own nest; one remains a German, even in exile."

It was evident that he was trying to probe me, trying to get me to commit myself on Germany. I answered him cautiously.

"I am an Austrian who had found a new home in Scandinavia. I do not believe that Hitler has contributed anything new. The Prussian Army and Pan-Germanism are simply reincorporated in him."

"I'd rather you didn't say anything against the Prussian Army. Its men were honest and had their own ingrained code of honor. We old officers look with contempt upon such things as Gestapo and storm troopers. But for us Germany would have splintered into a hundred small states. And, for your information, we Prussians have never been anti-Semites!"

He went on to speak of "refugee mentality." The refugees, he claimed, were misinterpreting Germany to the world. "It is unwise of them to close the door to all possibility of their ever returning," he observed.

I did not take him up on this. Instead I remarked that I knew Lieutenant-Commander Martin Bolte in Sweden— who at that time was already working as Pflugk-Hartung's agent. He gazed piercingly at me, trying to find out how much I knew. Then he remarked, "He is not a Nazi either. We old officers consider a monarchy the only decent form of government."

"What about a constitutional, democratic monarchy, such as we have in Denmark or Sweden?" I interrupted him.

Duel for the Northland 41

"Even that would be better than Hitler," he said with a theatrical gesture. Then he left me, evidently hoping he had impressed upon me that he was not working for the Nazis. He did not realize that even had he been able to convince me, I would have considered him dangerous. For I consider every German who is partial to Prussian militarism a permanent enemy of peace and of humanity.

As yet we have seen little of Pflugk-Hartung at work. We shall discuss his methods and his activities in a later chapter. It will suffice to remark here that shortly after he arrived in Denmark his great opponent, Wollweber, also turned up in Copenhagen, and the conflict between the two was taken up once more.

Denmark was at this time an international spy center. The country that had its agents shrewdly planted in Denmark knew about everything that went on in the Baltic, on the Kiel Canal, in the Skagerrak, the Kattegat, and on the mainland of Scandinavia itself.

Pflugk-Hartung's fundamental tasks in Denmark were to acquire complete control of merchant shipping in Baltic waters, to organize counterespionage against the Russians, to keep an eye on the work of political refugees from Germany, and above all—this as early as 1933—to prepare Denmark for the coming invasion.

Through the years Pflugk-Hartung constructed the greatest harbor spy system in Europe; he bribed police and army officers; he waged ruthless war against Russian espionage and virtually created a state within the state. Then, in 1939, the British Secret Service temporarily put an end to his work. Pflugk-Hartung was arrested and in January 1940 sentenced to five years' imprisonment for espionage. Three months later three German Army cars drew up before the gate of his prison and Heinrich Himmler in person entered his cell. Pflugk-Hartung was released and his visitor presented him with the uniform of a colonel. An hour later the man who had murdered Liebknecht and purloined Denmark's independence rode in an open car at the side of Himmler down Copenhagen's broad boulevards to celebrate the triumph of the Nazi invasion.

Himmler and Pflugk-Hartung drove to the Danish Palace of Justice, opened the bombproof cellar where the archives were stored, and took from it the documents relating to the case of Horst von Pflugk-Hartung. We shall discuss these documents in a later chapter, for they contained full details of his espionage work and marshalled the facts that the British Secret Service, the French Deuxième Bureau, and the Swedish Police had placed at the disposal of the Danish Government—facts that were sufficient to put this master spy behind bars for three months at least.

3. Jan Valtin's Boss

It was in Stockholm in 1937 that I first heard the name of Ernst Friedrich Wollweber. The place was the office of the Chief of the Alien Squad of the Swedish police.

It was a drafty, uncomfortable old building with hundreds of drafty, uncomfortable rooms; the kind of place you were happier leaving than entering. On the ground floor were the detention cells. The new Stockholm police headquarters, one of the most modern public buildings in Europe, was not opened until two years later.

The Swedish police had invited me to a hearing on Nazi agents who had been dogging the footsteps of foreigners in Stockholm and Gothenburg. The police thought I might have information that would give them stronger grounds for legal prosecution.

I shall never forget this particular November day. Stockholm was blanketed in snow; it was so cold outside that even the cold office felt warm and it was a luxury to have a roof over one's head. The hearing was over and I had just signed my statement when the police chief suddenly said:

"Just a moment. Since you know Germany so well you may be able to give us information about this person."

He showed me a picture of a big, stout man with thinning hair, and a swollen, alcoholic face. The man wore an open blouse without collar or tie, in the style of the proletarian youth movement of Germany. He must have been about forty-five years old. The face looked embittered and harsh, but that might have been the fault of the bad passport photo.

"Have you ever seen this man?" the chief asked me.

Absent-mindedly I turned the passport picture over and saw the rubber-stamped imprint of a hammer and sickle.

"You have no right to look at the other side," the police chief barked nervously at me.

"A German Communist?" I said inquiringly. "I've never seen him."

On the back of the photo I had caught a glimpse of the name Ernst Friedrich Wollweber.

"That man is a menace to society," the police chief said to me. "He's the head of Russian harbor espionage, a criminal who places bombs on German and Scandinavian ships. I suppose he's trying to strike at the Nazis, but he doesn't care how many innocent people he kills in doing it."

I replied that I had never heard the name of Wollweber and knew nothing about him, and the police chief dismissed me saying that I should report to him if I learned anything about Wollweber.

I soon learned that Wollweber was sought by the police of the three Scandinavian countries and of Finland, Spain, France, England, China, Japan and various countries in South America, and that his name is to be found even in the files of the FBI.

The man struck me as all the more fascinating when I found out that for eight years the police of half the world had been searching in vain for him. I discovered that he was one of the most important agents of the OGPU in Western Europe.

I had done my best to uncover Pflugk-Hartung's spy network. It now appeared that others were also interested in it, that agents who had the backing of the Great Powers were on the same trail. I learned that Wollweber was the man who planted bombs on Nazi ships in the harbor of Copenhagen—ships that were carrying arms to Franco in Spain. Now for the first time there dawned on me the significance of the newspaper reports of explosions in Scandinavian ports.

Ernst Friedrich Wollweber, the great antagonist of Pflugk-Hartung in the struggle for *Dominium Maris Baltici,* considered himself an officer in the army of world revolution. His commander-in-chief was Joseph Stalin.

What is the story of this Wollweber? It is an enigmatic and striking one for this man has lived more dangerously and mysteriously than most of the other spies and saboteurs of our time.

He is a man who fits into no system. If one were to call him a Communist, he might reply that he has never submitted to the Communist line; if one were to call him an Anarchist, he would reply that he believes in a strong central government; if a Socialist, he would probably say: "Call me what you will. I am a proletarian."

He does not follow Marx and Lenin; he is not a one hundred per cent Stalinist. His sole guide is his "proletarian instinct." He hates intellectuals with their finespun analyses of Marx and Lenin. He hates compromises. To him there is only black and white, capitalist and proletarian.

"If the Marxists had not bothered to write books, they would be in power everywhere today; instead they are eternally breaking up into splinter groups," he once declared. And when some of his friends died in the Russian purges, he said of them: "They talked too much about theories. In a revolution one must be able to obey."

Wollweber is the last man to obey, but the Russians have always overlooked his insubordinations. He is a professional revolutionary in the truest sense of the word.

He comes from a poor working class family, and knows what it means to grow up without milk or meat. He went to sea when still a boy, and the sea became his new home. His needs were few and he accepted the monotonous and ill-paid sailor's life solely in order to see the world. Eager to learn, he read more books than most men—in spite of his later precepts. When he declared to his friends, "Too much reading is unhealthy; it takes time away from the revolution," he was speaking from experience.

During World War I he was a stoker on the battleship *Helgoland*. He agitated within the German Navy and was largely responsible for its mutiny at the end of the war. In November 1918 it was he who raised the red flag in Wilhelmshaven and declared that the war was over. A few hours later Wendelin Thomas in Kiel followed his example. And a few days after that Ernst Friedrich Wollweber who—through reading—was the only one who had some conception of a revolution became leader of the workers and soldiers along the entire waterfront of North Germany. The Kaiser had fled, the generals and officials had remained. The new-founded Communist Party tried to accustom itself to parliamentarianism; but Wollweber felt uncomfortable in an environment that lacked fighting and revolution. Although he had sworn to avenge the murder of Liebknecht and Luxemburg, the Party put restraints upon him, warned him that a period of peace was needed in order to gain control by legal parliamentary procedures. The new economy of Russia had been brought to the point of collapse by the Civil War; the Russian Communists needed the cooperation of German democracy to survive the crisis. Consequently, the thoroughgoing German revolution had to be postponed for the time being.

Wollweber grew restless in Germany. "I ain't a desk revolutionary," he declared. His friends and comrades felt that he was a demoralizing influence; they began calling him an Anarchist.

This was more than he could stomach, He felt instinctively that the bureaucrats in Berlin and Moscow, who wanted to run the revolution from their armchairs, were not his kind. He went to sea again, refusing all offers of a seat in the Reichstag; he had a pet plan that he wanted to carry out. After several months he succeeded in putting his plan into effect. The year was 1920. Wollweber and his old friend of revolutionary days, Hermann Knueffgen, assembled some ten Communist leaders, concealed them in the fish tank of a trawler about to set sail, and then hired themselves out as sailors on the boat. Off Stavanger, in Norway, the two Communists opened the fish tank. The ten armed Communists came on deck, overpowered the captain and the helmsman and put them in the brig. They then informed the crew that the ship had been appropriated by the Communist Party. Without maps or charts, aided only by a compass, they sailed the ship along the Atlantic and Arctic coastlines of Norway to Murmansk. Here they presented their stolen ship to the land of workers and peasants.

The Russians gave them an overwhelming greeting. Lenin and Stalin were so impressed by the feat of the men who without any schooling in navigation had steered a ship without charts all the way to Murmansk, that they decided to see Wollweber personally. The theft of the ship proved more embarrassing than profitable to the Russians, for they were compelled to pay the owners for it; but Wollweber had attained his object. He saw Lenin and Stalin.

Later Wollweber boasted a good deal to friends about these conversations with the Soviet leaders. But we may believe his account that he spoke candidly to Lenin and Stalin, told them that the leadership of the German

Communist Party was made up of intellectuals who had no conception of what revolution was. He asked to be given work, real revolutionary work in Russia.

Stalin was taken with the forthright manner of this staunch revolutionary. He followed his suggestions, deposed the old leadership of the German Communist Party, and gave Wollweber a job he liked. Wollweber became chief of all sailors' organizations under Communist control in all parts of the world with the tide of chief of the Marine Division of the Comintern.

Stalin and Wollweber are still good friends. At Stalin's urging, Wollweber became a parliamentarian after all. Stalin pointed out to him that as a Reichstag Deputy he would possess immunity from arrest, which would be of great help in building up the Communist Sailors' Organization. Wollweber was convinced, but he refused to abandon his proletarian blouse. And so he appeared on the floor of the Reichstag without collar or tie. In time the deputies got used to it.

No sooner did Wollweber secure one of the Communist seats in the German Reichstag than he did his best to efface himself. He seldom spoke in the Reichstag and never in public. But he devoted himself all the more intensively to organizing Communist cells in all the important ports of Germany and throughout the world. He wanted the Communists armed against the day when "the Fatherland of the proletarians will be attacked."

Wollweber did not trust his own comrades. He told no one what he was about, for he knew the counterespionage services of Germany and other countries were on the alert. He himself caused rumors to be circulated that he had been elected to the Reichstag only because he happened to have been the first to raise the red flag in Germany. He gave his fellow deputies to understand that he was an illiterate who understood nothing of politics; that he was a fellow who preferred a good rousing drunk to attending a dull Reichstag session.

He played dumb very well. His role was successful until 1933 when the Gestapo was founded.

In his *Out of the Night* Jan Valtin has described Wollweber's underground work and told how Wollweber gave him his orders. There is little doubt that Valtin accomplished a good deal under Wollweber, though many of the author's opponents deny this. The fact is that the police forces of the Scandinavian countries not only had Wollweber on their "wanted" list, but also had listed a large number of his subagents, including Richard Krebs, alias Jan Valtin.

After Hitler came to power Wollweber had to switch to wearing collar and tie. This was part of his new tactics. He bought himself expensive suits in order to appear as a wealthy business man who traveled through Europe to sell textiles, iron ores, or what not. His resourcefulness was amazing, for though he traveled tens of thousands of miles in every country in Europe, he never owned a genuine passport.

The proletarian had become a bourgeois, and though his collar sometimes felt too tight and his well-tailored clothes hampered his movements, he wore them with a will, for it was his job. He had always possessed a certain peasant cunning, and this now stood him in good stead. The bourgeois drinks champagne, he reasoned; therefore, if he and his agents did the same, no one would ever imagine they were Russian spies. A simple trick, but it worked surprisingly well, perhaps precisely because it was so simple.

He knew that telephone lines could be tapped; therefore he made it a rule never to telephone. He knew that his sub-agents could be shadowed by the police; therefore he regularly avoided meeting them at the appointed time. He would shadow them, and if the police did not turn up, he would accost them as if by accident hours later.

He knew that he could never be arrested if his address were not known, and therefore he made it a principle never to tell anyone where he lived—except one or two women whom he trusted implicitly.

Although a devout Communist, he did not even trust his fellow Communists. He had always adhered to the "cadre principle" in politics; that is, he believed that only a few carefully chosen comrades should be permitted the honor of membership in the Communist Party. This principle had been abandoned long before; anyone who signed his name to an application and paid his dues could now become a member. "The Party is shot through with spies," he declared, and preferred to trust no one in it.

Consistently proletarian in everything, he refused to employ as an agent anyone who was not a worker. He hated intellectuals and considered them incompetent to do espionage or sabotage. Experience had borne him out in this. He also refused to accept petit bourgeois, for he believed they broke down when in the hands of the enemy. They would confess and betray everything. Only the worker would rather die than betray the names of his fellow spies. This theory proved false, for in after years Wollweber was betrayed not by an intellectual or a petit bourgeois, but by a worker who lost his nerve.

Dimitrov, the political head of the Comintern in Europe, was an intellectual, and Wollweber did not think much of him. In February 1933 the political leadership of the Comintern issued instructions that the Communists in Germany must print underground newspapers and organize strikes. As a consequence the Communists exposed themselves, and hundreds of them were arrested by the Gestapo every day. The best Communist agitators were thrown into prisons and concentration camps. In a rage, Wollweber refused to obey Dimitrov's orders and went to Moscow to speak with "his friend, Stalin."

At first he had difficulty gaining admittance to the Communist chief. But as soon as Stalin heard of his arrival he sent for him. Wollweber explained his stand: that the revolution gained nothing if all the Communists were cooped up in Nazi prisons. He pointed out that if all his men were arrested because of a few silly leaflets the harbor espionage system he had laboriously built up over the years would be destroyed. He thought the espionage system was more important than leaflets that only repeated what everyone knew: that the Nazis were robbers and murderers.

Wollweber suggested that all Communists become what he called "beefsteak Nazis"—brown outside and red inside. Every Communist was to join the Nazi Party and work inside the organization, striking where and when Stalin considered necessary.

Stalin, who knew so well what it had been like to work illegally under czarism, saw the wisdom of Wollweber's suggestions. He gave the sailor all the power he wanted, appointing him organizational chief of the entire Communist International in Western Europe. Otto Kuusinen was made political chief and later "president" of the short-lived "Finnish People's Republic."

Practically, this means that Wollweber was OGPU chief in Western Europe. Certainly, Stalin could not have found a better man. Wollweber was clever and imaginative, and he had already worked out plans for destroying the Nazis by sabotage and a counter-terror. One of these plans involved the murder of Hitler, Goering, Hess, Goebbels and the rest of the leadership of the Nazi Party during a Reichstag session or a Party Day. But his plans were rejected, allegedly because the Communists were opposed to individual terrorism. Wollweber was by no means convinced, but for once he obeyed Party orders. The reckless, hot-headed sailor had cooled off with the years.

At another time Wollweber tried to fulfil his oath to avenge the murder of Liebknecht and Luxemburg. For months he had Pflugk-Hartung followed every day, hoping to kidnap him in Copenhagen and take him on a Russian ship. But just before his plans were mature, Pflugk-Hartung fell ill and was sent to a hospital. Thus fate intervened, perhaps in order that the duel of destiny between these two men might not end prematurely.

But we shall speak of this later; here we are concerned only with Wollweber's personal life.

To be sure, Wollweber insisted that he had no personal life, that his existence was utterly devoted to the Party. Nevertheless, he found time to amuse himself now and then.

Hundreds of agents worked for him throughout Europe. Many of these agents were women, women who traveled as baronesses on false passports, women who were supplied with plenty of money and expensive clothing, "so that the stupid capitalist police will think they are bourgeois." Wollweber had many women, but they were all women of the people; even in the tenderer realm of emotion he remained true to his proletarian principles. Women party comrades and friends of his youth were his preference. He believed sincerely that revolutionaries needed women, many of them; in this respect he always pointed to Danton as his model.

And the women were loyal to him both as mistresses and agents. He is one of the few spies who can truthfully boast that no woman ever betrayed him.

After women, his great interest was the youth of the Party. In Sweden and Denmark he gave, under an assumed name, short courses in Communism for young people. He told the Communist youth: "You have enough teachers of theory. I want to show you how to fill cigarettes with dynamite and use them as bombs." He lectured only to selected young party leaders and made an unforgettable impression on the boys. Valtin describes him in his book as an impressive man, a man one did not forget, whether or not one agreed with him.

Then there was drink and food. Wollweber needs his ten bottles of beer daily and enormous quantities of food. Swedish smorgasbord and Danish aquavit could make even this master spy forsake his usual caution.

It is impossible to discuss this man simply as a common criminal and murderer, as the Swedish police chief had done in his conversation with me.

Wollweber is a man possessed. He is one of those great historical figures who murder, kill, rob and spy in order to help the tragic horde of the underprivileged. Such men, no matter how great their idealism and their piety, have always brought destruction upon themselves. Wollweber, the eternal revolutionary, will never be able to fit into civilian life. His life goal is world revolution, permanent class struggle, and he is wholly dedicated to this goal. In his way, he is a patriot of international fraternity, just as Pflugk-Hartung is a patriot of Greater Germany. Neither is interested in money or honor or fame; both perform the basest acts because they think them necessary for the freedom and the victory of their people. The two men have never spoken a word to each other, nor would they understand each other; they come from different social strata, but they have one prime trait in common: both would gladly sacrifice their lives for their ideas. Criminals though they may be—and both have many men's lives on their conscience—they are soldiers in great opposing armies; both will die a soldierly death, without ever feeling that their acts may have been criminal.

After six years of watching Pflugk-Hartung and his agents, Wollweber felt that he had enough information. He deliberately let his information fall into the hands of two British Secret Service agents who had their headquarters at the Hotel Angleterre in Copenhagen. It was no accident, therefore, that a British protest resulted in the temporary confounding of Russia's enemies in Denmark.

On April 9, 1940, when Heinrich Himmler freed Pflugk-Hartung from his prison cell and then drove to the Palace of Justice, the documents concerning Pflugk-Hartung were not the only ones they looked up. They also had copies made of the documents in the case of "Willy Schmidt alias Kurt Mueller alias Ivar alias Anton Berg alias Ernst Friedrich Wollweber." We shall have more to say about these papers in a later chapter.

4. Nazi Puppet-Masters

Admiral Wilhelm Canaris, a powerful man who is responsible only to Hitler, directs German espionage in World War II.

Hitler chose for his espionage chief a cold, tireless genius, a man utterly without heart or conscience, a man who is capable of working twenty hours a day and who has been trained as a General Staff officer. This man was one of Colonel Nicolai's most competent subordinates in the Imperial espionage service.

Admiral Canaris is one of the few high officials who are kept obscure in Nazi Germany. But although his name is relatively unknown, he has almost unlimited power. Responsible only to Hitler, his power behind the scenes is almost beyond conjecture; his work bears grim witness to the truth that knowledge is power. He is the Nazi super-spy. His is the brain that controls and directs the greatest mass espionage system ever conceived.

He might be called an engineer in the military sense of the word for in all instances of Nazi treason and conquest it was his sappers who first undermined the foundations of the opposing nation's defenses. It was only after he had done his work that the mechanized army moved to attack.

For years his office on the Luetzow Ufer has been collecting a catalogue of details on the personal habits, ambitions and weaknesses of potential Quislings in all quarters of the globe. In its files were notes on Bonnet, Laval, Marcel Deat and other betrayers of France. The files recorded which ones could be bought with money, which with women and which with promises of political reward. The records noted the neurotic frustration and extravagant ambition of Vidkun Quisling—Pflugk-Hartung had reported on him in hundreds of pages. It gave details on Guido Schmidt of Austria; it marked out Hacha of Czechoslovakia and Josef Beck of Poland.

In those files are ponderous briefs on Tanakoff of Bulgaria, Kosic of Yugoslavia, and Fritz Kuhn of these United States. The files analyzed and rejected Dr. Fritz Clausen of Denmark; they recommended that Premier Erik Scavenius take over his Quisling role.

When the time was ripe, the director of this office consulted his files. He chose the eight saboteurs who came to America out of his list of names. But his contribution to the Nazi effort is far more sinister than that. His adeptness in espionage technique, his genius in organization, are responsible for the terrible toll of Allied merchant ship sinkings. Not only did he organize the German espionage service into the greatest spy system in the world, but he also set up the "White Department" of the Japanese Secret Service. He trained Europeans in his spy school at Walchensee in Bavaria and placed them at the disposition of the Japanese—this in the name of preventing the "decline of the west."

Pflugk-Hartung, the professorial, gentlemanly spy, is his best agent, but even he is only a small link in the great chain of Nazi espionage. Nevertheless, there is a close bond between him and Chief Canaris. The men are friends, they started out around the same time, they are the same age and the same stature, physically and mentally.

But while Pflugk-Hartung may be considered a prepossessing man, Canaris has the face of the typical Prussian officer, a hard-bitten, tight-lipped man.

Admiral Wilhelm Canaris began his career like Pflugk-Hartung as a naval cadet, and was picked by Nicolai for espionage work. He was a lieutenant-commander in 1918; it was none other than Hitler who promoted him within a few months to Admiral.

Hitler knew perfectly well why he was advancing this man over the heads of so many others, and why he gave him blanket powers such as no other Nazi leader possessed. For the story of Wilhelm Canaris is inextricably bound up with the history of Germany's preparations for a war of revenge, and with the history of the German Secret Service from the Versailles Treaty to the Second World War.

The peace treaty had been signed. But the Prussian Army insisted it had never been defeated. It was "the stab in the back" that had given Germany over to revolutionaries like Wollweber; Socialists like Ebert, Scheidemann and the murdered Hilferding, had cravenly abandoned the struggle. The Prussian Army pointed out that Allied troops had never marched triumphantly through Berlin's Brandenburger Tor; the Victory Boulevard of the glorious kings of Prussia had not been trespassed upon even by the revolutionists and republicans and still bore witness to the fact that the Prussians were a superior breed of humanity.

The Allies had permitted Germany an army of only 100,000 men and fondly believed that thereby they had destroyed her for all time as a military power.

It is not Hitler who created the new German army, nor was he the founder of the great German espionage apparatus.

The German army was rebuilt by General Hans von Seeckt, one of Germany's great strategists. Out of defeat and decay he molded the most modern army in Europe, the army that was later to become the model for the Russian and Italian armies, and still later for the armies of the United Nations themselves.

Seeckt was a great believer in legality. The peace treaty had prohibited an army large enough to be of the slightest use and so Seeckt created a peacetime "cadre" army. An intelligence service was prohibited; so Seeckt created a department with quite another name.

The Allies thought Germany could not make war with a hundred thousand soldiers. It was years before they discovered that these 100,000 men were not being trained as common soldiers, or as lieutenants; every one of the 100,000 men in the German Army received the training of a General Staff officer. No army on earth has 100,000 General Staff officers—and that is one reason why there are forty-year-old generals in Germany today. Every one of those 100,000 men is a commanding officer in the present German Army. This was General Hans von Seeckt's gift to Adolf Hitler.

In 1920 General von Seeckt called Lieutenant-Commander Wilhelm Canaris to the War Ministry and informed him that he needed a capable intelligence officer of the last war to work in a new bureau that would have no connection with the Reichswehr. This new bureau required the utmost secrecy; it must be built up carefully and intelligently, and above all its true function must be kept secret from France and England. The Reichswehr would pay Canaris as a civilian employee, but he would have no official connection with the War Ministry; he had to disguise all his activities as those of a private person and must never admit—even should he be brought to court—that he was working as an agent for General Seeckt.

That September day in 1920 witnessed the birth of the new German Secret Service. Admiral Canaris became Chief of the Investigation Bureau of the "Black Reichswehr"—the secret army of 300,000 soldiers which had been organized in defiance of the Versailles Treaty and camouflaged under the guise of civil service.

The duties of the former Intelligence officer were multitudinous. And they were consistent with Germany's flagrant repudiation of her peace treaties. Ostensibly, Canaris checked Communist activities and fought Russia's OGPU. He traced other former officers of the Imperial armies to learn which ones could be enlisted against the Republic—and through his investigations found many of them leading the volunteer groups of "Free Corps" which were operating on the Polish border.

A further duty of Canaris was to locate all arms and munitions within Germany. All implements of war were supposed to be turned over to the Allies, but Canaris laid his hands on much armament, which he either gave to the Free Corps or held in readiness for the rapidly-growing illegal army. After Canaris had located the chief hiding-places of weapons in Germany and secured them for the Reichswehr and the Black Reichswehr, General von Seeckt, the newly-appointed Minister of Defense, set him to new tasks.

Colonel Liese of the Stettin Military District became Canaris's new superior. Liese requested Canaris to organize the *Grenzschutz,* or Border Guard, on all the German frontiers. Outwardly this organization was a harmless enough civilian defense group somewhat resembling our National Guard. But its membership consisted of such accomplished spies as Pflugk-Hartung and Manfred von Killinger, who commanded hundreds of unemployed army officers, Free Corps leaders, terrorists, putschists and would-be putschists. Colonel Liese, who received financial and moral support from the Third Military District of Reichswehr, became the military leader of this organization.

Freiher von Gablenz, today one of Hitler's generals, was Liese's adjutant; Canaris was the executive organizer.

With the utmost simplicity Canaris had established a new espionage organization. The civil head was the Commissioner of Public Order, and the agents appeared on the payrolls as civil service employees.

The *Grenzschutz* employed men like Heines, who later became Nazi chief of police in Breslau, and the "Hangman," Reinhardt Heydrich, who joined after the suppression of the Halle riots against the Republic, which he had incited.

Detachments of the *Grenzschutz* were posted on the borders of Poland, Czechoslovakia, France, Belgium, Austria, Switzerland, Holland and Denmark. Canaris visited each detachment in turn to give his espionage agents their instructions and to supply them with false passports so that they could cross the border. They were commanded to locate the most advantageous points for invasion, and above all to find sub-agents who would keep Germany informed of any new border fortifications in the neighboring country. Thus, Canaris and his spies kept abreast of the construction of the French Maginot Line.

The *Grenzschutz* served its purpose well until it was incorporated into the Investigation Bureau of Ribbentrop's growing espionage organization.

Canaris was, as ever, restlessly ambitious. He did his duty, but he hated his lowly status, which included not being permitted to hold an official position in the Reichswehr. His great dream was to return to the Army. It was this dream which led him in 1920 to take part in the Kapp-putsch; but the putsch failed and he was compelled to put by his ambition for a while.

After this failure he went to see Walter von Nicolai, his former chief, and requested him to help him obtain an official post in the Reichswehr. Nicolai's influence was great enough to persuade Seeckt, and so Lieutenant-Commander Canaris became Liaison Officer between the Reichswehr, on one hand, and the Black Reichswehr and the *Grenzschutz,* his own organizations, on the other.

Since Canaris was originally a Navy man, he was asked to lay the foundation for a new Naval Intelligence Bureau. He set about doing this, but his chief concern remained the organization of the Black Reichswehr and its espionage service.

In fact, the Black Reichswehr was expanding so rapidly that it became necessary to supply it with funds from new sources. The stratagems the leaders adopted were naive in the extreme. General Seeckt, the Defense Minister, presented Canaris with funds from the regular army allotment. Canaris invested the money in a large film company (Phoebus) which guaranteed a thirty per cent return on the investment. A first dividend was paid, but when Germany's inflation policy set in, the company was ruined. Canaris had bought for millions of marks stocks of the Phoebus Motion Picture Studios and the money was gone. The people wanted to know from what sources Canaris had received the money. In the ensuing Government investigation the scandal came out. In court, however, Canaris said to the judges: "I am not allowed to reveal my sources. This is on orders from the General Staff."

The investigation indicated that Canaris had worked in a camouflaged outfit called the "Department of Naval Transport" and nobody had suspected his money transactions. Canaris was discharged from the War Department, but he continued to operate from his home and received as his assistant Lieutenant-Commander Steffan, who later became under Hitler military attaché in Sweden, Norway, Finland and Denmark.

Furthermore the investigation indicated that men like Canaris are also personally unscrupulous, for he was shown to be a reckless gambler, overwhelmed with personal debts. Officially, General Seeckt's Reichswehr declared that such men besmirched the tradition and the noble reputation of the Prussian Army.

Nevertheless, Canaris had won the reputation of being uniquely qualified for espionage. As early as 1929 Goering convinced Hitler that Canaris was the right man to build up a first-class spy apparatus for the Nazi Party. Hitler decided to employ him.

Canaris's first job for the Nazi Party was wholly in the realm of personality research. Hitler asked him for a complete study of the political opinions, the private affairs and the economic status of all officers of the Reichswehr. For years before the seizure of power Canaris was thus busy rummaging for potential betrayers of the Weimar Republic in the Prussian Army. He must have done a good job, for the Nazi leaders won over to the Party one officer after the other.

Canaris and Papen prepared for the Nazis the fateful documents on General Schleicher. These were presented to Hindenburg and purported to show that Schleicher had undertaken "Bolshevist" experiments in distribution of land. It was Canaris who assembled the documents that sealed the fate of General Schleicher. These documents set forth plans for establishing the unemployed on the vast, unprofitable estates of the Prussian Junkers, and for breaking up these estates, which were subsidized by the State. These Prussian Junkers were Hindenburg's friends. These documents were the sum total of Canaris's "evidence" that General Kurt von Schleicher harbored secret plans to "bolshevize" Germany. Perhaps more than any other factor, these documents precipitated Schleicher's fall from Premier of Germany, and made way for Hitler's subsequent accession to power.

There is no doubt that Canaris could never have made such headway with his subversive activity within the German Reichswehr without the aid and protection of the Old Masters of German espionage, Colonel Nicolai and Franz von Papen.

Hitler, when he came to power, generously recompensed his faithful spy by entrusting him with the Nazi Secret Service. From now on the information in Hitler's files was no longer restricted to data on friends and foes within the German army. Canaris located the friends and foes of Nazism in all the armies and all the police headquarters of the world. The ambitious Admiral went to work with a will, for this was his opportunity to show his ability to organize espionage over the entire world for the coming global war.

For the present, however, Canaris was established as a department head in the Foreign Office whose Minister was Joachim von Ribbentrop, the former champagne salesman. Canaris was assigned to reorganizing naval espionage.

Ostensibly subordinate to Ribbentrop, Canaris began work on his own initiative, his work taking two forms that interlocked under some circumstances. At the beginning he devoted himself, as it were, to clearing the field for action, employing for this purpose only political and diplomatic agents. During his first years of military espionage, he was extremely cautious in his choice of agents, for during this period he had not yet subscribed to the principle of mass espionage. The few agents he chose were exceptionally competent. They were not the mythical spies with false beards and sham limps, with pebbles bouncing around in their mouths to disguise their voices. They were like the distinguished-looking Pflugk-Hartung, men of culture and good breeding, acceptable anywhere, often men with diplomatic immunity whose friendship was obviously desirable to many. For the present Canaris instructed his agents to listen carefully but not to act. Their duties were pure reconnaissance.

His objective was to place German observers where they could see and hear, and could transmit their information and receive new orders. Partly by sheer genius, partly by plain cunning, Wilhelm Canaris established a harbor espionage system that covered the entire world and yielded incredible results. At heart Canaris was a Navy man. He understood shipping and its vital importance both to the economy and the sinews of war. Other agencies in Germany were building with feverish speed the most effective instruments for ship destruction. It was Canaris's self-imposed task to be informed where and when enemy ships would be available for torpedo, mine or shell. On the face of it, the task was simple; every ship sails from a port and returns to a port, as a plane to its carrier or base. Actually this work was of enormous complexity, but not too great for the malevolent genius of Wilhelm Canaris.

Canaris's broad and diversified plans had one principle never departed from: all persons in this service, whether officials of the Reich or passing as private individuals, must have their places of business and residence as near as practicable to the waterfront.

Naturally, Canaris's first efforts were directed near at home. He set himself to work out plans for the destruction of the British North Sea and Russian Baltic Sea fleets.

His old friend and colleague of World War I days, Pflugk-Hartung, was called to Berlin and given his instructions. Canaris instructed Pflugk-Hartung to assign a German agent to every fifty miles of the immense Scandinavian coastline, so that no fact about the merchant marine of Britain, Russia, Poland and other nations would escape the eye of German espionage. In effect Canaris asked Pflugk-Hartung to transform the Baltic Sea into a

German "Mare Nostrum"; he wished to know of the arrival and departure of every ship, the names of all the Baltic captains, the number of crewmen on every vessel, the destination, consignor and consignee of every cargo. Such an undertaking was expensive, of course, but Pflugk-Hartung was given a blank check.

I investigated the Canaris harbor spy system from Helsinki to Helsingoer, from Esbjerg to the North Cape. Everywhere I found that German consulates or legations "happened" to be located on the seashore. Everywhere I found Scandinavians of German descent living on or near the waterfront.

The most obvious case was that of the German consulate in Malmoe, Sweden. From its windows one could observe with the naked eye, or with weak binoculars, every ship that passed through the narrow sound to enter or leave the Baltic Sea. It was some time before the Swedish authorities unmasked Consul Alexander Bogs as an agent to Canaris; Bogs promptly discovered that the climate of Sweden disagreed with his liver, and left the country.

In the harbor of Malmoe consulate windows gave a view of the traffic of the Baltic just as a house in Bay Ridge, Brooklyn, on the Narrows, may overlook Tompkinsville, or a house on the Staten Island shore may overlook the upper Bay and the Narrows.

Wherever it was feasible Canaris's agents bribed fishermen who were ideally situated to observe passing vessels.

Even after the outbreak of the war, Canaris contrived to keep his agents in every Scandinavian port.

He had many irons in the fire. As adviser of a Swedish refugee committee, I was visited one day by a fellow journalist. He was a small bald chap named Curt Haas who earned his living by acting as go-between in small affairs that were rather on the shady side. He told me his life story, showed me proofs that he had been arrested in the course of the Reichstag Fire Trial, and asked for aid. It was more or less a routine case. I promised to help the man. This promise evoked an outburst of confidences, and Haas told me of his unhappy love for Rosemarie Richter, whom I later met.

Rosemarie came from Hamburg and was married to a wealthy man whom she hated; she alleged that he was always drunk and used to beat her. She had turned to Haas for love and consolation. Since she herself was a beautiful woman, tall, blonde and expensively dressed, while the journalist was decidedly small, ugly and badly-educated, I was not a little puzzled by the relationship. But love knows no rules, I concluded, and did not worry about it.

The difficulty for Haas was that Rosemarie would not get a divorce. She feared poverty and had no inclination to share Haas's furnished room.

Her husband, George Richter, was the editor of a fairly well-known and rather well-edited technical newspaper for the fishing industry. The paper was published in Stockholm. George Richter traveled a great deal and published picture reportage of all parts of Scandinavia that were important to the fishing industry. Naturally, he had admission to all ports. He made a practice of interviewing everyone he met from shoal pilots to fishing captains. He knew every port, every fish canning factory and thousands of fishermen throughout Scandinavia.

George Richter finally made a slip. The Norwegian police arrested him just as he was photographing naval fortifications instead of fishing boats, and after the outbreak of the war in 1939 he was sentenced to several years' imprisonment.

Curt Haas, the lover of unhappily-wedded Rosemarie Richter, now had a chance to obtain a divorce. He hoped he would be able to marry beautiful Rosemarie. Indeed, he was particularly eager to marry her now, since shortly after her husband's arrest she had inherited a large sum of money. She explained that the Nazis had given special permission for her to receive this money from Germany, in spite of the existing restrictions against the export of money.

Haas, however, was an unlucky chap. The Nazis were afraid he knew too much about Richter. And so, one day, Curt Haas met with an accident. He was drowned while swimming. No one knew how or why; he simply did not return from his swim. His beloved Rosemarie disappeared at the same time. However, she was not drowned, for the following day Miss Rosemarie Koenig, daughter of the Colonel Koenig who works in Canaris's office, arrived in Hamburg. Rosemarie Richter-Koenig's mission in Scandinavia was over. Her husband was released from prison on April 9, 1940, and returned to Hamburg and the arms of his "unhappy" Rosemarie.

Canaris commands a many-tentacled organization. The following agencies work for him, directly or indirectly:

> The Office of Joachim von Ribbentrop
> The Office of Ernst Wilhelm Bohle (Germans Living Abroad)
> The Ministry of Joseph Goebbels
> The Political College (Hochschule fuer Politik)
> The Seminar for Geopolitics (Professor Karl Haushofer)
> Foreign Departments of the Nazi Party
> All Fascist parties abroad
> Army and Navy Intelligence Services
> The Special Investigation Divisions of every Governmental Agency
> Student Exchanges
> Anti-Jewish World League

Nordic Society
German Colonial Society
Embassies and Consulates
Last, but not least, the Gestapo.

The Foreign Division of the Gestapo has achieved world notoriety, and Heinrich Himmler is considered to be the great organizer of the Gestapo. But the man behind the scenes, the man to whom Himmler owes his fame, the real organizer of the Gestapo, is almost as unknown abroad as Admiral Canaris. This man is Dr. Werner Best, the most able agent Canaris possessed within Germany up to the end of 1942.

While Admiral Canaris is Germany's espionage chief in the realm of military and naval affairs, Brigade Führer Dr. Werner Best is Germany's chief detective in the government and in civilian life. Together, the two men control the entire espionage system of Greater Germany.

In chapter one we have already met Dr. Best in 1934, in Berlin, when he conferred with Carlis Hansen, the Danish Nazi who was to kidnap Wollweber.

Werner Best had distinguished himself in Germany when he was still a boy of fifteen. His father had fallen in France, and the boy hated France and the French occupation troops in the Rhineland with all his youthful ardor. In school, Werner Best had been an outstanding pupil, and his teachers forecast a splendid career for him.

For his extraordinary scholarship, Werner Best was to have received a medal. This medal was to be presented to him by a French occupation officer in the auditorium of his school, before the assembled pupils and teachers.

Dozens of French officers were present, when Werner Best unexpectedly refused to accept the medal with the words: "I will accept no medals from the enemies of my Fatherland."

The French officers sat in horrified embarrassment while a tremendous uproar broke out in the auditorium. Werner Best, the model pupil, was expelled from school.

Vowing revenge on the democratic government and the democratic educational system, young Werner joined the National Socialist youth group. He was accepted by another school and later attended the university, where he studied law. Naturally, he was one of those students who still clung to the old tradition of dueling and drinking. He was also a member of the Nazi Student League, and made a morbid habit of informing everyone that democracy had ruined his boyhood. Best had a rare capacity for hatred. He soon became a Storm Troop leader, then entered the Elite Guard and before long was Nazi leader in Hessen, although he earned his living by working for the democratic judicial authorities in Hessen.

In 1932 Werner Best made the headlines in all German newspapers, and received considerable notice abroad. At a secret session of Nazi leaders in Worms the talented Dr. Best had outlined an original blueprint for an uprising. The object of the plan was to give the Nazis sole power in Hessen. Best's plan contained detailed instructions on who was to be shot, who arrested, and who taken into the new government. He described how the police and army headquarters were to be occupied.

In the smoke-laden room of the restaurant in Worms where the meeting was held, a great deal of beer was drunk and the plan was accepted. The Nazi leaders decided to carry it out within a few weeks.

However, the Nazi Landtag deputy, Dr. Schaefer, became worried. He left Worms that night, brought the Police Chief of Frankfurt a copy of the plan, and thus betrayed the entire conspiracy.

Dr. Werner Best was arrested, but quickly released. A trial for high treason was proposed but never took place.

He was, however, expelled from the Hessian Ministry of Justice, and until Hitler took power he earned his living as a speaker for the Nazi Party at public meetings.

Immediately after the Nazis took power, Best was appointed organizational chief of the Gestapo. He was also made liaison officer with Canaris's Intelligence Bureau, and for years he was the only official of the Gestapo whose decrees were valid without Himmler's countersignature.

Today Werner Best is thirty-nine years old. He is a small man with dark, "non-Aryan" hair. He had compensated for the inferiority feelings stemming from his physical weakness by exercising brutal violence and terror upon all his enemies. In fact, he so distinguished himself for brutality that for years he worked as deputy of Reinhardt Heydrich. Best considers himself a scholar; he is inordinately proud of his legal and academic career. Now and then he writes pamphlets and articles. Thus, in June 1942, he wrote for General Haushofer's *Zeitschrift fuer Geopolitik* an article entitled *The Great Living Space and Its Administration*. Here he declared that the total annihilation of nations did not violate the laws of life if such annihilation were really total and no survivors remained.

For a short time he was police chief in Hessen; thus he was able belatedly to carry out the executions he had earlier planned. In 1935 he took the additional office of Chief of the "Justice" Department of the Gestapo. After the occupation of France Admiral Canaris requested his services for the occupied country and made him Chief of the Military Administration in France.

For Canaris, Best organized a widespread espionage network within conquered France. He then returned to his Gestapo work. In November 1942 Werner Best was appointed Minister to Denmark, though he had had no diplomatic schooling at all. This appointment made him virtual master of Denmark. Canaris had found it necessary to send Pflugk-Hartung to Rumania. Fearing an Allied invasion of Norway or Denmark, he sent his best man to this vital position on the "home front" as Pflugk-Hartung's successor. Thus, he assigned to the Baltic and North Sea District an espionage chief of great capabilities, a man whom the Allies dare not underestimate.

But this very act is significant. It signifies that Admiral Canaris is worried.

PART TWO
Something Rotten in the State of Denmark
5. Pflugk-Hartung at Work

The Germans, though their shoreline on the Baltic Sea is scarcely one tenth as long as that of Scandinavia and the Baltic States, have always referred to it arrogantly as the "deutsches Meer." With similar arrogance they paraded in the streets of Copenhagen in their green raincoats and green hats, disregarding the local traffic regulations and speaking German so loudly that one sometimes wondered whether the capital of Denmark was indeed a Danish city.

For many years Denmark was their favorite weekend resort, and with unabashed rudeness they made themselves at home. Before the invasion, dozens of weekend steamers came to Denmark, chiefly under the auspices of the "Strength Through Joy" movement. Though they were allowed to spend only ten "travel marks," the Nazis tried to gulp as much as possible of this Danish Eden. Danish butter, whose quality was famous throughout the world, had not been seen for years in Germany; unskimmed milk was unknown in the land of the Nazis. The Germans came to Denmark to eat and drink, and they did both with a will.

It was easy for Canaris and Pflugk-Hartung to stow away their subversive agents among the tens of thousands of visitors and tourists.

Denmark sensed the nearness of invasion, sensed the greedy, clawing hand of her great neighbor. But to the last the aging King Christian X rode daily through the streets of Copenhagen at seven in the morning to assure himself that all was well with his land. He rode alone, greeted jubilantly by workers going to work, by mail carriers, milk boys and all those whose business made them early risers.

The King of Denmark has always been a true democrat. He could well ride through Copenhagen unaccompanied. He needed no armored car when he appeared before his people; he was surrounded by no bodyguard when he visited the theater like any other mortal, or when he amused himself with all the rest of the world under the colorful lanterns of the Tivoli. He and Prime Minister Stauning were popular figures; King Christian was a servant of his people who happened to be King, but who would have served Denmark equally well had he been Mr. Jensen or Mr. Nielsen.

His son, the Crown Prince Frederik, went to the same school as other Danish children. Frederik, who has now relieved his aging father of many administrative burdens, played in the park or on the beach with the children of the people. Democracy is part and parcel of the Royal House of Denmark. Which is why the fat Danish Nazi leader, Dr. Fritz Clausen, reviles the king as "Chief Jew" and calls the late Prime Minister Stauning a "Bolshevistic Jew lover." A libelous tongue may say what it will in the shadow of the German army.

Premier Stauning was intelligent enough to foresee the fate of Denmark. In 1937 he declared in a bold speech to Swedish students of the Lund University that in spite of all the cooperation and friendship among the Scandinavian nations, in reality Denmark stood alone and would fall as the first victim, without the other Scandinavian countries helping or being able to help.

Stauning, who died in 1942, was considered one of the greatest social reformers of his country. Denmark called him the father of the "New Deal."

Duel for the Northland

Denmark possesses the richest and most highly developed agriculture of Europe; consequently this land was always an alluring morsel to its land-hungry neighbor of the South. In 1864 Hitler's Prussian predecessor, Bismarck, had fallen upon Denmark and Hitler intended to follow the precedent, for Denmark's strategic position was invaluable to German geopolitics. It faced England, and it controlled the channel that was the entrance to the great inland sea. Whoever controlled Denmark could bottle Russia in the Baltic, overrun the Baltic countries, decide what Finland would be allowed to import, and hold Sweden and Norway in check.

The Russians were not unaware of this; it is not surprising, therefore, that they made Copenhagen the headquarters of their secret service in Scandinavia. And this in turn made it necessary for Canaris's men to devote much of their time to counterespionage against the Soviet Union.

In Admiral Canaris's famous files there was a card bearing the name:

EILER PONTOPPIDAN
Lawyer
Copenhagen

On a summer morning in the year 1936, Pflugk-Hartung called at the well-known lawyer's office and went armed with all necessary information on Pontoppidan's life.

Pontoppidan was ambitious. He spent enormous sums of money on women; he wanted to enter public life, but found it difficult because the Danes disliked his pro-German sentiments. Admiral Canaris had first taken notice of him after he applied for the position of lawyer at the German Legation in Copenhagen and clearly indicated that he was interested in "collaboration."

Spies have been bought for the equivalent of $50—that is, 200 kroner. But Pontoppidan was more expensive; he demanded and got 20,000 kroner a year. (The purchasing power of 20,000 kroner amounted to far more than its monetary value of $5,000; it was a small fortune in Denmark.)

Pontoppidan is an ugly man, nearly sixty, with a double chin and pouchy cheeks. He wears dark spectacles over his baggy eyes, and carries a lawyer's briefcase wherever he goes. But he is a good lawyer, a clear and logical thinker.

Pontoppidan's task was to organize on a grand scale.

With his large clientele of criminals, Pontoppidan was ideally situated to recruit spies for the Nazis. A keen judge of men, he also chose those who had the greatest ability among the Danish Nazis and assigned them special tasks.

In the Danish Commercial Register for the year 1936 the name appeared of a new firm incorporated by three Danes. The firm opened offices in the Vesterport, in the center of Copenhagen, not far from the Raadhuspladsen, the City Hall. The new firm was one of many that imported radio sets from abroad. Its office had five rooms, and looked like a busy one. There was a large packing room and storeroom crammed with Dutch and American radio sets. For the Continental Radio Company did not deal in radios made in Germany. In fact, the firm participated in the boycott of German goods, and the sales people of the company, who traveled by automobile throughout the country, candidly told their customers that this was the firm's policy. They were well liked for it, since few people in Denmark wanted to buy German goods.

Agrarian Denmark possessed no native radio industry, and therefore depended on radios of Dutch, American or German make. However, the new firm did not do too well; although it employed six salesmen, the yearly gross did not amount to more than 10,000 kroner—although the books showed sales in the neighborhood of 100,000 kroner.

The technical directors of the firm were named Kyrre and Rambov, and the president of the company was a lawyer, Eiler Pontoppidan himself.

Thus the German spy headquarters were established in one of the most modern business buildings in Copenhagen—and incidentally next door to the offices of the Soviet Trade Delegation.

Kyrre and Rambov were talented electrical engineers. In court experts of the Danish Telephone Company professed great admiration for their skill. One night the two men broke into the office of the Soviet Trade Delegation. They carried out no search, examined no desk drawers, purloined no documents; all they did was to connect the telephone line of the Russian Trade Delegation with the office of the Continental Radio Company. The result was that for fifteen months the German spies listened to every telephone conversation of the Russian Trade Delegation, made stenographic copies, and sent them on to Berlin.

From time to time a gentleman named Dr. Erich Ring visited the office to buy radio sets. Ring, alias Pflugk-Hartung, enjoyed these visits. He would sit for hours in Pontoppidan's room, listening to Russian conversations. Canaris thoughtfully had sent three linguists to Copenhagen, since the Russians spoke virtually every language but Danish on the telephone.

Through this listening post Pflugk-Hartung was able to keep a close check on Russian trade in the Baltic area; he could unmask for himself Russian couriers and detect Russian espionage activity behind the cloak of Soviet diplomatic immunity. But he did not see or hear what he had hoped, for his great antagonist, Wollweber, never visited this official Soviet establishment. Quaintly enough, Wollweber had his office camouflaged as a brokerage firm—in the same office building. Indeed, he had suspected the radio company for some time, but had been unable to obtain definite proofs against it.

Having set up the radio company, Pflugk-Hartung assigned Pontoppidan to further tasks. He gave him a list of fifty agents in various ports of Denmark and on some of the small and minute islands that dot the coastline. These men were to receive American radio sets—six tube sets with which they could listen to Germany, if not to America. What was more important, they could also send intelligence to Germany by short wave. The sets were distributed to the agents just a year before the outbreak of the war.

For a time after this the radio company rested on its laurels. Pflugk-Hartung was running into difficulties, and had advised Pontoppidan to devote himself chiefly to his legal practice for the present and to run the radio firm as legally as possible. He wanted no risks taken. War was imminent, and his organization must be prepared for action. Since the salaries of Pontoppidan, Kyrre and Rambov were in no way reduced, they were not averse to taking it easy.

The year was 1937. Pflugk-Hartung, a man not easily discomposed, was betraying signs of nervousness. In his large study, with two walls lined with books and an immense glass wall that looked out over the sea, sat a Danish citizen. The Dane, a police official by the name of Max Pelving, was pale and trembling with fear as he declared to Pflugk-Hartung that this time he could not help him. Pflugk-Hartung's face flushed red; the veins in his forehead swelled, and he spoke loudly, which he rarely did. From Pelving's testimony in court later on, we can reconstruct the subject of their conversation.

A German Social Democrat named Heinrich Stau had arrived in Copenhagen. He was one of the thousands of refugees who had escaped at night in a small motorboat from the German Frisian Islands to Denmark.

Heinrich Stau, a good-looking man of about thirty-five, came from Luebeck. He had been an airplane engineer, and during the past several years had worked in the great Dornier factories at Luebeck. Among other things, he had constructed from the blueprints the latest Dornier warplane, and had devised certain parts for a new bomber.

Stau himself never realized how important he was to the Nazis. Secretly he worked in the underground movement; secure in his position as an engineer, he had helped many of his comrades in the underground movement to escape to Denmark, and had himself smuggled documents and funds of the suppressed Social Democratic Party to Denmark. The Nazis had at last become suspicious of him; warned, he fled to Denmark shortly before his arrest, leaving behind his wife and four children.

In Copenhagen old friends of Stau's helped him. Stau did not know that these friends had long since ceased to be members of the Social Democrat Party; they had abandoned their moderate liberalism and were working for Wollweber's Russian Secret Service.

These friends told Stau that a large Danish newspaper wished to publish an article on Dornier and desired a copy of the blueprints of the new warplane. His drawings from memory would suffice, they said. Stau, who was eager to find work in Denmark, had some drawings of his work with him; it was an easy matter to reconstruct the desired blueprints for the "Danish newspaper." Stau received a moderate sum in payment—enough to live on for several weeks. The article was never published.

The German counterespionage organization then got wind that Russia had obtained Stau's blueprints. Canaris sent a special courier to Copenhagen to start counteraction at once. At whatever cost, he directed, Stau must be brought back to Germany.

Max Pelving, the head of the Danish Alien Squad, was to help Pflugk-Hartung. Germany had already sent a request for extradition to the Danish police. The Luebeck police informed the Danish Alien Squad that Stau was wanted for criminal embezzlement; under mutual treaties between Denmark and Germany, each country was required to extradite those wanted on criminal charges. But Pelving pointed out to Pflugk-Hartung that Stau was a Social Democrat, a member of the brother Party to which Premier Stauning of Denmark belonged; there was no chance, he said, that the Danish Government would consent to his extradition.

Pflugk-Hartung insisted that Pelving arrest him; they would see then what the outcome would be. Pelving declared that the Ministry of Justice would never permit it, and that Stau would be released two hours after his arrest.

Taking no chances, Stau escaped to Sweden without waiting for the Government's decision upon the extradition request. Here he told me the entire story, expressing his deep regret that he had allowed himself to be tricked into aiding the Russian agents.

In Sweden he was arrested and brought to trial. The Swedish Court decided that he was innocent under Swedish law; only a German Court could decide whether he was guilty under German law. Swedish Foreign Minister Rickard Sandler saved the engineer's life by refusing to turn him over to a German Court for trial.

But what of Max Pelving in whose hands the fate of Stau had for a moment rested? He is a man of forty-seven, of large stature, with dark-brown hair and a high intelligent forehead. He has conspicuously protruding ears, a small mouth and bushy eyebrows. He habitually tries to disguise the rather comical effect of his protruding ears by wearing a stiff high collar and a dignified air. His lips are rather full and his jaw weak, and Pelving is indeed something of a weakling. Which is why we know so much about him and his activities.

Pelving was introduced to Pflugk-Hartung by Andreas Hansen, the Copenhagen Chief of Police. The introduction proved fruitful to the German spy master. Pelving and Pflugk-Hartung can claim to their joint credit a large number of the hundreds of people executed and the thousands thrown into concentration camps in Germany.

For Pelving was the man in Denmark who had the power to give or withhold permission for a political refugee to remain in the country. Every political refugee passed through his office. And Pelving required of each that he prove he was not a Nazi and give some evidence that he had worked in the underground movement against Hitler.

Pelving demanded concrete details. In what city had the refugee worked, what underground workers did he know, where had he hidden illegal leaflets or weapons? Every answer meant new arrests by Dr. Best and his Gestapo.

In court Max Pelving later confessed that he had sent reports to Germany in a total of forty-four cases; he denied the charge that he had sent copies of every single case that came into his office. The number of cases he confessed to exactly agreed, oddly enough, with the number of cases in which the Danish prosecutor, Harald Petersen, could prove that he had sent reports to Germany: forty-four. Assuming, however, that it was only forty-four, those forty-four cases resulted in some hundreds of arrests in Hamburg, Bremen, Luebeck, Berlin and other places.

Pelving's arrest was due to chance and to the stupidity of the Danish quisling, Dr. Fritz Clausen.

Fritz Clausen had been hailed into Court by Minister of Justice Steincke on charges of libelous defamation of character. Clausen had asserted that the Minister of Justice was systematically importing into Denmark "Jewish Communists and provocateurs" with the aim of Bolshevizing democratic Denmark. Clausen was, of course, merely following the international line of Goebbels' Propaganda Ministry, which had made similar statements about President Roosevelt.

In the course of the trial Clausen's advocate, Eiler Pontoppidan, Copenhagen's society lawyer, showed the court photostats of certain alien applications for permission to remain in Denmark; these applications showed that Communists of Jewish descent had asked for asylum.

The court could not understand where Clausen's lawyer had obtained photostats of police documents. The State Prosecutor ordered an immediate investigation.

It was discovered that the lawyer had secured the photostats from Max Pelving. Pelving was arrested and investigated. It was found that in 1924 Pelving had changed his name from Petermann. He was of German descent, and in 1918 had fought in the German and Finnish divisions against the Reds. He had even received a medal from Marshal Mannerheim. The State Prosecutor found out more and more; he was forced to conclude that the information given him by certain British agents (which came from Wollweber, of course) was a true description of the German espionage network.

Pelving had trembled before his chief, Pflugk-Hartung; he trembled also before the democratic authorities whom he had betrayed. He pleaded for mercy, pleaded that they understand the motives of his misguided conduct, and promised to tell all he knew. And so Max Pelving became a witness for the Crown against Pflugk-Hartung's entire spy organization. For a time Pelving dropped all his fear of the Nazis; terror made him brave, and in trying to save his own skin, he told all he knew. And he knew enough to give the Danish Court a fairly clear picture of how Pflugk-Hartung had carried on his work in Denmark.

He denounced his chief, Andreas Hansen; he told the court that Police Chief Hansen had worked for Pflugk-

Hartung. He, Pelving, could not progress in the police force without the aid of Andreas Hansen; since Hansen was a Nazi agent, he, too, must be one.

Pelving had secretly joined Clausen's Nazi Party. He admitted that he had been presented with an expensive camera with which to photograph the police files. Asked whether he had given copies of the files to Pflugk-Hartung, Pelving replied, "No."

He was telling the truth. Pflugk-Hartung had not wanted to be seen with Pelving and had therefore frequently contacted him through a man named Nils Aage Jensen, another member of Clausen's Nazi Party, and through lawyer Eiler Pontoppidan. Pelving knew, however, that the money he received from these men actually came from Pflugk-Hartung.

I was fortunate enough to be present at the trial when Pelving, and later on Pontoppidan, admitted their collaboration with Pflugk-Hartung.

Pelving recounted in a nervous whisper how Andreas Hansen, the Police Chief, had introduced him to Nils Aage Jensen, and how Jensen had taken him to the luxurious apartment of the lawyer and spy Pontoppidan, where the deal was closed.

The Judge, Jorgen Berthelsen, asked Pelving whether he knew that Jensen had informed his German boss that Pelving was in financial difficulties.

"Yes," Pelving replied, "but I had not asked him to tell Pflugk-Hartung."

"Did you not receive 200 kroner a month from Pontoppidan?"

Pelving tried to evade the question by saying that he had not received the money regularly.

The Judge then asked:

"Why did you give information to Pontoppidan and Pflugk-Hartung, if not for money?"

"To get other information that I needed for my police work."

Pelving was finally compelled to admit that he had received regular bribes. The Prosecutor produced several receipts for 400 kroner signed by Pelving; according to the notation on the receipts he had received this money to cover "traveling expenses," although as a police official he had a free pass for all railroads in Denmark.

When these receipts were produced, Pelving broke down completely. With tears in his eyes he asked the Judge whether he could not make amends. He pleaded for a chance to make good the harm he had done. From this point on he confessed freely.

Pflugk-Hartung's spy network in Copenhagen and within the police force had been built up as follows.

Police Chief Hansen was his chief aide. Hansen brought in Pelving, so that the alien squad was under Pflugk-Hartung's control. Pelving later brought in Inspector Kaj Yttesen, the man who had been so clever as to arrest the intended victims rather than the kidnappers during the earlier mentioned Wollweber kidnapping episode in 1934. He had been the liaison man between the police and the Danish Nazis; his activities gave the clue to the mysterious talent all leading German or Danish Nazis had of being "out of town" shortly before they were to be arrested. Yttesen had ample opportunity to request information and dossiers from the various police bureaus of Norway and Denmark. However, the Swedish police had suspected Andreas Hansen for many years and were more than cautious. The Police Chief of Norway, Jonas Lie, had of course long belonged to Pflugk-Hartung's band of corrupt police officials.

From Pelving the State Prosecutor proceeded to examine the case of Eiler Pontoppidan. He discovered that the lawyer's role was an extremely important one. Pflugk-

Hartung played the part of newspaper man and professor, of the gallant Prussian officer who moved in the highest circles of Copenhagen society. Pontoppidan was the man who did the daily chores for him, who met his underlings, executed Pflugk-Hartung's orders and prepared the reports which the chief examined at his leisure.

I saw Eiler Pontoppidan on March 29, 1939 in the Copenhagen Court. Where Max Pelving had been frightened, Pontoppidan was composed and aggressive. He admitted every charge the State Prosecutor made against him, and gave the impression that he could have admitted much more. He did not deny that he had received copies of police documents from Pelving and passed them on to the German Secret Service, but he refused flatly to mention Pflugk-Hartung's name.

The Prosecutor asked him whether he, like Pelving, had fought with the Germans and Finns against the Russians in 1918. Pontoppidan replied that he had, and was proud of it.

Prosecutor: Did you retain your interest in political affairs afterwards?

Pontoppidan: I was at that time not interested in Danish internal politics, but in the international Communist movement; I hoped to find out the courses it would employ to attain world revolution.

Prosecutor: When did you begin gathering information on particular persons?

Pontoppidan: Since 1930 when the great international depression began. I tried to discover what persons had been sent to Denmark by the Communists and with whom they were collaborating in Denmark.

Prosecutor: In other words, you built up your personal archives?

Pontoppidan: You might call it that.

Prosecutor: Who helped you to gather information and make investigations?

Pontoppidan: Young men who shared my views.

Prosecutor: Did you carry out investigations in Communist Party headquarters and in private houses?

Pontoppidan: What does the Prosecutor mean to establish by this question? In two cases my friends placed microphones in houses, which is why I am on trial today.

Prosecutor: About what persons did you gather information?

Pontoppidan: About Communists like Wollweber, a man named Richard Krebs, all Danish Communists, and many others.

Prosecutor: Did you give money to Max Pelving, former chief of the Alien Squad?

Pontoppidan: Yes.

Prosecutor: From whom did you receive this money?

Pontoppidan: I refuse to answer that question.

Prosecutor: Your refusal does you no good. We have ample material about you, including copies of your correspondence and of your contract.

That contract deserves a place in a museum of criminology. The Nazis were so sure of their safety in Denmark that Pontoppidan kept in his home a copy of his contract with Pflugk-Hartung. The two agents signed a written contract in which they agreed on the following points:

1) Pontoppidan was to install microphones in Russian Government offices.
2) Pontoppidan was to found an innocent-seeming business as a front for Nazi activities.
3) Pontoppidan was to keep watch on Communist refugees and tap the telephone line of the Emigrant Home in Copenhagen.

4) Pontoppidan was to negotiate with Max Pelving, to receive copies of police documents from him and to forward them to a certain address.
5) Pontoppidan agreed to admit that he had done everything on his own initiative; he was never to confess before a Court that he had worked for Pflugk-Hartung.
6) Pflugk-Hartung would pay him 20,000 kroner annually.
7) Pontoppidan was given a German passport.
8) In case the lawyer was arrested, Pflugk-Hartung would pay him an extra 20,000 kroner, and an additional bonus for any term of imprisonment.
9) In case flight became urgently necessary, Pontoppidan was given the right to remain in Germany as long as he pleased.

This six-page contract which bore the signatures of Pontoppidan and Pflugk-Hartung had fallen into the hands of the Danish authorities. It resulted, of course, in an investigation of all Pflugk-Hartung's activities. Every new arrest demonstrated more convincingly that the Prussian had built up a magnificent spy network. The Great Powers were too vitally interested in the spy scandal to allow it to be hushed up. And so, in spite of all the efforts of German agents in Denmark, the spy ring was broken.

6. Round-Up of Enemy Agents

"There are persons who at no great cost are willing to aid you . . . and as for the informers, you may observe that they are far from being exorbitant in their demands; a little money will satisfy them. My means, which, as I am sure, are ample, are at your service, and . . . here too are strangers who will give you use of theirs . . . Simmias the Theban has brought a sum of money for this very purpose . . ."
Crito to Socrates in Plato's "Dialogues"

The year was 1939. Nothing was done to Pflugk-Hartung, for his agents in the Danish police gave him a clean bill of health, declaring that he had never acted otherwise than as a model newspaper correspondent. But difficulties for him were once more inspired by the Social Democrats.

The Social Democratic Party possessed documents proving that through friends he had bought farms near the German-Danish border. Thus he was able to station German soldiers on Danish soil, soldiers whose farmhand's costume did not disguise their military bearing. The Social Democrats were planning an interpellation in Parliament. Moreover, they had obtained other documents of even greater importance.

On orders from Admiral Canaris, Pflugk-Hartung had undertaken the registration of the four thousand Germans living in Copenhagen, and of all Germans and all Danish Nazis in the provinces. With his usual efficiency, Pflugk-Hartung had prepared a questionnaire to obtain information that would be useful when the invasion came. These were some of the questions:

Do you live near the sea?

Do you live near an airport, railroad station, gas works, electric factory, government building? If yes, where?

Do you own: automobile, motorboat, sailboat, rowboat, motorcycle, bicycle, truck, or other means of transportation?

Are you prepared to place your automobile, motorboat, sailboat, etc., at the disposal of the German Legation?

Do you know any persons in the government?

Do you have any knowledge of Danish industrial plants and communications, or do you know persons who have such knowledge?

The Social Democratic Party turned this evidence over to the press, creating a national sensation. The case of Pflugk-Hartung was now brought up in Parliament. The German Legation glibly explained that it hoped to borrow automobiles and boats for summer picnics of German tourists, and that the questions on industry and communications were devised with a view to improving German-Danish trade relationships.

This latter explanation won over the semi-Nazi, conservative Peasants' Party, whose members depended largely on exporting to Germany, for England and the other democratic countries had introduced high tariffs on the import of foodstuffs.

Nevertheless, the matter worried Pflugk-Hartung. He wanted to find out how much the Danish Social Democratic Party knew about him and his connections with

Pontoppidan and the police. He therefore called a conference with his agent, Carlis Hansen, who had been on the "wanted" list since 1934, for his part in the attempted kidnapping of Wollweber, and had reason to be cautious. Nevertheless Carlis Hansen promised to obtain friends from the Clausen Nazi Party who would do the job for 100 kroner per man, and he it was who organized the robbery.

Hans Hedtoft-Hansen, who was looked upon as the successor to Prime Minister Stauning, never dreamed that anyone would dare break into his office. A man without secrets, it did not occur to him to lock his desk or his files.

The Social Democratic Party Headquarters was on the outskirts of Copenhagen, in the Rosenoerns Allé. The Danish Socialists were loyal monarchists who would have felt deeply insulted had they been accused of trying to overthrow the monarchy. They called themselves republicans, but this was a traditional way of speaking rather than a conviction.

Five men, all members of Dr. Clausen's Nazi Party, broke into the headquarters late one night. Carlis Hansen's friend, Inspector Yttesen, was in command of the Copenhagen police that night; this meant that everything was fairly safe. The robbers took their time. They entered the unguarded building with skeleton keys. They found the Party Chief's office unlocked.

The five Nazis were, like most of their ilk, good thieves; but they did not know which letters among the thousands they found in the files were important. They therefore decided to take along as much as they could and let their employers sort out all this material. Some money in one of Hedtoft-Hansen's desk drawers vanished at once. Books, pictures and placards in the room were torn up. A little incidental vandalism was always a tonic for the Nazi soul.

Pflugk-Hartung was well-pleased with the results of the nocturnal visit. The stolen material was fairly interesting, although he found little about himself among the papers and letters. He learned, however, that the Danish Social Democrats were working out plans for the fortification of the Dano-German border, and for laying a large number of land mines along the frontier.

He also found correspondence with the Social Democrats of Iceland, who warned that the Nazis were erecting secret radio stations on their island. And he found copies of letters to Swedish and Norwegian parliamentary deputies which showed that a widespread pan-Scandinavian anti-Nazi movement was in full swing.

Pflugk-Hartung took his discoveries very seriously. Next day, while the entire Danish press was raising a hue and cry against the robbery, he flew to Berlin. A murderer returning to the scene of his crime, he went directly to the Eden Hotel. Here Canaris visited him, for he wished to speak with his old friend in private.

Canaris had already received the stolen papers; he was in excellent spirits, laughed heartily at the coup, voiced his admiration for the efficiency of the spies in Denmark, and suggested that the Social Democrats might have some difficulties if their entire correspondence should disappear. But Pflugk-Hartung was in no mood for laughter. His days in Denmark were numbered, he said: he was already suspected by many, and the police would be unable to protect him forever.

Canaris is said to have laughed jovially, ordered a whiskey, and replied, "Horst, you're getting old."

Horst replied that he had no inclination to inspect the inside of a Danish prison.

Canaris tried to cheer him up. From the court records we can infer that he must have said something like this: "You must remain in Denmark until we march in. If you or your men are arrested sooner, it will be so much easier for us to present an ultimatum." Canaris promised him—on the word of a Prussian officer—that he would never desert him, and that "everything is ready; only the exact day has not yet been determined." This was early in 1939.

Canaris instructed him that from now on waterfront espionage was of primary importance, for war in Scandinavia meant sea warfare with England. Before his departure Pflugk-Hartung was awarded the Cross of Merit, First Class, and returned to Denmark with fresh funds and fresh tasks.

Every spy must reckon on detection. Pelving, Pflugk-Hartung's most important agent in the police, had been arrested. The trial of Pontoppidan, recounted in the last chapter, had resulted in the exposure of his radio company; this in turn had led to the revelation that Kyrre and Rambov had tapped the telephone line of the Emigrant Home in Copenhagen as well as of the Russian Trade Delegation. Pelving and Pontoppidan were now behind bars, and Pflugk-Hartung daily awaited his own arrest. It came finally after the outbreak of the war, toward the latter part of 1939, when the British and Russian Secret Services supplied the Danish Government with the proofs that the Danish police could not or would not find. Great Britain protested vigorously against Pflugk-Hartung's spy network. The protest was so vigorous that it approached an ultimatum. Great Britain threatened Denmark that she would take steps to insure that the Danish coast no longer harbored spies. The Danish Government was more than disturbed; it was deeply shocked.

Suddenly it found itself in the possession of proofs that Pflugk-Hartung had employed two hundred agents in the country and virtually lined the Danish coast with German spies.

Now Pflugk-Hartung's master stroke recoiled upon him. The story sounds as though it had been plagiarized from some operetta; it appears fantastic and utterly incredible in this era of the Second World War. But Pflugk-Hartung was perfectly willing to employ the methods of fiction if they served his ends.

He had known a capable good-looking young man named Ernst Grueber who had been born on the German-Danish border. The man was unemployed and seemed to Pflugk-Hartung an excellent prospect. The spy master therefore sent him to the espionage school in Berlin. Grueber passed his examinations with flying colors, and Pflugk-Hartung was well pleased with him. In 1936, Pflugk-Hartung assigned him to a simple task; he spent the summer, on Pflugk-Hartung's money, at the well-known bathing resort on the Island of Bornholm. All he had to do was to busy himself with learning as much as possible about the island and its inhabitants.

Sunburned, wearing white flannel trousers, an expensive tie and dapper hat, the young vacationer put in his appearance at Pflugk-Hartung's Strandvejen Villa and reported to his employer.

"Do you know where Admiral Tuerck's villa is situated?" Pflugk-Hartung asked him.

"Yes. On the east side of the island. It has a large garden and is close to the sea."

"Can you drive a car?" was Pflugk-Hartung's next question.

"No, Herr Kapitaenleutnant."

"God knows, those fools in Berlin might have taught you that." This was the end of the conversation. For the next two weeks Grueber did nothing but practice driving for eight hours a day. After he had learned how to drive he again reported to Pflugk-Hartung.

"The Tuercks have a chauffeur," Pflugk-Hartung informed him. "The chauffeur is going to get sick or have an auto accident. Mrs. Tuerck will be looking for a new chauffeur, and you will apply for the job."

Grueber returned to Bornholm. And two weeks later an advertisement appeared in the local newspaper; Mrs. Tuerck was looking for a chauffeur. Her old chauffeur had been run over by a truck.

Mrs. Tuerck was taken with the handsome, sun-browned young fellow who told her he was a fisherman, but would like to change trades; he said that he could also do odd jobs as a handy man.

Mrs. Tuerck asked him how long he had been at sea. Grueber answered, "Three years," which happened to be the truth.

"Well, then, you will feel at home here. My husband is Admiral Tuerck, you see."

With these words Grueber was hired.

For months he worked efficiently for his employers and for Pflugk-Hartung. He bribed and won over to the Nazis dozens of lighthouse guards, fishermen and dock workers. He soon showed that he was destined for higher things than a chauffeur's job, and one day Mrs. Tuerck came to him with the suggestion that he work as her private secretary—he had contrived to let her know that he was an excellent typist.

For a time Grueber was Mrs. Tuerck's private secretary; then he began writing letters for the Admiral. And soon Berlin knew everything of importance that went on in the Danish Naval Staff. Tuerck was active in promoting Scandinavian cooperation, which gave Grueber further chances for gathering information about Norway and Sweden.

Bornholm lies close to the German island of Ruegen, and Grueber frequently received visitors from Ruegen. Should the Admiral ask about them, they were old friends of his fishing days; in reality they were German Naval Intelligence officers, who inspected landing-points, lighthouses, and so on. Grueber also regularly secured copies of passenger lists of boats and planes for the Nazi Intelligence Service. All this material was too important to be sent through Pflugk-Hartung; it was transmitted to Germany via Ruegen.

Pflugk-Hartung now had the police and the Navy under control. But he also needed agents within the Danish Army.

He bribed two young officers, Captain Nils Garde and Captain Winding Christensen. The British, though they knew so much about Pflugk-Hartung's activities and had given the Danish Minister of Defense a great deal of information, knew nothing about these men. But Wollweber had found out about them. His friend, Communist Deputy Aksel Larsen, declared in Parliament that the two traitorous captains had been in Kiel to negotiate with leaders of the German Navy. They were to arrange for the German fleet to make an unopposed landing on the Island of Fuenen. Here the Nazis intended to build a naval and submarine base.

A week later the two officers were dishonorably discharged from the army; they then entered the German Army. Newspapers, radio and Parliament discussed the case without once mentioning the name of Pflugk-Hartung. Later, when he was at last arrested, he admitted that the two captains had been his tools.

Enemy agent after enemy agent was arrested, and all were found to have worked for Pflugk-Hartung. There was Max Rasch, editor of the pro-German newspaper *Bladet,* which was published in Schleswig-Holstein. Receipts were found in his possession for money he had paid lighthouse keepers and fishermen for information on shipping. Rasch had stupidly forgotten to get rid of the receipts, and had kept them in his home. He was proved to have been District Head of the border territory, and one of Pflugk-Hartung's most important agents. It was he who bought the frontier farms and planted German soldiers in the guise of farmhands on them.

A singing teacher named Max Voight was also arrested. His choral group had given performances in all harbor towns. In his possession were surveying instruments, telescopes, an expensive camera, and all necessary technical equipment for surveying the coastline. Voight was a close friend of Hermann Wildfeuer, who was doing similar work in Sweden.

Two exporters had regularly supplied information on ship movements. They were found to have been in collusion with Heinrich Wiedemann and his son Christian—relatives of the same Consul Wiedemann who blessed us with his presence in America.

The center for all Danish harbor espionage was in Copenhagen. Here a man named Rudolf von Wistinghausen served as the front; he had a large office devoted to arranging exchanges of German and Danish students.

As more and more enemy agents were arrested in Denmark, an ever ghastlier picture of corruption was unfolded. Among the arrested men was a bank clerk named Niels Johannes Nielsen. He was a secret agent for the modest Danish Intelligence Service. On the side he had sold copies of his reports to the French Deuxième Bureau—and second copies to Pflugk-Hartung.

Dozens of members of the Danish Nazi Party were arrested. Pflugk-Hartung, it was learned, had contributed 20,000 kroner for Clausen's last election campaign. Clausen himself, however, was not arrested, for he had seen to it that his secretaries and lieutenants assumed all the actual work of espionage.

At last Pflugk-Hartung himself was arrested and brought to trial in November 1939. He appeared altogether unchastened, and declared that he had done his duty as a German officer and that Germany was endeavoring to protect Denmark from British Imperialism. He said he loved Denmark and had never done anything not in the interest of that country.

The trial took place behind locked doors. Pflugk-Hartung and twenty of his agents were found guilty and at once sentenced. The sentences were made as mild as possible—from eight months in the case of the lesser agents to five years in Pflugk-Hartung's case.

Little Denmark had dared to pass sentence on the spies, but every spy, from Max Rasch to Ernst Grueber, who requested amnesty, was granted it and deported to Germany.

The case was destined to give rise to a last mystery. Nineteen spies made a plea for amnesty; Pflugk-Hartung preferred to remain in prison. All sorts of rumors circulated in Copenhagen about his decision. In the end two theories prevailed. One school had it that Pflugk-Hartung was afraid to return to Germany; he was after all a monarchist, rather than a Nazi, and feared Hitler's reward for failures. The other school advanced the most logical explanation: that Pflugk-Hartung was ordered to remain in prison. For among the inmates of the Copenhagen jail were several agents of Wollweber. This was Pflugk-Hartung's great opportunity to penetrate into the secrets of the OGPU; he had more chance to learn about Russian espionage in jail than outside of the gray walls.

Pflugk-Hartung remained in jail from January to April 1940, when Heinrich Himmler came to release him. By that time he had obtained enough material to start a great trial against "Wollweber and his comrades" in Copenhagen. Wollweber escaped, but many of the comrades were caught. This was Pflugk-Hartung's revenge for the trick Wollweber had played on him when he turned over to the British his information on Nazi harbor espionage.

PART THREE
Norway Resists
7. What Quisling Told Me

CANARIS, the master, and Pflugk-Hartung, the disciple, won the Battle for Norway, at least temporarily, and after Norway had been overrun and King Haakon VII (whom the Norwegians now name Haakon the Great) and his Government had fled to England, Pflugk-Hartung was ready to harvest what he had sowed.

Vidkun Quisling and his Chief of Police, Jonas Lie, demanded payment for their work of treachery. From far-off Rumania, Pflugk-Hartung, who had "discovered" them, could watch with satisfaction their rise to power, glory and infamy. Pflugk-Hartung has several dozen letters from Quisling which he likes to show to friends; they date from the time when Quisling was asking him for work and eagerly offering his services. Pflugk-Hartung rather enjoys the feeling that he has placed his tools upon the throne. And it was the place on the throne that fascinated Quisling; it did not matter to him at all who had raised him to it. If the throne of power could be acquired only through treason, then Quisling chose treason.

On July 18, 1887 in Telemark in Southern Norway there was born a traitor the like of whose history has not been seen since the days of Herostrates and Judas Iscariot. This man is Vidkun Abraham Lauritz Quisling.

No one prophesied at his cradle that he was to become the greatest traitor of our age, that he would spend his life in service to his country's powerful southern neighbor—as a spy.

Fyresdal, the valley where he lived until his twelfth year, is situated in wild remote country formerly reputed to be a haunt for bears. There is amusing significance in the remark of one of his Nazi biographers that "Quisling's childhood memories are largely concerned with the general terror of the bears. Even in daytime the people of the district never felt safe from bears."

This childhood fear left its traces in Quisling's character; so also did the unhappiness of his schooldays. The boy spoke an uncouth country dialect and was, of course, teased by his schoolmates. Having entered school late in the year, he was put directly into the second grade, although he could not yet read or write. Consequently, he was at the foot of the class for some time and, as the Nazi biographer puts it, "the marks of this humiliation burnt themselves upon his memory." Finally, "he was always homesick. He disliked the town and all it stood for. His sole desire was to go home to Fyresdal."

Fear, loneliness, injured pride, and the feeling of being one against many, are often characteristic features in the personality development of the would-be dictator. Quisling's hurt pride and bitterness was the same as Hitler's, the same as General Haushofer's, the same as Konrad Henlein's, the betrayer of Czechoslovakia; we have seen these same traits in the personalities of all German agents from Canaris to Pflugk-Hartung, from Manfred von Killinger to Jacques Doriot.

Quisling was a brilliant student. He was graduated with high honors and entered upon a military career. In the Military Academy he was considered the most promising of the cadets, and two years later was graduated from the

Military College with a "recommendation to the King," a citation which had never been given before.

In 1911 he became a probationer on the General Staff. He was promoted to captain in 1917. During World War I his sentiments were pro-British. After serving as military attaché in Leningrad in 1918, he was for two years military attaché and secretary of the legation at Helsinki. Here he met the great explorer and philanthropist, Professor Fridtjof Nansen, and at Nansen's request directed the International Russian Relief Organization in the Ukraine and the Crimea during 1922-23. He also assisted Nansen in 1924-26, during Nansen's great relief work in Russia and Armenia under the auspices of the League of Nations.

Quisling unquestionably did good work and Nansen, in the preface to his book on these missions, has expressed gratitude, though in a rather non-committal fashion, for Quisling's assistance.

Nansen was one of Norway's greatest men, and one of the noblest who ever lived. He received the Nobel Prize for his humanitarian work; he also won fame as an explorer of the North Pole and the Arctic regions. In him were combined the faculties of the great scientist and the spirit of the great liberal. Quisling was proud to work with Nansen, and under his influence was wont to declare that liberal democracy is the only government that can bring human happiness and that fascism of Mussolini's sort would utterly destroy the peace and security of Europe. For many years, too, Quisling was an admirer of Soviet Russia; he stayed some time in Moscow. In 1923 he married a Russian girl from Kharkov, and later had to go to some pains to assure his Nazi friends of his wife's "Aryan" descent.

When diplomatic relations between Great Britain and Soviet Russia were broken off in May 1927 he was appointed secretary of the Norwegian Legation in Moscow, charged with the duty of guarding British interests in Russia. He, who was to become the arch-hater of Great Britain during this war, was awarded the Order of the British Empire for his services.

In 1928 he retired from active military service, as the General Staff refused to give him further extension of his leave. For this "unjust treatment" Quisling harbored a grievance against the military authorities. He stayed in Russia until 1929.

In an autobiographical note written in 1930 Quisling said: "My strong, and perhaps predominant, interests are politics and science. In politics it is chiefly Russia that has interested me. With this nation my activities have been closely connected for the last twelve years. In the field of science I have, apart from military science, studied history, languages and natural science, as well as mathematics, which was once my favorite study. In recent years these diverse interests have drawn toward a unity embodied in philosophy. The question of a universal explanation of life, based on knowledge and experience and reconciling religion and science, has of late been more and more my consuming thought apart from necessary daily duties. Disturbed conditions of life and other unfavorable circumstances have hitherto prevented me from making public my literary and scientific labors. But I hope that I shall yet be able to say my word, before the great stillness descends."

This vainglorious little piece is a complete give-away of Quisling's character.

When Quisling returned from Russia in 1930 he found himself out of a job and receiving half pay as an officer in the reserve. We can comprehend the tragedy of a man of his high gifts, of equally high ambition, who, returning from great enterprises abroad, finds that his abilities are spurned at home. Very likely he overestimated himself and was unwilling and unable to cooperate with superiors. Be that as it may, Quisling soon became convinced that he was the victim of wrongs and persecution.

In compensation he decided to create the career for which he believed himself destined, no matter how desperate the means. He was prepared to give himself to any political party or group that could bestow on him the role of leader. Once he suggested to the Socialists that he form "Red Guards" and become the Trotsky of Norway. Of this there is documentary proof. He actually wanted to organize armed workers groups to initiate insurrection and revolution after the Soviet manner.

Communists and Socialists rejected the suggestion with some fierceness. Both were positive Quisling was a British agent; surely a man with a British Service Medal would not turn to radicals without a concealed motive.

If Quisling had been accepted by the radicals he would certainly have risen to be a formidable leader. History provides a similar case, that of Mussolini being expelled by Italy's Socialists. Years later Lenin had to confess that "the biggest error the Italian Socialists committed was their expulsion of Mussolini."

Rejected by Communists and Socialists, Quisling had no other haven but the circles of conservative and semi-fascist elements in Norway. A pamphlet of his written in 1931 shows Quisling's strange views on the necessity of saving the Norwegian people from "a mortal disease which leads it toward anarchy and disintegration." There is also a smattering of Nazi-influenced racial theory. He says, "The Norwegians, together with the other Scandinavian peoples, form the core of the great tribe which represents the most valuable racial strain of humanity, the great Nordic race."

When, in May 1931, the new Government of the Farmers' Party made Major Vidkun Quisling Minister of Defense, he was still scarcely known to the public. Nevertheless, he was received with a good deal of approval. For the first time in many years the Ministry was to be headed by a professional soldier. Quisling's brilliant intellectual record became known, and his work with Nansen in Russia was given due credit. Moreover, he was without a past as a politician.

Quisling's function in the new government was to carry out a drastic reduction in Norway's defense expenditures. This pacifist policy had been resolved upon before his time, but he had the duty of putting it into effect. This he did, and this is worth remembering since the Quisling propaganda in Norway lays all the blame for the later catastrophes upon the labor government of Johan Nygaardsvold. The slogan used against the labor government is that it preferred butter to guns. By a whimsicality of history, it was in Quisling's time that an ordinance was passed to provide butter instead of margarine for soldiers during their training period.

Quisling was an efficient Defense Minister who kept his papers in order, but otherwise it was difficult to form an opinion of him. It was as hopeless a task to find out what he thought as to make him look one straight in the eye. He gave the impression of being a silent, lonely and not too happy man. All at once the dignity that draped his secretive and vague personality was suddenly torn away by the famous "assault case" in the Ministry. I narrate it according to his own account.

On the evening of February 2, 1932 Quisling went to his office. As he was passing through a darkened room, someone suddenly threw pepper in his eyes, stabbed at him with a knife and beat him on the head so that he lost consciousness. The culprit was never found, and the affair soon became a subject of rumor and speculation. It was suggested that the attack had been arranged in order to get publicity, or that it was connected with some love-affair. Officially the case has never been solved, but the Chief of

Police Intelligence has privately stated that "it is a swindle, pure and simple."

But the case received widest publicity, and everyone in Norway became aware of Vidkun Quisling, who had narrowly escaped assassination. What part Quisling himself played in the assault is equally obscure; it was not he, but an enterprising friend of his who reported the case to the police. The affair roused such a sensation that for months afterwards the name of Quisling made the headlines on any pretext.

The Swedish Nazis adopted Quisling's trick to get publicity for their new party. A year after Quisling's little drama a Swedish Nazi was shot in the shoulder and the grave of Karin Goering was desecrated. Swedish Police Commissioner Torsten Soederstroem brought proof that the Swedish Nazis had committed both these acts themselves, simply to create a martyr like Horst Wessel and provoke tremendous publicity about the desecration.

Vidkun Quisling utilized the rather embarrassing pepper-and-knife episode as the motive for an incendiary speech he made in the Storting about two months later. The speech came as an utter surprise to his colleagues in the government. He spoke darkly of the activities of subversive and destructive forces, hinting that he possessed conclusive proofs that the leaders of the Socialist Party were guilty of high treason and were on the payroll of the OGPU. Everyone was alarmed. He was asked to produce his evidence, and a special investigating committee was appointed. The evidence proved to be certain antiquated documents from the archives of the Defense Ministry and the police. Quisling himself could not muster any new or plausible contribution. The committee, alas, could make only a very bare report. They concluded by saying that they felt the Minister's strange speech should be forgiven and forgotten. Not even the members of the Minister's own Party would commit themselves further. The scandal shook his position, but he was permitted to remain in office.

When Quisling, together with the other Ministers of his Party, left politics, he must have realized that he would never again be invited into the Government, by his Party or by any other party. The dubious pepper-assault was not forgotten, and public opinion had marked him as a scandalmonger and alarmist.

His only recourse was to start his own movement. There was only one man who would understand him and employ him. Quisling paid a visit to Berlin. After an interview with Hitler, the Nasjonal Samling (National Union) was born; this occurred in May 1933. It presented candidates at the general elections held in the same year. In not a single constituency did the Party receive more than a fraction of the votes necessary to secure a seat in Parliament under Norway's system of proportional representation.

From the very beginning Quisling's Party copied Nazi methods: uniforms, marches, strange emblems, espionage groups and, above all, the "führer" principle. It never had any followers among mature responsible citizens, but like many other mystical and foggy political creeds it succeeded in gathering a group of the youthful and uncritical around Quisling's person. For the 1936 elections the Party staged a tremendous propaganda campaign, having received considerable funds from Germany and the Nordic Society. It pretended to such importance that its opponents were surprised when the election results were published. Not even two per cent of the votes went to the Nasjonal Samling, and again the Party sent no representatives to the Storting. After this disaster the Party began to disintegrate. The few clever and ambitious men within the Party now deserted it, telling Quisling that he had caused the defeat by his incompetence and inability to cooperate.

After this defeat Vidkun Quisling vanished into oblivion. The Norwegians ignored him completely. Only his weekly newspaper, *Fritt Folk* (*Free People*), remained.

I wanted to see this defeated man. I recognized, of course, that at the moment Quisling did not loom as a danger to Norway. But I knew also that he was only a tool of Hitler's; if he had dropped out of sight for the present, it was in order to prepare secretly for the future. Moreover, I was convinced that Quisling and his men were engaged in espionage activities for Pflugk-Hartung and Canaris. They kept watch on German refugees and spied on Anglo-Norwegian affairs.

Folket i Bild, a Swedish magazine, had sent me to Norway to interview Leon Trotsky. I decided to profit by this chance and obtain an interview with Vidkun Quisling.

When I entered his small newspaper office, I found him sitting behind a desk covered with newspapers. He greeted me with the words, "Well, what kind of lies do *you* want to concoct about me?"

I replied I would write only the truth and asked why a man like himself preferred to work with the Germans rather than with the Norwegians.

Quisling showed signs of interest. He asked me whether I considered him a traitor, as everyone else did. I countered that I could answer that question only after the interview. A frown spread over his plump, swollen face, but he began to talk freely. I took notes of what he said to me and later entered them in my journal.

"To tell the truth," Quisling began, "I don't give a damn what people say about me." He explained that Norway was a small country and must inevitably remain tied to the apron strings of the Great Powers. Germany had entered on a period of rejuvenation. To be sure, the rejuvenation necessitated brutality and concentration camps, but if one had seen as much as he had—famine in Russia, extermination in Armenia—one was forced to believe that the majority of mankind were illiterates, that the people could not rule themselves and that it was essential for a few chosen intelligent men to take over the business of government.

"I've seen the Labor Party send a charwoman to Parliament. What did she know about politics?"

Quisling was embittered. He hated the entire world and probably, at certain times, he hated himself. During the two hours I spent with him I did not once see him laugh or smile.

Quisling went on to say that it was rank injustice to call him a traitor, unless one applied the same epithet to Knut Hamsun, the Nobel Prize winner, who shared his views.

Knut Hamsun was at that time already pro-Nazi. An embittered man with strong sentimental attachments for Germany, the "blood and soil" theory of the Nazis appealed profoundly to him. Hamsun's electoral district had delivered only one vote for Quisling; that vote was Hamsun's. Not even Hamsun's wife voted for the future traitor. Later, Hamsun became one of Quisling's chief supporters.

In analyzing the reasons for Hamsun's defection from democracy, some have recalled that his books sold in tremendous editions in Germany, whereas in Norway he could not expect more than a small sale. Another cause may date back to the time he spent in America in his youth. He suffered in America a number of unpleasant experiences, and ever since has harbored a hatred for the Anglo-Saxon world and subscribed to the theory of "nordic" hegemony.

Both Quisling and Hamsun are fond of Norwegian schnapps in large quantities, and have often drunk together. Hamsun has become a heavy drinker in his old age. It is sadly repulsive to hear coming from the toothless mouth of a senile man, who was once a great writer, propaganda speeches in praise of Hitler and Quisling.

At this point in our interview Quisling became theatrically demagogic, declaring:

"We represent the New Europe, the Europe of Youth. We want new methods, and the methods of Hitler will bring us to our goal. If I pronounce myself for dictatorship, I do so irrespective of Hitler, simply because I believe dictatorship is the form of government that will prevail in the future. I have studied history; whenever a liberal age failed, as it did in Greece and Rome, dictators came to rescue the people. Did not Napoleon save France from dissolution?"

Quisling tried desperately to convince me that he had not been bought by Hitler, but that his own personal ideas and interests had led him to Hitler.

"But you cannot rule against the will of the people, can you?" I asked. "And the people rejected you in the last elections."

This was obviously Quisling's sore point.

"When I come to power, and I will come to power, elections will be abolished," he declared. "Are women whose talents are limited to the art of cooking to have power over me? Are workers whom the capitalists consistently exploit to govern? No, I do not need the people."

Quisling's theory envisaged an intellectual aristocracy whose function would be to rule. The people, in his eyes, were an unteachable rabble too low in the scale of evolution to think. "And now you may agitate against me all you please," he said in conclusion.

I departed convinced that Quisling was a megalomaniac who genuinely believed in his asocial ideas of power. He was a sick man, an abnormal man, who could bring only misery to humanity.

When I told my friends in the Labor Party about him, saying that such a man ought to be put out of harm's way, they gave the usual reply that a democracy must practice tolerance and commit no injustice and that men are innocent until they have committed their crimes.

Two months before the invasion of Norway *Fritt Folk* suddenly became a daily newspaper. Quisling had been to Berlin and received new funds. But no one bothered much about it, nor about the fact that in the winter of 1939-40 Quisling made several trips to Germany. The purpose of these trips has since become tragically clear, but the Norwegian Intelligence Office had no hint of what was afoot.

Quisling knew about the coming invasion and was even informed of some details. He himself wrote leaflets and proclamations which were printed in Berlin. The Führer-elect spent the night of April 8-9, 1940 at the Hotel Continental in Oslo, where the Germans were to make their headquarters the following day. Throughout the early hours of the morning he walked restlessly in his rooms, nervously awaiting those who were to meet him here. And in the evening his name was announced over the radio as the new Prime Minister. This was the first great mistake the Nazis made in Norway.

Premier Quisling established himself in the Storting. He published a list of ministers—with many posts unfilled. Many of those included in the list promptly announced that they would have nothing to do with the traitor. Even Dr. Gulbrand Lunde, who was later to become the "little Goebbels" of Norway, remained in Stavanger and declared he had nothing to say. The new Premier could be seen sitting all alone hour after hour, staring into space. His one official act was to issue a treacherous order cancelling mobilization; it did not prevent thousands of young men from slipping through the German lines to join the Norwegian Army. He gave another order to all Norwegian ships to go to neutral ports; the order was not obeyed by one ship in a thousand.

The German authorities soon realized that the situation was impossible. Strikes were breaking out; there was sabotage everywhere. When a number of leading Norwegians formed a committee and demanded Quisling's dismissal, the Nazis yielded and allowed an "Administrative Council" to be set up.

To disguise Quisling's defeat he was given the task of supervising "demobilization." His goose seemed cooked—which was the only natural consequence of his good offices. "The treachery is sweet, not so the traitor."

Quisling, in desperation, left for Germany. Throughout the summer of 1940 there were frequent rumors that Quisling was in deepest disgrace among the Nazis. It was said that he was in a kind of "honorary concentration camp." However, he was recognized by some Norwegians when they saw him in the basement of the fashionable Hotel Adlon during a raid on Berlin—and this, of course, is not very far from inner circles. Actually there is reason to believe that Quisling is backed by Hitler himself, and that he has won the confidence of Alfred Rosenberg. With the German military authorities in Norway he has always been unpopular and despised as a traitor. It is said that they insistently demand that Quisling be dropped, since he hardly abets the task of the Germans in Norway; on the contrary, he arouses burning hatred in all Norwegians. Nevertheless, on September 25, 1940 he was given a second chance by his German masters, when they created a new Nazi puppet Government. Quisling was given no place in it, but as "führer" of the "State Party" he was theoretically inferior only to German Reich Commissioner Josef Terboven in the internal administration of Norway.

It was not until 1942 that Hitler decided to employ pure terrorism in Norway. Other methods had failed to pacify the country, and his generals were warning him of the possibility of an Allied invasion of Norway. Consequently, Vidkun Quisling was at last given his reward. He was appointed Prime Minister of Norway.

One of the first laws that Quisling passed countermanded the most elementary of decent customs. By decree he removed the obligation imposed on physicians honorably to guard the secrets of their patients. This infamous decree soon turned against himself. The head of a Norwegian hospital where Quisling had been a patient informed the Norwegian Government-in-Exile that Vidkun Quisling had suffered from a grave case of syphilis of many years standing. When the disease reached the third stage he had been attacked by paralysis, accompanied by mental symptoms, and for some years had been a dangerous megalomaniac.

The Norwegian doctors had prescribed the malaria cure as Quisling's only hope. The cure had worked, but his megalomania had remained, a fateful residue of the disease.

And this megalomania was constant with him. He celebrated his birthday in the palace of King Haakon VII and reviewed his marching storm troopers. He imitated Goering by stalking about in an endless variety of uniforms. One of these has a wine-red military jacket with a girdle of silver and white; among the drabber uniforms is one which is merely a variation of a Nazi uniform. He makes no effort to conceal how his fame delights him, and openly shows his pleasure in watching parades and listening to the "Heil Quislings." This diseased would-be dictator has chosen for himself one of the finest mansions in all Oslo. He has confiscated castles in the country and turned them into summer residences, like all the Nazi leaders in

Germany. The reconstruction of the Grande Villa in Oslo cost 100,000 kroner, which included a private bombproof cellar. When the dedicatory ceremonies were held, a panicky feeling spread among the assembled Nazi leaders; some patriot had cut the electric wires and the festivities had to be conducted by candlelight.

Quisling cannot walk the streets of any Norwegian town unguarded. In 1942 fifty men watched over him day and night; in the national budget 120,000 kroner were provided for the salaries of these men. Certain of the bodyguards have had to be discharged because they sold rationed foods on the black market—stuff they stole from Quisling's houses and castles where, of course, there is always more than enough for a good table.

The Norwegian Nazi puppet has built for himself a new sixty thousand dollar "Northern Berchtesgaden" near Oslo, where he now lives under the increased protection of one hundred and fifty guards who man machine-gun posts twenty-four hours a day. The story of Quisling's new fortified retreat was revealed in January 1943 by a Norwegian who arrived in England after carrying on extensive counterespionage as a member of "Premier" Quisling's inner circle.

This reliable counter-agent said Quisling now is a haggard, weary man who lives in constant fear of death by assassination. He maintains one hundred and fifty storm troopers on duty constantly both at his new retreat and when he moves about the country. Fearful of poisoning, he refuses to eat or drink, until the food or liquid has been tasted by someone else.

His "little Berchtesgaden" is located on the beautiful Bygdoe Peninsula, a finger of land that juts into Oslofjord about a half dozen miles from the city. In addition to machine-gun nests around the house, antiaircraft guns have been mounted in the vicinity. In the basement of the house is a concrete-reinforced air raid shelter where Quisling takes refuge when the RAF comes over Oslo.

The house is a rambling forty-six room structure with bullet-proof stone walls. It had been used for some years as a meteorological station, and is topped by a high tower from which Quisling gets a view for miles around. Eight nearby villas have been taken over to house Quisling's guards and staff.

The house is known as "Gimble," a name Quisling excavated from an old Norwegian saga.

The house is furnished with property confiscated from Norwegian patriots. Quisling has a number of masterpieces on the walls of his estate and a large library comprised entirely of books seized by the Germans and his own storm troopers. The task of putting the house into shape for Quisling was carried out by a force of two hundred men conscripted by the "Premier" and placed on twelve hour shifts from 9 a.m. to 9 P.M.

Quisling has fitted up a small astronomical observatory in the tower of the house, where he spends much of his spare time observing the stars.

On Quisling's various journeys through Norway he is guarded with especial care, traveling only in armored cars with military escort.

Quisling has even demanded that his portrait be placed in schoolrooms and affixed to stamps; but here he was overruled by Terboven, who declared that Adolf Hitler's portrait was sufficient.

Quisling tells the Norwegians—who hate him more than any figure has been hated throughout the heroic history of Norway—that he is the successor to the king and that Haakon VII will never return to his people.

The most crucial point of Quisling's career came in February 1942, when the Nazis at last realized that the entire population of Norway, after two years of German occupation, still considered themselves at war with Germany. They gave Quisling full powers to organize a typical Nazi regime of terror. Quisling promptly declared himself both Prime Minister and Führer of Norway. In German fashion, he considered it appropriate to hold a torchlight procession in honor of the new order. But even while he was celebrating his coronation as Norway's hangman, the railroad stations of Oslo were burned, there were bomb explosions throughout the city, and fires burst out in many important Nazi offices. In the midst of his celebration Quisling was compelled to declare a state of emergency in Oslo. His Minister of Police, Jonas Lie (whom the Norwegians always refer to as Judas Lie), had to excuse himself from the festivities and hasten to his office to restore order in the city.

After Quisling, Judas Lie is the most hated man in Norway. Although he has had a remarkable career, he is one of those men whose ambitions are never satisfied. He had been police chief in democratic Norway, but he had never been happy. Always there had been money troubles and difficulties with women, and he was compelled to search constantly for new sources of income. He wrote detective stories under the pseudonym of Max Mauser, and was undoubtedly one of Norway's best detective story writers. He had always been sympathetic toward Germany, but no one considered him in any way suspect; he seemed to be merely another of the many Norwegian officials who wanted to keep on good terms with Germany in order to maintain their country's neutrality.

When the Norwegian Government was rescuing refugees from the occupied Sudetenland, Lie was sent to Prague to supervise the giving of visas. It was also he who got the assignment to lure Trotsky on to a ship and when the ship was in mid-ocean to inform him that he was being taken to Mexico, having been expelled from Norway. The voyage with Trotsky gave him the idea for an excellent novel, *A Shark Follows in the Wake,* that later was awarded a prize.

After the Nazi occupation and the appointment of Quisling as chief of state, Lie hesitated. He wanted to wait and see whether the British won the battle around Narvik. Later on, however, he offered his services to Quisling—and was all the more ardent a Nazi to cover up his earlier equivocations.

Jonas Lie has invented methods which outdo the stories of Torquemada's tortures under the Spanish Inquisition. Lie proved to be a star pupil in the School of Terror. When Himmler visited Oslo, he examined Lie's work and found it good; subsequently, he invited him to Berlin, where Lie was given a rapid course in Gestapo methods and introduced to Reinhardt Heydrich. He proved to be a worthy disciple of both these men.

Jonas Lie strutted through the streets of Oslo in a German Elite Guard's uniform. He organized Norwegian troops to fight in Russia and himself fought in the Balkan campaign as a colonel. He returned with an Iron Cross, and shortly afterwards participated in the punitive expedition against the Lofoten Islands.

The two British-Norwegian commando raids on the Lofoten Islands in Northern Norway had been unusually successful. The Allies found extremely important documents, captured Nazi soldiers and Quislings, and took a great many Norwegian boys on the islands back to England as volunteers. Jonas Lie was sent to punish the populace. He arrested all the men on the island and burned down the homes of all families whose sons had gone to England with the British warships.

From 1940 to 1942 Quisling and Jonas Lie organized a first-rate spy machine in Norway and abroad. The Norwegian ships that had been caught in Swedish ports were desperately trying to break through the Nazi blockade in order to reach England. The spy apparatus set up by Quisling and Lie denounced these ships to the German submarines. Some were torpedoed, some forced to flee back to Sweden, and only a few succeeded in reaching England safely.

This secret service of Jonas Lie's worked in close cooperation with the Swedish Nazis and received money and constant aid from them.

The idea of organizing a Norwegian Secret Service was Lie's own; his suggestion was at once taken up by Admiral Canaris. But aside from the affair of the Norwegian ships in Sweden, Jonas Lie has had little to show for his efforts. He even experimented with espionage in America, among people of Norwegian descent, but accomplished nothing. Or almost nothing.

The files of the FBI contain a mysterious case that has never been cleared up. It concerns the President of the Norwegian Seamen's Union, Ingvald Haugen, who has charge of 25,000 Norwegian sailors employed on board 1,000 Norwegian ships in the service of the United Nations. These ships represent Norway's great contribution to the war at sea.

Haugen had secured information on Nazi sabotage and Nazi espionage on the waterfronts of the United States. His material dealt principally with the experiences of Norwegian sailors on Norwegian ships. Haugen intended to present this material at a meeting of shipping experts in Brooklyn.

Haugen never arrived at the meeting. On a street in the Bay Ridge district of Brooklyn he was kidnapped. Two unknown men threw pepper into his eyes, dragged him into an automobile, blindfolded him and drove around for several hours. Then they brought him to a room whose only furniture consisted of a bed, a table and two chairs. The kidnappers refused to say a word to Haugen. They took his documents and kept him imprisoned for two days. Then he was again forced into a car and driven to woods on the outskirts of the metropolitan area of New York. Haugen had to walk for several hours before he reached a populated neighborhood.

8. How Norway's Gold Was Saved

The day was April 10, 1940, one day after the landing of the Germans in Norway. The German General Staff had set up its headquarters in Oslo's Continental Hotel, only a short distance from the Storting and the palace of King Haakon.

Vidkun Quisling, the traitor, had so far found little employment, for in critical situations the Nazis trusted their own forces much more than native sympathizers.

But at last the call had come. A German colonel who spoke excellent Norwegian had excitedly asked to see Quisling. Quisling was only too happy to receive the summons; for a while it had appeared that his beloved Germans had forgotten him.

The German—Colonel Ernst Kretschmer—wanted information from Quisling. Kretschmer was the former secretary of the German Legation in Norway, a man whose fame had hitherto rested on his murder of General Kurt von Schleicher, Hitler's predecessor as Chancellor of Germany.

Kretschmer gloomily informed Quisling that the battleship *Bluecher* had been sunk by the Norwegian Coastal Defense, and that consequently the Gestapo men and the military and naval intelligence agents had not arrived in Oslo with the rest of the occupation troops.

The Norwegian counterespionage later learned that between 1,300 and 1,600 Secret Service officials were on board the *Bluecher* when the battleship was sunk. Only eighty-six escaped drowning. Some of these were captured by the Norwegians. The prisoners from Canaris's Intelligence Bureau and Best's Gestapo were carefully questioned.

The Germans revealed small courage. Trembling, they made their confessions. They revealed that every one of the agents on the *Bluecher* had had an address in his pocket, to which he was to go and inform the Norwegian officials that he was the new head of their office. In this way, the railroads, postal service, telephone, telegraph, banks, and so on, were to be taken over at one stroke. The entire plan had been worked out years before by Canaris's espionage bureau.

The new masters knew precisely how each office operated. They knew something about the personality of the Norwegian head, had lists of the names of their subordinates, and were prepared to become the directors of these functions and institutions months before they set foot in Norway. But this time they were out of luck. Colonel Kretschmer asked Quisling where the Norwegian gold reserve was concealed.

Quisling was unable to help; he had not thought of the matter at all. He guessed it might be in the "Riksbank" in Oslo. Kretschmer laughed scornfully; the Germans had already searched the National Bank and found no gold.

This was the beginning of a Norwegian epic. It is the story of the flight of one man who, with the help of a few Norwegian soldiers, wandered up and down the country for months, passing through burning villages and mined fjords, to save a quarter of a billion kroner in gold from the hands of the Nazis.

Duel for the Northland

Pursued by Nazi troops, airplanes, warships, the Gestapo, the Secret Service and by Quisling's traitors, this man fought his way through the entire German war machine and slipped through the net cast for him by General Nikolaus von Falkenhorst and Admiral Wilhelm Canaris.

Fredrik Haslund is small for a Norwegian, no more than five feet six, with honest, sparkling blue eyes and an ardently patriotic heart. He had never had much military training. Originally he had been an engineer, had studied in Germany, in fact; but with the years his chief interest defined itself as the social development of his country. He joined the Labor Party; soon afterward he became secretary of the Norwegian parliamentary fraction of his Party. In Norway he was considered a walking lexicon on social and economic problems.

Haslund was the man who drafted some of Norway's most important social legislation. He also organized aid for the fighting loyalists of Spain, and took part in numerous international congresses.

The night of the invasion Haslund received a telephone call asking him to go to the Storting at once. He was with King Haakon and the cabinet members at the time that the German Stukas attempted to facilitate Nazi occupation of Norway by exterminating the constitutional rulers. That same night the government officials, together with the King and the Crown Prince, took flight. They were almost captured by parachute troops in the vicinity of Dovre.

The German Secret Service, though it arrived late, arrived in time to discover the whereabouts of the northward fleeing Government. King and Government were pursued day and night through forests buried under deep snow; the chase moved ever northward into colder regions. The fugitives, including the aging King Haakon VII, were subjected to the greatest physical trials of their lives.

The Nazis were all the more eager to capture the Government because they thought the King and his party had taken the gold with them. However, the prudent Minister of Finances, Oscar Torp, had had the entire gold reserve loaded onto trucks early that morning. It was transported out of Oslo to a well-guarded concrete cellar somewhere north of the capital. This place had been built by Torp years before, in case an invasion made it necessary to hide the country's gold.

Haslund left the retreat of the King and his Government and taking an army car, escorted by a single soldier, returned a few days after the invasion to the vicinity of Oslo, which in the meantime had been completely occupied by the Germans.

He drove through German lines so fast that he was not stopped.

His task was to rescue fifteen hundred cases of gold, worth a total of two hundred and forty million kroner. Haslund did not know that precious time had been gained through the fortunate sinking of the *Bluecher*. He knew only that the Nazi military authorities were, for the moment, following a false trail, and this gave him his chance. Strictest secrecy was maintained. Only the few highest treasury officials were enlisted to help save the gold.

Norway had mobilized for war and for two months battled the Nazis. In the midst of that battle Fredrik Haslund and thirty Norwegian soldiers careened about the country with 240,000,000 kroner in gold.

The town where the gold was hidden lay asleep. Not a light showed; the blackout was complete. The group of soldiers waited and waited in the icy night air, for even in April Norwegian nights are freezing cold. The wind howled around them; the soldiers gritted their teeth and stamped their feet. Then came the sound of distant motors. Friend or foe—how were they to know? Had the Nazi spies discovered the hiding place of the gold?

Then the soldiers heard low-voiced commands. They breathed easier; the commands were in Norwegian. Armed policemen surrounded the area. Then truck after truck arrived over the dark road, bringing the loading crew. None of the workmen knew what they were loading, and none asked. The police and soldiers stood with naked bayonets flashing in the moonlight.

Fifteen hundred boxes were loaded on the trucks and taken to the nearest railroad station. Here a train stood ready, the locomotive puffing smoke. The boxes were unloaded and loaded again into the train, while the checkers strained their eyes in the darkness to count the boxes. Armed soldiers accompanied the train. For hours they rolled over the gleaming tracks, their confidence mounting because no Nazi planes passed overhead. As daybreak approached, when the German searching planes would surely be abroad, the train which had reached a valley in central Norway, ran off on a spur to await the protection of night.

The parachute troops out to capture the King were still haunting this valley through which ran the only railroad line to the coast. But during the day the Norwegian troops rounded up all of the parachutists, and by nightfall the train was able to proceed. It moved slowly, for no one knew whether the Nazis might not have mined the railroad line. The troops went ahead, searching every inch of the right-of-way.

The following morning Andalsnes, the first stopping-place, was reached. But if Fredrik Haslund and his faithful followers thought their difficulties were over, they were bitterly disappointed. The British had just landed in Andalsnes and Goering's Luftwaffe was concentrating its forces upon the town. Bombs fell incessantly.

Haslund at once reported to Finance Minister Torp that Andalsnes was too dangerous a place for his precious cargo. He was ordered to proceed several miles to the south and there await a warship which would transport the gold to Britain.

The Norwegians took their train to a small railroad station in the vicinity and waited. They waited and waited, while their distant superiors negotiated with the British Secret Service and the British Admiralty. The station was, fortunately, so unimportant that the Nazis paid no attention to it. All Haslund and his group could do, however, was to wait for a telephone call from Andalsnes. A member of the party, one of Norway's best-known younger poets, Nordahl Grieg, sat for hours at the telephone.

The little party were in the valley between Romdalshorn and Trolltinnene, hemmed in by mighty precipices. Above the mountains constant air battles raged, and one day two heavy bombers swooped into the valley to destroy the railroad. The bombs just missed the train and destroyed a section of the track. A railroad employee and ten soldiers repaired the damage in three hours.

At last, one night, the opportunity came to transfer some of the gold. A British warship moved in to the dock at Andalsnes. While the British troops were disembarked and all the equipment of warfare was being unloaded, some of the boxes of Norwegian gold were carried on board.

Fredrik Haslund himself has described that night:

"A peculiar mood prevailed. The snow-covered peaks gleamed like blue gems in the clear air of this spring night. All about us was the profound night silence of the mountains. But the tiny center formed by the ship seethed with activity. The cries and the rumbling of our work went on and on. At last, when day broke, we had to stop and the cruiser was able to depart."

Once more the rescuing of the gold had not gone according to program, for only a small part of the gold had been loaded aboard the cruiser. Andalsnes had become too dangerous; the Nazis were raining bombs upon the waterfront installations, and the cruiser did not dare linger after dawn. In fact, the Germans were intent on sinking every British warship they sighted, for they had meanwhile got wind that the gold was somewhere in the vicinity of Andalsnes and would be taken aboard a British vessel.

That May morning Haslund learned that the Nazi ground forces had broken through the Norwegian lines in the valley. He received the alarming news that the Germans might enter Andalsnes at any moment. Again he must take flight, and this time he did not dare to employ the train. An unprotected train was too big an objective for the German bombers to miss a second time. All the preparations in Andalsnes had been in vain, since only a small part of the gold had been shipped on the British cruiser.

The only chance was to load the remaining thirteen hundred cases of gold on trucks and follow the coastal road northward. Haslund set about requisitioning trucks that were intended for the transport of munitions.

Within half an hour Haslund had rounded up twenty-six trucks. The drivers had not slept for twenty-four hours; they were near collapse, and now they were being asked to drive for at least another twenty-four hours. One complication succeeded another. The coastal road was broken by various fjords; ferries would be needed to get the trucks across these fjords.

The trucks drove several miles apart, so that the Stukas would not find them too easy prey. But they had been underway scarcely half an hour when four Nazi planes appeared, dived low, and spattered machine-gun fire at the column. Fredrik Haslund, driving a private car at the head of the column, sought cover in a thicket on the side of the road. Together with Nordahl Grieg, the poet, he crawled under a bush. During the worst of the machine-gunning, the Norwegian poet spoke to him of the beauties of approaching spring as symbolized in a small white flower that had bloomed too early above the snow.

The Nazis did not suspect that the trucks contained the long-sought Norwegian gold, and so they abandoned the attack after some three-quarters of an hour of strafing. No one in the column had been injured, and the convoy of gold was able to proceed.

The trucks still had to pass through Andalsnes, which had become a no-man's land. As the first cars entered the town, a building was struck directly by a heavy bomb. Great blocks of concrete and sections of brick wall were hurled across the road. The men had to stop and clear the way before they could continue. Finally the road was clear, and they went on, despite the roar of planes overhead.

In the afternoon they reached the first ferry crossing, but there was no ferry in sight. The only ferry had been bombed the day before, they were informed, and there was no other to be had.

By frantic telephoning, Haslund arranged for two small passenger ferries to come to their aid from another point.

The drivers and accompanying soldiers were utterly exhausted. Now they had six hours' rest, for Haslund had decided not to risk ferrying the gold across until nightfall. For the interval, the trucks were driven into the woods and camouflaged.

The two ferries took six hours to transport the twenty-six trucks across the fjord, since each ferry could take only two trucks at a time.

Once across, other difficulties developed. The trucks that had been hastily assembled were, for the most part, intended to carry loads of no more than a ton and a half.

All of them had been loaded with two or three tons of gold. Soon one of the overloaded trucks broke down. There was nothing to do but unload it and place even more weight on the others. The Norwegian coastal road is both curving and narrow, and each breakdown caused the halting of the entire column until the road could be cleared.

Their goal was Molde, in the Northwest, where they had been expected for the past twelve hours. A concrete cellar had been prepared here to hide the remaining gold.

The journey began with twenty-six trucks. Four broke down on the road; three replacements were secured. In spite of great obstacles, all the gold arrived safely in Molde.

The truck drivers, although they had scarcely slept for days, returned to the vicinity of Andalsnes to continue their task of transporting munitions. The rest of the group waited for an opportunity to get their gold to a ship. Their vigil took place in a burning town, for the Nazi planes had bombed Molde unmercifully. For five days they waited, while all around the town was reduced to rubble. Molde, once known as the "City of Roses," was wrecked as thoroughly as Warsaw and Rotterdam.

In Oslo Jonas Lie, the new Chief of Police, conferred in the first days of May with Vidkun Quisling and the German Army Staff on the problem of intercepting the shipment of gold to England. The Germans suspected that it was somewhere in the vicinity of Andalsnes, where it had last been located. Fifty Nazis planes were assigned the mission of discovering the hiding place.

In Molde a British warship lay at anchor in the burning port, receiving aboard King Haakon and the members of his Government. Haslund hoped he would be able to transport the gold on this same ship. But all the piers had been shattered or burned by bombing; there seemed to be no way to get the gold aboard the 10,000 ton cruiser. At last he decided to bring the gold alongside the ship, using small boats.

Meanwhile the German planes were steadily attacking the cruiser. The British felt concern for the safety of the King, and urged haste. The loading and unloading of the small boats was proceeding with painful slowness.

Haslund decided to risk driving four trucks out on a burning pier. Through shattered, littered streets the trucks fought their way and at last reached the dock. But the cruiser had already weighed anchor and was leaving the port. From the ship one of the government members cried out encouragingly to him, "You must try to get through to the north."

Haslund gathered a new fleet of trucks. He later wrote that he did not know how they drove the trucks out of the city through flames and an incessant hail of machine-gun bullets. But at last his convoy reached the open road, and headed northward.

After several hours' journey along the coast, they came upon a small passenger ship that was taking refugees on board. Haslund insisted on requisitioning the boat.

His small group now had no orders, nor any information. The King and the Government were on their way to England; Haslund had no idea how far north the Germans had already driven. He concealed the cases of gold in the woods and arranged for the loading to be done at night.

In the course of the day the small ship was bombed and driven aground. This ship was their last hope. Haslund and his men resolved to attempt repairs and float the ship again. After frenzied labors by men who knew little about ships, they succeeded. The gold was loaded on board, and then began a journey in June down hundreds of Norwegian fjords. The ship had no radio; no one knew what districts were already in the hands of the Nazis. Haslund wanted to go to Namsos to establish contact again with the British,

Duel for the Northland 129

but on an island he was told that Namsos had been abandoned by the British.

Meanwhile, the Nazi Secret Service, now at work at last, had learned that the ship with the gold was under way. Seaplanes were sent to attack it. A captured Norwegian torpedo boat was manned by Germans and lay in ambush in a fjord for Haslund's ship. But the Norwegian Secret Service discovered the trick in time, and informed Haslund.

At last, on an island in one of the Norwegian fjords, Haslund obtained two small fishing boats from Norwegian patriots. The remaining five hundred and fifty cases of gold were placed aboard these boats, and again the flight began.

The two fishing boats sailed northward. Planes circled overhead, but saw no more than two shabby and harmless small vessels and did not attack the Norwegian "fishermen." Another time the boats passed within twenty feet of a U-boat, which also did not attack. Haslund took the risk of hastily going on land and informing the Norwegian naval command in the area, which had not yet been taken by the Germans. A few hours later the submarine was sunk.

At last the expedition reached Tromsoe and from there the gold was shipped directly to England.

This is the story of a modern Viking, a modest man whose amazing feat is hardly known. In the summer of 1940 he came to America to direct the activities of the brave Norwegian merchant marine which had contributed over one thousand vessels to the cause of the Allies. Haslund has charge of some twenty-five thousand Norwegian sailors. When he has some time for himself, he works on the problems of post-war reconstruction in Norway.

9. Sabotage and Counterespionage in Norway

The moon is not down in Norway. Norway, because of her long coastline and her steady contact with England, is in a position to offer greater resistance to her rulers than any other of the occupied countries. It is true that Ernst Friedrich Wollweber, the OGPU master mind, has struck tremendous blows against the Nazis in Norway. But it would be utterly wrong to overlook the fact that not Wollweber, but hundreds of thousands of Norwegian patriots, guided by their exiled government in London, have organized the chief work of sabotage and counterespionage against the enemy in their country.

Norway is an ideal land for hidden sabotage and counterespionage activities. Thinly populated, with scattered settlements cut off from one another by mountains, fjords, forests and swamplands, adequate military or police supervision is physically impossible. To patrol every mile of the long Swedish-Norwegian border would require more soldiers than the Germans can spare for such work. And the rugged, fjord-indented coast offers endless opportunities for small boats to make the trip to England and back in comparative safety, especially during the Arctic nights.

"Ruteboat" is what the Norwegians call these craft; they make their voyages virtually on schedule, at least once a week, passing between Norway and England. They transport short wave radios, military information and recruits for the Free Norwegian Army.

Admiral Canaris, the Nazi spy-master, had spent years creating his system of mass espionage controlled from a single center. Norway boasts a quite similar system. It is not, to be sure, controlled centrally, but every Norwegian considers himself a member of it. He does not know his superiors, but he does know that his duty is to "pass on" whatever information he gathers about the Germans. Through the so-called "grapevine" the intelligence is whispered from neighbor to neighbor, until at last it reaches a member of the authoritative counterespionage group, who sends it on to London.

When a Norwegian discovers that a schoolhouse in the vicinity of Narvik has been confiscated by the Nazis and turned into a munitions dump, he relates the story; it is told and retold until at last it comes to the ears of someone who can check up on it and then inform the Norwegian Government-in-exile in London.

Secret radios have been distributed throughout the country, despite Nazi threats and penalties, despite the fact that several score of Norwegian martyrs have been executed after short wave transmitters were found in their possession.

Every member of the Norwegian underground has been warned not to take needless risks. Sabotage and counterespionage are punishable by death; the Norwegians are instructed to undertake such activities only when the chances of discovery are exceedingly small. The "Quisling traitors" receive their just due only when they present an opportunity for a virtually "perfect crime."

The Norwegian counterespionage has a peculiar advantage; not only is every Nazi and every Quisling office under observation by loyal Norwegians, but patriots are stationed in the offices themselves. On May 10, 1941 the General Secretary of the Quisling Hird Storm Troopers founded a secret espionage division. It was arranged that all informers would be paid liberally for their services, and that arrests would be made by Quisling troopers instead of Germans. The stratagem proved valueless because it remained secret exactly one day. The following day the London radio broadcast warnings to the Norwegian people describing all the features of the new spy organization.

The Nazis find the London radio a sharp thorn in their side. Indeed, Governor Josef Terboven must listen to it to keep himself informed about conditions in the country he rules. Vidkun Quisling has never been able to fulfil his promise to restore order in Norway. Because he is afraid to confess his defeat, he conceals a great many unpleasant facts from his German masters. To check up on Quisling, Terboven listens to the London radio every day.

One day the actors of Oslo went on strike. Terboven's first news of the strike came from the BBC. Quisling had balked at admitting the extent of his impotence.

Three times Quisling attempted a coup d'état to seize complete power for himself. Each time he was betrayed by the counterespionage agents within his own ranks. Quisling had wanted to establish a so-called *Riksting,* a new parliament to be elected on a class basis. This new parliament would promptly make peace with Germany, depose King Haakon, and mobilize all able-bodied Norwegians for military service against the Allies. In other words, Quisling hoped to transform Norway into a full partner of the Axis.

After the London radio informed the Norwegians of this plan, Quisling found it impossible to persuade any Norwegian statesmen to attend the preliminary conference. The Norwegians smiled at Quisling's lame apologies in which he said that he had conceived of the *Riksting* merely as an economic conference having nothing to do with politics.

When the British and Norwegian commandos raided the Lofoten Islands, they were met by native members of the Lofoten underground. These natives led them to the official and the secret offices of the Gestapo and the Military Intelligence. Hundreds of letters and instructions were found, and proved of the greatest value to the Allies.

When heavy cannon were mounted on the northwest coast of Norway, London knew about it a few hours later. For the counterespionage service informed London at once via radio that Maginot Line cannon had just arrived in northern Norway and that German workers were being used to install them.

The Germans do not trust Norwegian workmen. While all the occupied countries of Europe are sending slave labor to Germany, the reverse is true in Norway. There are only 5,000 Norwegian forced laborers in Germany—and 100,000 German workers in Norway. The reason is simple. Norway holds the record for sabotage; Terboven and Quisling are helpless to stop it.

Here is one of many significant examples.

Norwegian workmen were forced to build fortifications in the vicinity of Kirkenes and the North Cape. It was winter and bitterly cold, too cold to keep strict supervision of the laborers. The cement for the fortifications was mixed with three times the required proportion of water. In the intense Arctic cold the water and cement froze splendidly; the cement works looked as sturdy and solid as could be desired. But when the water began to thaw in the spring, the Nazi masters found that the entire fortifications were crumbling.

The Germans never permit Norwegian bus drivers to take charge of busses transporting German soldiers. The occupation troops still speak with horror of the two

Norwegian bus drivers who at top speed drove their busses, each containing seventy-five German soldiers, over a precipice into a fjord. The drivers and every one of the soldiers were drowned.

In the fall of 1942, when the Oslo headquarters of Gestapo Chief Paul Rediess was bombed, the British fliers found the hated building through light signals flashed by Norwegian counterespionage agents.

The Nazi espionage system has had a consistent run of hard luck—or bad management—in Norway. There, in the land of the true "nordics" the myth of Prussian efficiency has been dispelled once and for all.

It was not until April 20, 1940, eleven days after the invasion and the *Bluecher* incident, that the second squadron of German administrators and espionage agents arrived in Norway.

The Norwegians were surprised to find that some of them were old acquaintances. There was, for example, the talented German-Norwegian, Rolf Schuettauf, a quiet man who had been a flutist with the Oslo Philharmonic Orchestra. Schuettauf had played the world's greatest music under the world's greatest conductors. Now he had exchanged his flute for a rubber truncheon and stepped forth as a robust Gestapo bruiser, taking great delight in beating and torturing the victims of Nazi inquisitions. The man who had once played the prisoners' songs from *Fidelio* under Toscanini and Bruno Walter, now listened to the cries of prisoners under the lash.

All the Germans in Norway were organized after the pattern by which Pflugk-Hartung had organized the Danish Germans. Every German-Norwegian was suddenly promoted to office, and betrayed his own best friends. The examples of Norway and Denmark have convinced me that the members of the German-American Bund in the United States were being trained for the same sort of foul work.

The captured Canaris spies also told the truth about the institution of the "Wiener-Kinder"—the Viennese children. Wiener-Kinder were the half-starved children, mostly Austrians, who had been taken to neutral Scandinavia by philanthropic Norwegians during World War I. Each of the children was placed with foster-parents, given a good upbringing, and above all decently fed—while millions of children whose fate was to remain at home in Germany and Austria suffered from malnutrition.

The children spoke Norwegian perfectly, and after the war made a practice of visiting their foster parents almost every year.

Long before Hitler took power the Wiener-Kinder had had a club in Vienna. When the Nazis occupied Austria, the membership list of the club was checked and each Wiener-Kind—now a grown man, of course—was carefully trained for the eventual invasion of Norway. They were questioned on their acquaintances in Norway, and for several years before the invasion some of them were employed as espionage agents, spying upon their foster-parents.

The Wiener-Kinder were sent to Norway upon the transport *Kiel,* there to be used for espionage work and terrorism. Some of the men—all now German officers—betrayed their own foster parents.

In fairness, it must be said that Vienna's children were not all unnatural. There were also Wiener-Kinder in Nazi uniform who committed suicide rather than perpetrate deeds of criminal ingratitude against the country of their foster-parents.

There were other ingrates in Norway, who repaid generosity with treachery. Out of the 1,500 political refugees in Norway, three proved to be traitors; the rest were more than loyal, and never forgot what they owed to the country that had given them asylum.

Duel for the Northland

That there were only three is astonishing when we consider that Judas Lie, the Quisling Chief of Police, had personally controlled the rescue of refugees from Czechoslovakia. He, together with the Nazi-phile Chief of Passport Control, Richard Konstadt, had selected the refugees that were to be admitted to Norway. Despite such foresight, they were able to smuggle in only three spies.

Konstadt can be most quickly identified as the Norwegian version of Max Pelving. Pelving spied on the refugees in Denmark for the Nazi Secret Service; Konstadt performed the same function in Norway. Cross and double-cross permeated their work.

On April 9, 1940, the day of the invasion, a German refugee who walked with a limp visited Richard Konstadt. He offered his services to the new masters. I may not reveal the real name of this refugee, for his work is not yet over, so let us call him Hans Schwalbe. Schwalbe had formerly been a well-known Communist in Germany, and was said to have worked with the OGPU. In 1937, after the Moscow Trials, he went over to the Communist Opposition. This fact was known to the Norwegian police. Since 1933 he had been living in Norway; earlier he had been in a German concentration camp, where he had received such severe beatings that his leg was permanently injured. This was the cause of his limp.

Konstadt needed the good offices of traitors in order to capture the remaining 1,497 loyal refugees and turn them over to the Nazis.

A few days afterward Schwalbe, in Nazi uniform, was installed in the main office of the Oslo Gestapo. At first he acted merely as interpreter; later on he examined prisoners, drew up reports and carried out investigations on his own.

Schwalbe rose swiftly in the ranks of the Gestapo. His fellows spoke of him with bitter hatred, and the Nazis, who at first had distrusted him, had become so fond of him by 1942 that he was permitted to enter the Nazi Party.

Schwalbe was freely admitted to all German espionage offices. He organized much of the Nazi counterespionage system in Norway; he also had connections in Denmark and Sweden, and used these connections for espionage. Soon he was honored by a personal interview with Himmler, when the Gestapo Chief visited Oslo. To Himmler he declared, "I starved long enough as a refugee; now, at last, I'm doing sensible work, and I'm doing it to the best of my ability."

Himmler, impressed by the reports of Schwalbe's superiors, remarked that his abilities were of a high order.

The Norwegian agents, who knew Schwalbe well from the days when refugee committees had supported him and given him the chance to build up a new life, reported his new activities; and the Norwegians' bitter resentment against the Judas increased. But at the same time confusing reports were flowing in to the Norwegian authorities of the Government-in-exile. Schwalbe was said to have smuggled information out of prisons and passed it on; Schwalbe was said to have given warning to Norwegian patriots when they were about to be arrested. Apparently, Schwalbe was a man of two aspects: one was the merciless Gestapo man, and the other the "guardian angel" of underground patriots.

Norwegian patriots, both in London and Oslo, were in a quandary. The Oslo underground members who tried to sound him out by going to him and soliciting favors, were treated harshly. There seemed no way to find the truth about Schwalbe; the Norwegians decided to wait and be cautious. A prominent leader of the Norwegian underground escaped to London and reported that Schwalbe was definitely a Nazi spy; he declared that his "favors" were cunning devices to win the confidence of the members of the underground, in order to destroy them.

At last Schwalbe himself provided the solution to the mystery. On New Year's Day, 1943, wearing a full Nazi uniform, he drove openly to the Swedish-Norwegian border. Then he vanished. In spite of his injured leg, he walked miles—in civilian clothes—through the forests of Norway and escaped to Sweden with a large briefcase crammed with Nazi documents.

Schwalbe, the man who had broken with the Communist Party, sent these documents of the German espionage service to Russia. He was one of Ernst Friedrich Wollweber's best agents. In working for the Gestapo from 1940 to 1943 he was acting on Wollweber's "beefsteak" order that every Communist must join the Nazi Party and spy on it. Schwalbe has made an immense contribution to the work of the Russian Secret Service, but his identity must not be revealed because his work is not yet over.

Guenther Kern, a pious language teacher who acted as the Nazi master mind in Norway and had done the most to prepare the country for invasion, is now living out his days in obscurity. He had been entrusted with giving light-signals to the Nazis when they invaded and then deposed.

Guenther Kern was a dangerous man for the Allied cause, for he saw more clearly than his superiors. He warned dozens of Nazis against Quisling, whom he considered wholly incapable of mastering the situation. Quisling, however, proved himself the better salesman; he succeeded in selling his incompetence to Hitler. Kern suffered the same fate as Konrad Henlein, who was cast off as useless by the Nazis after the murder of the Czechoslovak Republic. For years little has been heard of Kern. In 1942 he left the church, stating as his reason that "I do not believe in God;

I believe only in Adolf Hitler." Today he lives quietly in Berlin, a fallen angel.

The struggle in Norway is a battle of time bombs and dynamite, of grit and liquid poured into machinery, of axe and firing squad, of guillotine and gallows, of smuggled literature and denunciations to the police, of lights flashing fitfully in the darkness to show waiting submarines the location of their prey.

Few realize the full meaning of the life-and-death battle waged daily by the Norwegian saboteurs and counterespionage agents.

I kept a diary of this battle, intending some day to publish parts of it. The diary recounts the story of Norwegian sabotage from 1941 to 1943; it indicates in bare outline the heroic epic of one of our allies—the epic of the Norwegian patriots who, without benefit of espionage and sabotage schools, successfully defeated the highly-trained spy machinery of Germany. Perhaps some quotations from this diary will give a picture of their work.

In this silent war the most remote events may have a close tactical connection. A train is derailed, a bridge collapses, fire sweeps an oil-well, a handful of emery clogs essential machinery in a munitions plant, a ship blows up, a woman's mutilated body is fished out of Oslo harbor, a German brigade is poisoned by a shipment of Norwegian herring, an avalanche hurtles from a mountain peak and crashes upon the rails below just as a Nazi transport train passes. . . .

During one stormy night the strategic Oslo-Bergen line was interrupted in no less than ten different places. In spite of heavy penalties the German Army's telephone and telegraph lines were constantly cut, holes were drilled in the bottom of Nazi freighters, road signs disappeared. The German counterespionage agencies were helpless.

Duel for the Northland 141

Norwegian sabotage is now so extensive that the Nazis have been forced to place a guard every 200 yards along the railroad from Oslo to Lillestroem. They have ordered that, should the line suffer damage at any point, the two nearest Norwegian guards are to be shot.

The Nazis arrested and shot members of the Norwegian underground, but each additional punishment merely engendered new sabotage. To the Nazis, the underground movement was like the hydra: when one head fell, two new ones appeared in its place.

At first the underground was extremely cautious, but as it grew steadily stronger, it ventured more and more. In place of spontaneous minor acts of sabotage, there came sabotage and counterespionage that was carefully planned and centrally directed. The weapons of the underground were fire, dynamite and short wave radio. Radio transmitters were smuggled into the country in every imaginable manner, with superb daring and cleverness. For patience, there is the example of a Norwegian patriot who landed in Norway by parachute and in landing damaged the short wave transmitter he was carrying. Returning to England on the "rute boat," the famous "ferry to England" of the underground movement, he obtained another set, flew to Norway once more and again parachuted down to the soil of his native land. The second time he was more successful and delivered the radio to its planned destination, so that it might take up its work of sending vital information to England.

It was this one—out of hundreds of short wave transmitters—that broadcast to the Norwegian Government in London the fateful message that the German battleship *Bismarck* had left the port of Trondheim. Not many days afterwards the *Bismarck*, the most modern battleship of Germany's fleet, was sent to the bottom by the British

Navy. That sinking can be credited directly to Norwegian counterespionage.

Innocent hostages are shot; Norwegians suspected of sabotaging or spying on German military installations are shot; and nevertheless the wave of sabotage and counterespionage surges onward. It cannot be stopped.

The Nazis frankly admit the sabotage. Everywhere in Norway hang posters warning that the death penalty will be exacted from saboteurs, and hostages will be seized in the communities where sabotage occurs. The *Deutsche Zeitung,* published by the occupation authorities, rants against the sabotage and publishes proclamations of Quisling requesting the people to be peaceful and orderly. When this did not help, proclamations signed by Knut Hamsun were published; in February 1943 one of Hamsun's proclamations was distributed throughout the country. Hamsun implored the youth of Norway to come to their senses and not be tempted into sabotage or counterespionage, which would merely bring more suffering upon Norway.

In my journal of Norwegian sabotage and counterespionage I noted hundreds of acts of resistance and sabotage. It is impossible to recount them all, but I must mention some of the more important ones.

At least thirty separate acts of sabotage were directed against the Sola airport, near Stavanger. The Nazis have built up a first-rate air base here. This is quite natural, since it is the point in Norway that is closest to England. Sola was an important base during the air "blitz" on London. At least three times Norwegian saboteurs cut all the power cables leading to the German airport. When the RAF bombed the air base, school children with flashlights pointed the way for the British fliers. Eleven children were arrested. The underground hangars of the Sola airport were completely wrecked. The extent of the damage may be calculated by the German reaction: the population of Stavanger was four times sentenced to pay heavy fines. The first fine amounted to 30,000 kroner; the fourth to six million kroner.

Sabotage against Hitler's vulnerable spot, the transportation system, is a heroic story in itself.

On July 30, 1941, a magnificent summer day, six hundred railroad workers at the Oslo Freight Yards were arrested. A time bomb had exploded on the tracks just outside the yards; a German munitions train was brought to a halt just before it reached the wrecked track. The saboteurs were never found. The six hundred hostages were later released, since there already was a shortage of railroad workers.

On September 5, the Oslo railroad workers had better luck, for this time a German munitions train was successfully blown up. Thereafter, Oslo workmen would say to one another, "We all work six hours for King Haakon and two hours for Quisling." In other words, six hours a day they sabotaged Nazi factories by slowdowns or direct interference with the machinery; no more than two hours out of every shift were devoted to actual production.

The greatest railroad disaster occurred on February 1, 1942. On this day, the "coronation day" of "Premier" Quisling, Oslo's Central Railroad Station caught fire. The fire burned for seven hours. Only two of the thirteen tracks remained in operation. All trains for Germany had to be halted.

Around this time, fires were blazing up everywhere. During one week in February there were at least twenty fires at different railroad stations.

On March 21, 1942, the United Press reported that saboteurs had blown up railway bridges that were links for the transport of munitions and soldiers to Finland. In consequence, General Dietl was much handicapped in his campaign against Murmansk and was forced to depend solely upon supplies by sea.

The Nazis shot Norwegians for sabotage against the U-boat base at Trondheim; they shot Norwegians for destroying military installations, for cutting power lines, for blowing up power plants, for sending to England blueprints of secret air and submarine bases. But the united efforts of Admiral Canaris's and Quisling's spy services could not cope with the relentless momentum of the underground movement.

Most of the German factories in the Vestland district have been wrecked. Cities like Fredrikstad, Arendal and Haugesund have earned a place on the honor roll of sabotage. In all places "civil guards" were organized to help protect German military establishments against sabotage. Nevertheless, the Nazi flag was torn to tatters and every German poster in the towns ripped down. The Mayor of one of these towns was ordered to give the Nazis the names of ten citizens who were to be shot. The Mayor listed ten leading Quislings.

Norwegian sabotage continued during 1942 and 1943 as vigorously as ever. A sulphur factory in Astvedt near Bergen was burned down. There was a tremendous explosion, and seventy tons of sulphur were consumed—the fifth sulphur factory to burn within two years.

There was a great fire in the Anne Kures Hotel on the Voksenkollen, a favorite skiing place of Norwegian boys and girls in pre-war days. The Nazis had taken it over for winter quarters. The hotel was completely gutted. Again the cause of the fire was unknown. Several soldiers received severe burns and most of their belongings were lost.

When the Nazis confiscated a fish filet canning factory in Bodd in Northern Norway, the factory caught fire and burned for two days. It was a total loss. Machines valued at a million dollars were destroyed. Several factory workers

Duel for the Northland

were arrested, but the cause was not discovered. This was the second time the Nazis had ill luck with Norwegian fish.

Indeed, the Nazis have had persistent ill luck with fish. Several thousand German soldiers have been poisoned by bad fish. At one time three German fishing vessels transported a stolen fish catch from Norway to Hamburg, only to find that wax had been poured over the entire cargo, rendering it inedible. Another time the Norwegians hawked fish in the streets with the cry:

> "Herring, herring,
> Fat as Goering."

There was a certain macabre humor in the cry; the Nazis soon learned the grim fact that the Norwegians knew only too well. The fish were especially fat that year from feeding on the corpses of torpedoed Germans.

The newspapers played many pranks on the Nazis. One courageous Danish editor published a story that an RAF raid had done considerable damage—a factory had burned for an entire day. The editor was warned; no damage had been done, the Nazis insisted, except that a few cows had been killed. The following day the newspaper printed a retraction. "No damage was done. A cow burned for four days." The editor was promptly arrested.

One of the most thorough acts of sabotage in the German-Norwegian war shows evidence of such careful planning that there is no doubt it was the work of an organized group. A fire destroyed a million gallons of gasoline stored in tanks at Bergen. The fire lasted for several days.

Children who laughed and bantered about the fire were arrested. School children in Norway greet each other inevitably with the word *Klump*. It means "Kongen Leve ut met Pakket"—"Long Live the King; throw out the gangsters."

Fires aboard ships were started in the tried-and-true Wollweber fashion. The Norwegian ship *Stensaas,* which was sailing under the Nazi flag, was set afire by its own crew. The sailors sprang into the icy water and swam ashore to Sweden. Well may we say that the blood of the Vikings still flows in the veins of such men.

Norway is still a great whaling country. Whalers from all over the world come to Norway for training. The Nazis, who know little about whaling and still less about building whaleboats, forced the Norwegian Nylands Mekanisk Verkstad in Oslo to build five whaleboats. Normally, such boats take about a month and a half to construct. These boats were five months in the building, and after a few weeks all had to be sent back for repairs. The German naval espionage authorities demanded a sabotage investigation, but nothing was proved.

It is impossible to detail all the sabotage, great and small, that has been committed by the Norwegians in their struggle against the enemy. It is clear, however, that all Norwegians, from schoolchildren to graybeards, are in revolt. The Japanese system of mass espionage and sabotage, which Admiral Canaris regarded so highly, has been developed to perfection by the Norwegians. An entire nation is fighting underground, not only with words and strikes in the schools, the churches and the factories, but also with explosives, short wave radios, and fire. It is an epic worthy of the ancient nordic mythology—an epic written not only in blood, sweat and tears, but in hatred also. It is the epic of Haakon the Great and his great people.

The Norwegian people cannot speak openly. Their bishops are in prisons, their teachers in concentration camps. But these acts of sabotage speak their own language. Some of the sabotage is trivial, but all of it is disturbing and confusing. In sum, it has forced the Nazis to realize that they have not really conquered Norway.

There has been no guerrilla fighting in the hills of Norway; the Norwegians are only too well aware that armed resistance now would be incurring mass suicide. However, it is no secret that there is an army in Norway, training like Commando troops, for the day when guerrillas can assist the invading Allies or protect the Norwegian civilians from a retreating and demoralized German army. German Military Intelligence is fully aware that only a fraction of the light arms of the Norwegian army was turned in; every so often they stumble upon caches of hunting rifles, dynamite and home-made hand grenades, while the youth of Norway has gone in for intensive physical training as never before. Rumors in Norway say that as early as Christmas, 1940, the secret army had progressed sufficiently to hold "winter maneuvers" near Oslo. To date, however, the principal problem of the secret army has been to keep young hotheads from shooting before the time is ripe.

The most maddening thing of all to the Gestapo is their utter failure to lay hands on any of the leaders of the Norwegian underground. They have executed scores and thrown thousands more into concentration camps, but to no avail. After each mass arrest the organization gives evidence of being stronger than before. The search for the Master Mind goes on, for the Germans are convinced that there must be a Master Mind, a Leader with powers of organization and ingenuity surpassed only by Der Führer himself. That an organization can spring into being from the universal desire of a democratic people for freedom so that one leader can be replaced by another equally capable and sincere is beyond their imagination. They do not comprehend that Norwegian democracy was not something imposed from the top upon a docile people conditioned by two hundred and fifty years of Prussian drillmasters and Prussian schoolmasters. There is organized resistance in Norway today, but the organization sprang from the people, not from a power-mad little Führer.

When Norway capitulated to the superior might of the enemy, after a struggle that lasted sixty-two days, she was forced to release the German prisoners she had taken —there had not been shipping space to send them to England. But the Norwegians hid the weapons they had captured in safe places, in readiness for the day when they will be able to use them.

Today Norway's organized and unorganized army of saboteurs is waging war against Hitler more intensively than ever. The Germans need 400,000 troops in Norway to guard the land against attacks from within and without; despite his desperate need for men to maintain his Russian front, Hitler dare not withdraw these soldiers. For in the final analysis he knows that neither Quisling nor Terboven is dependable; it is the army alone that can keep order in rebellious Norway.

PART FOUR

Intermezzo in Iceland and Greenland

10. Germany's Secret Service in Iceland and Greenland

Now that British, Norwegian and American troops are garrisoning Iceland, it is legitimate to reveal the unsuccessful plan of Pflugk-Hartung's agents to conquer Iceland and Greenland.

The conquest of Iceland was on Hitler's schedule, and had he not lost half his fleet in the battle of Norway he would undoubtedly have invaded Iceland. The sixty-two day struggle of the Norwegians against General Nikolaus von Falkenhorst was a longer battle than either Poland or France put up, and those sixty-two days were also the salvation of Iceland.

Norway had fought a heroic battle. It was due to the spontaneous resistance of the ably-led Norwegians that the Germans suffered such tremendous naval losses, as well as army casualties of some 60,000 soldiers and officers.

The master-plan of the conquest of Iceland was concocted in the offices of Admiral Wilhelm Canaris and Joachim von Ribbentrop. Its administrators were Pflugk-Hartung and a German "scientist," Professor Paul Burckhardt. They were designated to lay the groundwork for the surrender of Iceland in conjunction with the fall of Denmark; both of these men had been working for years to establish Germany's spy system in Iceland.

It was General Haushofer himself who once stated: "The Power that holds the Finnish Aaland Islands would have a revolver forever pointed at Sweden." He made a similar statement about Iceland and Greenland, asserting that the Power that held these two countries would have its revolver covering England, Canada and the United States. The brisk intervention of Great Britain and the United States in Iceland and Greenland effectively knocked that revolver out of the hands of the Nazis.

To tell the story of the plot against Iceland and Greenland we must embark first on a long and sentimental love story. Pflugk-Hartung had selected a girl to be one of his agents, a girl who was to fall in love with his chief organizer in Iceland, Professor Burckhardt; without this the plan could not be realized.

Pflugk-Hartung's task was to arrange the boy-meets-girl detail. Then he was to withdraw from the romance, the rest being in the hands of his sub-agent. But he hoped he would eventually be called upon to give them his blessing.

She was about twenty-eight; Burckhardt was not quite fifty years old. They met for the first time in Copenhagen in 1938. Gudrun was an actress. Born in Iceland, she spoke perfect German, in addition to Danish and her native Icelandic. She was a handsome girl with vivid red hair, not very tall and none too slender. Gudrun had no great opportunities for a career in Iceland, a country of only 116,000 inhabitants, of whom some 34,000 live in the capital, Reykjavik. Consequently, Gudrun had gone to Germany to study, and later on she was given the opportunity to play larger roles in Copenhagen. There, quite by chance, at a dance sponsored by the theater organization, she met this German professor. There were quite a number of Nazi diplomats present that evening, including Pflugk-Hartung—the Nazis have always been eager

Duel for the Northland

to form close ties with the men and women of the stage world. Canaris and Pflugk-Hartung have a weakness for the old-fashioned idea that nothing surpasses a Mata Hari for espionage work.

Burckhardt, who was about to go to Iceland at the head of a great archeological expedition, was introduced to all Icelanders present at the party. This included, of course, Gudrun.

Burckhardt made love to Gudrun—quite successfully. That very night he suggested to her that she come with him to Iceland as his companion. They would have a wonderful time together, he promised, and since he needed an interpreter he would, in the bargain, pay her a thousand crowns a month for six months.

Gudrun wanted the money. Her life was rather lonely, and she had no disinclination toward adventures. Still, she would have been reluctant to accept this precipitate offer if Burckhardt had not thrown in the promise that he would afterwards take her to Germany and get her into the *Reichskulturkammer,* the Nazi union for all intellectuals. He said he could place her in one of the theaters of South Germany, where he had good connections.

All this Gudrun accepted. All expenses were paid by Pflugk-Hartung, leaving her several thousand crowns to put away as savings. In any event, why should she be cool toward this German professor who was good-looking and who did not behave like a professor, at least not according to her notion of a German professor?

Admiral Canaris and Pflugk-Hartung had had everything prepared months before. While Gudrun had been in Germany studying dramatics she had mentioned to some Nazi friends that she knew virtually all of high society in Iceland, as well as people in key Government positions. Gudrun prattled that she was not interested in politics, but that if politics would help her career she would not mind taking part in it. She also mentioned that her father owned part of the Icelandic fishing fleet. The sum of it all was that her name was typed upon one of Canaris's filing cards, and now her role was ordained.

Gudrun had no idea what the game was. She did not know that Professor Burckhardt was a high-ranking officer of Himmler's Elite Guard; she did not know that Professor Burckhardt had a Copenhagen bank account of some 100,000 kroner to draw upon—the account was under another name, that of Lars Larsen, who was a puppet and sub-agent of Pflugk-Hartung.

The archeological expedition set out. It comprised ten men and one woman, and was supplied with scientific instruments, tents, winter equipment. The voyage began auspiciously with a wonderful sea passage along the beautiful Norwegian coast toward Iceland.

While still on the boat Gudrun mentioned to Burckhardt that there was a man in Iceland he simply must meet. He was more or less a sympathizer with the new Germany; Professor Alfred Wegner, a famous German geologist, had visited this man a few years ago and had been very well received.

Wegner was a brilliant scientist. He had explored unknown territories in Iceland and Greenland and drawn maps. During the First World War he had been an officer of the Queen Elisabeth Grenadier regiment and was wounded twice. Later on Kaiser Wilhelm used him for meteorological war tasks. His first Greenland expedition had been organized as early as 1906; at that time Wegner was one of the balloon pioneers and there was no one in Europe who equaled his intimate knowledge of Iceland and Greenland. In 1924 he published in New York a book, *The Origin of Continents and Oceans;* he had visited the United States and Mexico and worked as late as 1928 with the American Association of Petroleum Geologists.

In 1930 Wegner had erected several weather stations in Iceland and Greenland.

Burckhardt was quite agreeable to visiting Professor Wegner's friend who turned out to be one of Iceland's most distinguished personages, the sculptor Gudmundur Einarsson. Einarsson is not only a sculptor, but one of the foremost authorities on political and economic conditions in Iceland and Greenland. He was extremely flattered by the visit, especially since Burckhardt, perceiving that Einarsson could be very helpful, improvised a host of lies on the spot. He told Einarsson that he came bringing greetings from the German Ministry of Culture, and that he himself, in his capacity of director of the Nordic Society in Luebeck, wanted to ask if Einarsson would permit the Society to hold an exhibition of his works in Germany. Einarsson was delighted. He was cheaply secured.

He asked Burckhardt what he could do to show his gratitude for this honor. Burckhardt replied that he was a scientist and would like to be introduced to Iceland, both in a social and scientific sense. Einarsson was glad to oblige. He gave banquets for Burckhardt where the German could meet Icelandic society. Gudrun made the personal introductions. Everyone was delighted to meet this charming professor who consistently maintained that he was no Nazi, merely a good German. He assumed the character of a conservative German who did not care for Corporal Hitler. It was a pose that most Icelanders believed only too easily.

Einarsson also arranged secret meetings with Iceland's small group of fascists. These men Burckhardt quickly organized into a branch of the German espionage system; the Icelandic native fascists were soon providing Burckhardt with reports on the location of weather stations, the possible operation of secret radios, and so on.

During his six months' stay in Iceland Burckhardt did not limit himself merely to cementing social contacts. On the contrary, he drew up a careful analysis of the sources of raw materials and the industrial possibilities of the country and sent his reports to Pflugk-Hartung. At the same time, this very activity helped his social relationships. Because of his zeal in exploring the island from one end to the other, everyone considered him a real lover of Iceland. Gudrun accompanied him everywhere and introduced him to everyone who counted. Burckhardt had promised to marry her; the poor girl was, of course, unaware that he had a wife and children at home in Berlin.

Burckhardt had with him German General Staff maps of Iceland; on these maps he sketched in the plan of each significant air base and landing field. In addition, he drew up a great many weather charts with exhaustive data about weather conditions in Iceland. He founded a reliable Nazi spy group and then, having secured the archeological and geopolitical information he wanted, he left with Gudrun for Berlin. A few weeks later Einarsson arrived in Germany; he was admitted for special training in the spy school at Walchen Lake in Bavaria. Gudrun was rewarded with a role in one of Munich's theaters. More Burckhardt could not do for her, since he had decided—he informed her—that it was best for them both not to marry. He paid her the compliment of telling her that Germany's friendship with Iceland had been established solely through her aid.

In Berlin Burckhardt prepared in 1939 a report several hundred pages long. This report was delivered to Admiral Canaris, and Burckhardt himself took Ribbentrop and Himmler their copies—Himmler had, after all, financed his trip. At Pflugk-Hartung's suggestion he also prepared a manuscript called *My Trip Through Iceland*. Pflugk-Hartung argued that if he published a book on Iceland it would prove that his journey had been a genuine scientific mission. Burckhardt was utterly incapable of writing such a book—it would have to be full of strange adventures in the country of sagas and steaming geysers. But Himmler had already arranged a publisher, and there was no getting out of it. Professor Burckhardt did not dare admit that he was incapable of writing such a book. Instead, he decided to look up an old classmate of his named Arthur who had attended the University of Berlin in the days when Jews were allowed to enter German universities.

Arthur was Jewish; he was a writer, and the times were very hard on him. His wife was under arrest and he himself faced deportation to one of the ghettos in Poland. Burckhardt visited him and asked him if he would be willing to write a book on Iceland. The man answered that he was on the deportation list to Poland and could not do it. Burckhardt arranged everything; the man was not deported and continued for some time to be Burckhardt's ghost writer. Arthur studied hundreds of books on Iceland and wrote a new one. In a charming, easy-going style Burckhardt's collaborator described his experiences as a tourist in Iceland and characterized Iceland as "the paradise of Nordic culture." Later, a similar book was published on Greenland. From Sweden I have received reports that Swedish journalists have seen Professor Burckhardt in the Gestapo headquarters on the Prinz Albrecht Strasse in Berlin, acting as head of the Iceland-Greenland Section of the SS Espionage Service.

One by one the members of his secret Nazi group in Iceland were invited to Germany to undergo their "basic Nazi training." The group was still operating in Iceland when the country was occupied by British troops.

Canaris and Pflugk-Hartung were more than satisfied with Burckhardt's "scientific work." A few weeks before the invasion of Norway and Denmark they gave him another assignment. He was to establish a new airline between

Germany, Bergen, Norway and Iceland, and another new airline between Germany, Bergen and Greenland. Burckhardt had speculated a good deal on an ideal airline, the airline of the future, connecting Germany-Norway-Iceland-Newfoundland-the United States. This plan came near to being put into effect by Burckhardt and the Lufthansa, but was upset at the last moment by the Allied occupation of Iceland.

The Nazis had plans for using Iceland as a springboard toward England and America. They had actually worked out in careful detail methods for launching an invasion from Iceland against Cape Cod. This was to be timed simultaneously with a landing by Japan on our West Coast. The Allies, however, by refusing to take chances by leaving Iceland unoccupied, reduced these detailed plans to idle speculations.

The Nazis utilized their Nordic Society as an agency to propagandize Iceland on a vast scale. The Icelanders were told that Iceland belonged to Northern Europe, to Scandinavia, to the Nordic bloc and not to the Western Hemisphere, as Vilhjalmur Stefansson, President Roosevelt's adviser on Iceland, had claimed. When the Danish king recognized Iceland's independence, and when Sven Bjoerzson, former Icelandic ambassador to Denmark, was inaugurated Regent, the issue was sealed and Iceland was brought into the United Nations. The alliance is traditional; in the First World War Iceland and Greenland were also dependent upon the United States, although then belonging officially to Denmark. And while Denmark and Norway, cut off by the blockade, suffered severely, Iceland received cargoes regularly from the United States.

Icelandic friends of mine remark that they are happy to be the recipients of the good will that used to be solely the portion of the Scandinavian countries. "After all," they said, "we are the most peace-loving nation in the world. In

Duel for the Northland

a thousand years we have never had an army, nor has there ever been an Icelandic soldier."

As for their relations with the United States, they refer us to olden times, to the year 1000 a.d., when the Viking, Leif Erickson, discovered America.

Iceland calls herself the oldest democracy in Europe. And indeed, Vilhjalmur Stefansson, America's foremost authority on Iceland, has called the country the first American Republic. Europeans, however, have continued to look upon Iceland as part of Northern Europe.

Whenever the flames of war flared up in the world, Iceland was cut off from Europe and in consequence the Icelanders endured great hardships. In 1807, during the Napoleonic Wars, when Europe was dominated by one man as today she is dominated by Hitler, England took over the Danish fleet. From then on Iceland had virtually no contact with Europe. During the entire year of 1808 not a single merchant vessel came to Iceland. How defenseless and helpless the country was may be judged by what happened to the unhappy land in 1809. On June 25, 1809 a Danish pirate named Jorgen Jorgensen landed on the island with his band of pirates, and proceeded to take over the government and make himself master of Iceland. He called his band of buccaneers "Hird"—the same name Vidkun Quisling now uses for his storm troopers. The pirate dictator ruled for two months until a British expeditionary corps restored order and deported Jorgensen and his "Hirds" to Tasmania. It is with an effort that we recall that this happened only one hundred and thirty-five years ago.

During World War I, Iceland was never wholly severed from Scandinavia, for by this time it possessed its own merchant marine. But without British protection and American food supplies the island could not have maintained itself. For then, as now, German U-boats torpedoed vital shipping to and from Iceland.

In the last hundred and fifty years Iceland has transformed itself from an almost medieval state into a modern community, and during the last twenty years this process has been greatly accelerated. Iceland has one of the most modern cooperative movements in the world and their domain is wide; the cooperatives in Reykjavik, for example, have erected model houses. Under the personal union with Denmark the Icelanders were very content. Assurance of their independence was extended at the same time that President Roosevelt, upon the request of Henrik de Kauffmann, the Danish Minister to the United States, undertook the protection of Greenland. Thus, in the course of this global war, the bond between Iceland and America has been forged so firmly that henceforth Iceland will undoubtedly be in closer relationship to the Western Hemisphere and the Western Democracies.

Hitler has never secured the valuable Icelandic fishing fleet, despite the efforts of Pflugk-Hartung and Canaris. When Hitler realized that his battle for Iceland was lost, Burckhardt was instantly ordered to organize an attempt against Greenland. The Danish Minister to the United States, Hendrik de Kauffmann, had shortly before committed Greenland to the protection of President Roosevelt, but Hitler thought he might nevertheless try his fortune. One fine summer day in June 1940, shortly after Hitler's final victory in Northern Norway, Burckhardt prepared to put his plan into action.

It was a plan based on an ancient agreement of 1814, when Denmark was forced to cede Norway to the Swedish Crown. The treaty allowed Denmark to retain Greenland, Iceland and Faeroe Islands, all of which had been settled by Scandinavians. The loss continued to rankle among Norwegian nationalists, and became a burning national issue when Norway was made independent of Sweden in October 1905. The question was considered settled in

1933, when the Hague Court upheld Denmark's right to Greenland. At this time Norway's Government accepted the outcome of the arbitration, but asked for and was granted the right to operate a meteorological observation post and radio stations on the east coast of Greenland.

Shortly after the invasion of Norway, Vidkun Quisling, the arch traitor, claimed urgently that Greenland was Norwegian and should come under his rule. Quisling, Professor Burckhardt, and Josef Terboven, the Nazi Governor of Norway, outfitted invasion vessels, the *Busko* and the *Furenak*. They set out on a voyage with fifty German spies who purported to be meteorologists intending to visit the Norwegian radio stations in Greenland.

The *Busko* sailed, but the British-Norwegian counter-espionage agents were quick to find out about the projected coup. The *Furenak* encountered the Royal Norwegian gunboat, *Fridtjof Nansen,* and an American Coast Guard cutter, one of the many stationed in Arctic waters after the invasion of Scandinavia, seized the *Busko* and brought her to Boston, Mass. The ships carried elaborate short wave radio apparatus designed to reinforce existing stations on the island and guide Nazi planes to a happy landing on Greenland's airfields, which were so scattered as to be otherwise difficult to locate.

Greenland is vaster than is generally conceived. If the southern tip of Greenland were placed on the Gulf of Mexico, the northern extremity would extend as far as Manitoba, Canada. Its 736,518 square miles equal the area of all the twenty-six states east of the Mississippi. And all that great area is populated by only 17,000 Eskimos and some five hundred whites, mostly Danes who are government employees of the island's administration. The patrolling of such an area is a steep task for American Coast Guard cutters, assisted only by small Norwegian forces. Those who are familiar with the situation as it stands are consequently convinced that the Nazis might try to smuggle secret agents into Greenland, equipped with short wave transmitters. Iceland and Greenland are fortresses in the battle of the Atlantic and they are half-way houses for all our operations. From the fjords of Greenland it is only four hours by air to Newfoundland, five hours to Nova Scotia, New Brunswick and to the province of Quebec, and only six hours to New England. The distance from Julianehaab (Greenland) to Reykjavik (Iceland) is only 950 miles and from Reykjavik to the Faeroe Islands it is only 500 miles.

On the strength of the experience of these flights Greenland and Iceland may obtain a new importance in postwar years, providing a link between Russia and Scandinavia and the Western Hemisphere.

For air bases, the practically level top of Greenland's ice-cap—the only large relic of the last ice age left in the northern hemisphere—forms a continuous landing field, 1,500 miles long and up to 600 miles wide. And although 84 per cent of Greenland's area is snow-covered in mid-Summer, the snow-free area amounts to some 130,000 square miles, an area larger than that of the British Isles. All this area will be used for airfields and Arctic experts say, "Imagine trying to find an airdrome, which is probably well camouflaged, in all that expanse." The answer is, "It can't be done."

The above incidents were not the only attempt the Nazis made to land spies in Greenland. As early as 1937 Pflugk-Hartung endeavored to smuggle radio operators into Greenland. The Nazis seemed to have little difficulty in persuading Mr. Adolf Hoel, head of the "Ishavskontoret" (Norwegian Arctic Office), to admit to Greenland three German scientific observers, the vanguard of a larger

Duel for the Northland 161

"scientific" expedition. This was the more remarkable since for years Greenland had been jealously guarded from foreign eyes.

The three scientific observers of Greenland were no strangers to Admiral Canaris; indeed, they were old friends of his. There was Vitalis Pantenburg, whom we shall meet later in Finland. The others were Paul Burckhardt, the expert on things Icelandic, and Horst von Pflugk-Hartung, master-builder and espionage chief of the Arctic.

Greenland has long been familiar territory to the Nazis. The man whom the Germans consider their Lindbergh, Wolfgang von Gronau, made three flights across Greenland in 1929, 1930 and 1931. Moreover, one of the generals of Goering's air force spent several months in Greenland. The pretext was a familiar one. The German film company sent an expedition to Greenland to get shots for the picture *S.O.S. Iceberg.* This expedition spent many months filming the fjords of Greenland and the sites of possible airfields. Among the members of the cast were Leni Riefenstahl, the actress who was once very close to Hitler, and Ernst Udet, hero of World War I and one of the founders of the German air force—he died not long ago, allegedly in an air crash.

There is no doubt that, wittingly or unwittingly, the beautiful Leni and General Udet were spying for Admiral Canaris.

A thorough survey of Greenland was undertaken by Germany's greatest geologist, Alfred Wegner. Wegner's experience was not restricted to the realm of science; during the last World War he had been a member of the Prussian Aeronautical Institute, and he had spent five years as chief of the Nazi Coast Guard.

Wegner established meteorological stations on both the west and east coasts of Greenland, and on the peak of the icecap. Through these stations the Nazis were supplied with weather forecasts that were invaluable to their program of bombing Britain.

It happens that Greenland provides the only known commercial source of cryolite, a flux used in the production of aluminum from bauxite. Years before they embarked on war the Nazis imported huge quantities of this mineral from Greenland. Yet their supply cannot last indefinitely. For this reason alone the Nazis would certainly have landed in Greenland had not the well-organized counterespionage system in Norway promptly thwarted every one of their attempts. The fact is that not a single ship leaves a Norwegian harbor without the ship's movements being quickly reported by Norwegian patriots via short wave to the combined Free Norwegian, British and American patrol boats.

About a year after the Nazi occupation of Denmark the Germans had tried to land expeditions in the eastern part of Greenland. It was at this time that the courageous and farsighted Danish Minister, de Kauffmann, concluded an agreement with the American Government regarding the defense of this important island.

By this agreement the American Government obtained the right to construct and use for the duration of the war air and naval bases in Greenland. In return, the United States guaranteed Danish sovereignty over the island.

No extensive occupation of Greenland has taken place, and its entire administration remains in Danish hands.

The Dano-American Greenland agreement, which was concluded on April 9, 1941, the anniversary of the invasion of Denmark, has proved of the greatest military value to the Allied cause.

Not only did it thwart a threatened German invasion, but it prevented the Germans from exploiting the meteorological stations they had succeeded in establishing on the island.

Weather reports from Greenland and Iceland provide some of the most important data for forecasting the weather over Europe. The German General Staff has badly felt the lack of these readings, for knowledge of the weather over Europe is essential to the activity of the Luftwaffe. Meteorological information from Greenland is, of course, now available only to the Allied Command.

More important, the agreement makes Greenland a bastion in the Battle of the Atlantic and the Battle of the Arctic. Greenland, like Iceland, is a stepping stone in the causeway between Great Britain and the United States. Patrols operating from the air bases on Greenland protect the huge convoys crossing from the United States to Britain and to Murmansk in Russia.

Hendrik de Kauffmann had signed the Dano-American agreement on Greenland without the permission of the Danish Government in Copenhagen. The Nazis in Denmark compelled his Government to dismiss him and to vilify him as a betrayer of Nordic unity. But de Kauffmann today is extremely popular among the Danes—so it is reported to us on the word of Denmark's Minister of Trade, Christmas Moeller, who recently fled to England. De Kauffmann and Moeller are today the leading figures in the Free Danish Movement; they assist the activities of the Free Danish merchant marine and of the Danish pilots who fight on the side of the Allies under the Norwegian flag.

Kauffmann also prevented the Nazis from obtaining any of Denmark's money abroad, for he is controller of the funds of the National Bank of Denmark, and these funds are in America. Some day they will be employed to rebuild the Denmark that Germany has plundered.

PART FIVE
Spies and Saboteurs in Sweden
11. The Wollweber League

For fifteen months the Nazis had been masters of Scandinavia. Sweden alone was still fighting its desperate battle to protect its neutrality, while in Norway and Denmark the new masters had made themselves at home, which meant that they had systematically plundered both countries. The Danish farmers had been forced to slaughter half their cattle; the Norwegian fishermen saw their fishing catches vanishing in the direction of Hamburg and Kiel, while they themselves went hungry. Finland had become a war partner of Hitler; aged Marshal Mannerheim promised his people German food and coal that were slow in coming.

Fifteen months earlier, Jonas Lie, Heinrich Himmler, Pflugk-Hartung and Thune Jacobsen, the collaborating Danish Secretary of Justice, held an important conference in the Palace of Justice in Copenhagen. Pflugk-Hartung took the floor. He had with him all the documents concerning Wollweber. And he demanded that Wollweber be captured. He pointed out that as early as 1938 the Inter-Scandinavian Police Conference had characterized Wollweber as the most dangerous of the Russian agents. Now he wanted the documents on Wollweber to be reexamined with the utmost care. Every clue, every suspect, was to be reinvestigated. What the democratic police of Scandinavia had not been able to accomplish, the united forces of the Gestapo, Jonas Lie and Thune Jacobsen must do. Efforts must also be made to secure the cooperation of the Swedish police. It was time, Pflugk-Hartung declared, to annihilate both Russian and British counterespionage once and for all.

For fifteen months Wollweber's sub-agents were shadowed. The three months Pflugk-Hartung had spent in the Copenhagen prison proved very valuable, for there he had learned the names of some of Wollweber's aides, and these were now hunted through all of Northern Europe. For fifteen months the Nazis and their traitorous collaborators prepared a monster case against "Wollweber and comrades." At last the case was brought to trial in Denmark. The trial dealt with fifty OGPU agents. But thirty could not be located, thirteen were acquitted; there remained only seven victims. The chief offenders were Anton Schmidt, alias Ernst Friedrich Wollweber, and Richard Krebs, alias Jan Valtin, whose book, *Out of the Night,* had given the Nazi prosecutors much valuable information. But Jan Valtin and his former chief were safely out of the reach of the Nazis.

As in the Reichstag Fire Trial, the entire Nazi propaganda apparatus was mobilized to publicize the case. For this trial was to justify the Nazi occupation; the Germans hoped to show the Danish population that the Russians had wholly undermined their country and that Germany had come to protect it in the nick of time. The trial was intended to show also that the Russian and British Secret Services had cooperated, and that England had plans to invade Denmark; in other words, to reveal that King Christian and his people had cause to be grateful for Germany's paternal hand.

The propaganda trial began on July 7, 1941. The large courtroom of the "Landsretten" was overcrowded; on every hand Nazi troops and Danish police were in evidence.

Pflugk-Hartung attended in his Elite Guard uniform, Dr. Werner Best in the black uniform of the Gestapo, Carlis Hansen in his Danish uniform; "Fat Fritz" Clausen and members of his Nazi party, and all the elite of the Nazi occupation forces were on hand. It was a triumphal spectacle of the conquerors. Among the audience were Eiler Pontoppidan, whose face had grown somewhat baggier, and even Elsa Andersen, who had once bought the villa in Charlottenlund as a headquarters for the spy ring. The only one who was missing was Admiral Wilhelm Canaris, who was evidently too busy to leave Berlin.

The victims were six Communist workers and one woman; their faces were gray from long imprisonment and they showed signs of many beatings. Victims is the accurate name for them, since the verdict was predetermined.

Although Danish judges were compelled to play their parts in this spectacle, there were remarkably few Danes among the spectators. The Nazis had the courtroom to themselves.

The accused were:

Richard Jensen, treasurer of the West European Bureau of the Comintern. He had provided Wollweber with the funds he needed for his work of "total sabotage." Jensen was also a member of the Copenhagen City Council. Large sums of money had been found in his possession, although he himself was a man of small means. To the bemedaled, scornful audience Jensen had declared simply:

"Nazism and Communism are deadly foes. I have done my duty and would do it again tomorrow." He was given sixteen years' imprisonment.

The second offender was the most interesting of them all: a tall, tough, middle-aged sailor named Gustav Langfors who for years had been Jensen's secretary and adjutant. He was Jensen's and Wollweber's most trusted courier; a man thoroughly experienced in all forms of sabotage. He was sentenced to twelve years.

The third was a Danish sailor, Kaj Geil, who had done most of the rough work and with Jensen received the heaviest sentence: sixteen years.

The other three were men from the waterfront: a vigorous longshoreman, Kjeld Vanmand, who was given six years for transmitting information on Nazi ship movements to the Red Baltic Sea fleet; a lighthouse keeper, Harry Rasmussen, who informed Wollweber which of his colleagues were in the pay of Pflugk-Hartung and who also had informed the Russian Secret Service of Nazi ship movements—Rasmussen was given the relatively light sentence of a year and a half; and Alberti Hansen, also a sailor, who had placed dynamite on German ships. He received ten years.

The seventh offender was a woman, Elsbeth Mollerup, who had allegedly helped Jensen by permitting him to use her address to receive mail. She was sentenced to three years, but acquitted by an appeal court.

The six agents of Wollweber were responsible for explosions or fires on sixteen German, three Italian and two Japanese ships.

The Nazi officers in the courtroom forgot their manners and hissed loudly when these statistics were announced in the court. They were particularly incensed because all sixteen German ships had been sabotaged *during the period of ostensible German-Russian friendship*. Thus, although they were victors here in court, the Nazis felt that Wollweber had "pulled a fast one." They had, to be sure, caught some of his most trusted aides, but he himself was at large and his work went on in the territories they had occupied.

The twenty-one acts of sabotage, which had resulted in the total loss to the Axis of two ships, and extensive repairs on all the others, had all been committed from

Duel for the Northland

1938 to 1940 in Danish ports. The accused men naturally denied that they were responsible for similar acts of sabotage in France, England, Norway and Sweden, but the suspicion remained.

Among the most curious items brought to light by this trial were two unsuccessful attempts to blow up the giant Polish liner *Batory,* which fell into German hands in 1939.

Jan Valtin's former boss, Ernst Friedrich Wollweber, had hidden twelve incendiary bombs aboard this ship as it lay in the port of Copenhagen, but only one small fire broke out, which was promptly extinguished. In another instance, a charge of fourteen pounds of TNT was placed in the hold, but failed to go off.

The Nazi Secret Service was particularly interested in obtaining details on ship sabotage after the invasion of Denmark, for this was a menace they were still combatting. Shortly after the invasion of Denmark in April 1940 a German troopship, the *Marion,* with four thousand men aboard had set sail for Norway from a Danish port. It blew up in mid-ocean, and only a few hundred of the four thousand men reached the Swedish shore.

Pflugk-Hartung and his friends were, of course, especially interested in learning where the OGPU men got their dynamite—whether from Sweden or Russia—and where they kept it hidden.

Jensen's right-hand man, Gustav Langfors, was cruelly tortured, but refused to reveal the hiding places of the dynamite. He talked freely, however, about matters that could not endanger the present activities of Wollweber's organization. He revealed "ancient history," and his revelations were highly interesting, though utterly useless to the Nazis.

Langfors recounted, as had Jan Valtin, that Wollweber had organized his shipping espionage all over the world, that his best agents were men and women who held good positions in civil life, and who would never be suspected of espionage. They all employed false names, he said, and he gave two of the aliases: Josef Schaap, a Dutchman, and Ernst Lambert, a German. Neither of the two was ever found; the Nazis were at last forced to conclude that Langfors had set them on a false trail.

Langfors freely told his own life story. He had been a sailor all his life, and had early entered the labor movement; he had joined the Communists after he concluded that the moderate Social Democrats were merely "appeasers" of capitalism.

Richard Jensen, his employer, had been leader of the Danish Communist Party in 1934. He had requested Langfors to undertake an important mission for the Party. Langfors, whose devotion to the Party knew no bounds, was willing to go anywhere and do anything.

Jensen explained that he had orders from Moscow to send one of his best men to China. He felt that Gustav Langfors, who had traveled much, spoke several languages and was hard-headed and self-assured, was the man for the job. Jensen gave him a large amount of money, a cleverly forged passport which he was instructed to use only in an emergency, and secured him passage on a boat bound for China.

Langfors became Wollweber's liaison man in China. His task was to organize espionage and sabotage against Japan.

The Nazi officers in the courtroom pricked up their ears. This would be extremely interesting to their Axis partner.

"I let people know I was tired of seafaring," Langfors said, "and that I wanted to settle down somewhere for good. And so I bought the International Bar in Shanghai from my savings. People believed my story. Before long I had one of the most profitable bars in Shanghai."

Langfors' story was so interesting to both the court and the audience that no one interrupted him—though what he was saying was hardly pertinent to the trial. The courtroom was utterly silent.

The International Bar in Shanghai had become the headquarters of the OGPU. Communist sailors, agents and couriers from all nations delivered their reports there: information on shipping, trade and Japanese armament. These reports were then sent by Langfors through sailors and other sub-agents either directly to Russia or to Richard Jensen in Copenhagen, who in turn transmitted them to Wollweber.

But the Langfors bar was more than a spy center. From it Communist literature was smuggled into Japan, sent to America, distributed throughout China. And weapons were sent to Red troops in China and to comrades in Japan. Dynamite was unloaded from Russian ships and sent to its destination on ships flying other flags.

At this point the Danish Judge interrupted to ask whether dynamite had been sent from China to Denmark. Langfors replied meaningfully, "It could be got from places closer to home." He refused to expand this statement.

Langfors made no attempt to conceal that he had received thorough training in China in the technique of sabotage. Chinese and Japanese Communists had showed him how to carry out bombings of bridges, railroads, ships and planes. He had learned in China all the tricks of guerrilla warfare.

Without implicating any of his arrested comrades, Gustav Langfors told the Court all about his past.

In Shanghai he had also learned how to manufacture incendiary bombs that could be concealed in cigarette cases or even in cigarettes. Chinese and Koreans, he recounted, could blow up a bombing plane with a single cigarette skillfully planted.

Until 1937 Langfors was the OGPU's most important man in China. Then he was recalled. He "did not know" the name of his successor, nor where his successor had located his headquarters after the sale of the International Bar.

Langfors returned to Copenhagen and Richard Jensen took him to meet the chief himself. Wollweber was pleased with his work; he now wanted Langfors to become an instructor. He was to induct Wollweber's agents into the secrets of explosives, and to experiment with the construction of automatic fuses so made that the risk of discovery would be lessened. These instructions were never given to classes, but to individual comrades. There is no doubt that Langfors was telling the truth when he declared that he did not know the names of his pupils and they did not know his name.

At this point the Nazis introduced a surprise. The Gestapo officers handed the State Prosecutor "proofs" that the bombing attempt in the Munich Beer Cellar in November 1939, which had been aimed at killing Hitler and Hess, had been organized by Wollweber's and Langfors' men. This was obviously part of a build-up by the Gestapo of a case against Russia in order to prepare Hitler's way for a declaration of war on Russia. At first Himmler had declared that the bombing had been organized by Otto Strasser, who had left the Nazi Party in 1930. When, however, the Swiss police affirmed that they had had Strasser under constant surveillance, another version was given out; the Gestapo then asserted that British secret agents had arranged the bombing.

Their story was that three British Intelligence officers, Richard Henry Stephens, a Mr. Best, and a mysterious citizen of the Netherlands, had secretly entered Germany—not been kidnapped, as the British press averred. These intelligence officers had received the dynamite for the bombing from Langfors and Wollweber. The Gestapo

Duel for the Northland

men declared that the three British Intelligence officers had previously had connections with the OGPU when they were spying on Germany from Copenhagen. Wollweber, they said, had given these officers information that led to the arrest of Pflugk-Hartung in 1939.

The truth or falsehood of this statement will remain unknown until after the war. The Danish judges, however, declared there was insufficient evidence, and the charge was dropped. Probably the Nazis attempted the maneuver in order to have Langfors extradited to Germany. For at this time Denmark, though occupied, still maintained a fictive sovereignty and could refuse extradition. After Premier Stauning's sudden death his successor, Dr. Erik Scavenius, dropped these last formalities and made no protest when the Germans set up their own Nazi Courts in the country. Dr. Scavenius gave his permission without asking either the Danish Government or the King, and thus the last remnant of Denmark's independence vanished.

Wollweber's agents were sentenced in the aggregate to fifty-nine years' imprisonment. Undoubtedly, this represented a significant victory of the German Secret Service over Russian counterespionage. But the chief organizer had eluded them.

During the trial the figure of Wollweber was evoked repeatedly. Proofs had been obtained—to Pflugk-Hartung's chagrin—that Wollweber had located his headquarters in the same building as Pontoppidan's radio company. On the door of his office had been the name "A. Selo & Co., Broker." It is amusing to imagine the encounters that must daily have taken place in the elevators of the building. But the Nazis had not found out until too late; their prey had been so near and yet so far.

It was known also that the six prisoners had carried on virtually no activity after the invasion; Wollweber must have chosen a whole new set of agents. In the course of the trial one of the witnesses stated that Wollweber had fled to Norway and was now probably in Sweden.

This assumption was correct. The master of Russian espionage was in Oslo when Herr Josef Terboven, the new Governor, entered the city; he was in Norway while the Nazis and Quislings began their reign of terror in the land.

Wollweber was farsighted and so astute that he was misunderstood by most of his comrades. In 1940 he gave the same orders he had given in Germany in 1933. Every Communist was to turn color overnight and work with the Quislings. The German-Russian Pact was still in force; therefore the Communist line was to be that the King and the Labor Government had cravenly deserted the country. Norway was now a Republic and must collaborate with Germany; otherwise the people would suffer severely.

Communists who had been ardent anti-Nazis were stricken with dismay. They left the Communist Party, crying that the EX.R., Anton, was a traitor. EX.R. meant Executive Committee Representative, and Anton was the name Wollweber was using in Norway. But Wollweber's trusted followers asked no questions and obeyed; in any event, his course was the easiest to follow.

Quisling, always in desperate need of followers, accepted the former Communists. It was at this time that the world learned with amazement that notorious Communist leaders had turned Quislings overnight; that trusted trade union leaders had accepted posts in the organizations of the "Nasjonal Samling," the Quisling Party. In return payment, Quisling placed the trade unions under Communist leadership, and for some months even permitted the Communist press to publish, although all other newspapers were either confiscated or "coordinated."

Newspaper correspondents such as Leland Stowe reported that Norway was overwhelmed by Quislings. In reality, ninety-nine per cent of the Norwegian population was always against the Quisling regime. The Communists that joined Quisling's Party abhorred him and the Nazis. They were not renegades; they were simply donning Wollweber's clever masquerade costume.

These "Trojan Horse" tactics were carefully worked out. For example, Wollweber sent the leader of the Swedish Communist Youth, Sven Landin, to Denmark and Norway to report on the "new conditions." In the Swedish Communist newspaper Landin published a series of articles that raised a turmoil among Swedish Communists. He described the freedom accorded to the Communists in Norway and denounced the "crimes" of the Norwegian labor movement; the Labor Government and King Haakon, he said, had simply stolen the country's gold and taken it to "Imperialist" England. Only cowards deserted their people. These and similar utterances were the burden of the articles.

The Nazis and Quislings were highly pleased by these fresh demonstrations of Nazi-Communist cooperation. And this was precisely what Wollweber wanted, for he needed time to rebuild his spy apparatus in Norway and Denmark. The West European Bureau of the Comintern had meanwhile been transferred to Stockholm. The Swedes were horrified, but Wollweber could not be located.

Sweden was struggling bitterly to maintain her neutrality; she wanted to give the Nazi aggressors no motive for eventual invasion. For she knew well that her army of 600,000 men could not hope to stop Hitler's war machine.

Sweden placed her confidence in King Gustav V, or Mr. G. as he was known during his tennis tournaments. Gustav had visited Hitler and Goering in Berlin several times, employing all his diplomacy to give Sweden a breathing spell. Meanwhile the country rearmed feverishly; a state of semi-mobilization had been declared. Consequently, men like Wollweber were more undesirable than ever, for they seriously compromised the country's foreign policy. The Government felt that it was bad enough the Communists had legal status, for in democratic Sweden there was no way to ban them—this was among the advantages and disadvantages of a democracy.

Sweden, with her five-hundred-year-old Parliament, is proud of her democracy and believes that democratic principles are the best bulwark against Nazism or Communism, whether foreign or native in origin. King Gustav is as democratic as his neighboring ruler in Denmark. The Social Democratic Prime Minister, Per Albin Hansson, daily rides to the "Kanslihuset," the Ministry of State, in the street car. He lives in an old mansion on the outskirts of the city; his wife keeps no servants and does all her housework alone.

Per Albin once stated his policy to me in the course of an interview:

"So long as we pursue the middle way and stave off all economic crises, our people will not become desperate. Only desperate men join the Nazis or Communists."

The Swedish Communists, who might have been Wollweber's helpers, have experienced the blessings of the Swedish cooperative system and of Swedish social legislation as well as all other citizens of the country. In consequence they believed only in methods of strict legality. If Wollweber were to obtain their assistance, he would have to change his methods. The Swedish Communists were unwilling to take any risks. The Communist International has always looked down scornfully upon the Swedish Communist Party. Wollweber was highly amused by the story told in Stockholm of how the Swedish Communists had postponed the May Day parade of 1929 because of rain. Communists who deferred a demonstration because it rained were not Wollweber's kind. But he had to get along with them, and so for a time he became a devotee of legality. He quoted in this connection Goebbels' *mot:* "We are legal to the last rung of the gallows, but the hanging will take place."

Sweden's Communist Party profited by this temporary legality of Wollweber's. The chief paid for a new headquarters, new presses and obtained fresh funds from Russia for propaganda.

He published a newspaper in German, *Die Welt,* which appeared openly as the organ of the Comintern. The newspaper was guarded in its language, and only two issues were confiscated—something of a record for Communist newspapers. *Die Welt* attacked the Norwegian Government-in-exile. The bewildered Nazis decided to let the Communists in Norway alone for the present.

At the same time Wollweber was building up his forces in Finland, and instructing all his agents to keep under cover until the signal to strike was given. Then came fresh orders from Moscow. War with Germany was unavoidable, and Wollweber was to strike at the Nazis wherever possible.

Soon a great wave of sabotage swept over Norway, reaching its height in the winter of 1940-41. Most of these acts were directed against the railroad system and were so managed as to resemble damage wrought by the forces of Nature. Never before had the strategic Oslo-Bergen line suffered so much from "landslides," "avalanches," and similar mishaps. In spite of heavy penalties, the German Army's telephone and telegraph lines were constantly cut, holes were drilled in the bottoms of boats carrying freight for the Nazis, tanks of gasoline were found to be diluted with water, road signs were removed or upset, and so on.

Not all of these operations, of course, were carried out by Wollweber's men. Many of them were the work of Norwegian patriots fighting the might of occupying force with every means possible. But the Communists had more experience, and they showed greater recklessness in sabotage than any of the other Norwegian parties fighting the Quisling regime.

In looking back upon the trend and development of these sabotage acts, one cannot fail to perceive that they followed a graph exactly parallel to the progressive worsening of German-Russian relations during the latter part of 1940 and the first half of 1941. We know, in particular, that Moscow was deeply concerned about the massing in Northern Norway of a formidable force of Nazi shock troops. The Russians did not credit the German explanation that these troops had been gathered there for an invasion of the British Isles. They knew that everything was being prepared to strike east, not west.

Accordingly, Wollweber received word from Moscow to double and redouble his efforts. His men broke into the warehouses of the Swedish iron ore trust at Kiruna and made away with large quantities of dynamite and TNT. One night they carried off a hundred pounds, and the next night sixty more. The booty then was smuggled into Norway little by little by men going on skis across the forbidding ranges of the Kölen mountains. Some of it also was used to manufacture time-bombs which were placed aboard the German freighters carrying iron ore from Luleå and Oxelösund to Stettin or Danzig. Quite a few Nazi ships which were reported to have run into mines actually met their fate in this manner.

The situation became so serious that late in November 1941 the Nazi Minister of Propaganda, Joseph Goebbels, and Gestapo Chief Heinrich Himmler flew to Oslo to investigate. They were not long in finding out whence the trouble originated. It emanated from Sweden, where Wollweber worked in comparative safety. They summed up their findings in a report that was officially forwarded to the chief of the Swedish police. To make it more forceful, the former German Minister in Stockholm, Prince Friedrich zu Wied, called on Foreign Minister Christian Guenther and stated that the Reich would hold Sweden responsible for any further acts of sabotage organized by Wollweber. In the report Wollweber was described as "the most dangerous OGPU agent still at large anywhere in Europe outside of Russia."

When the Swedish authorities disclaimed official knowledge of Wollweber's presence in the country, the Nazis went one step farther; they offered to hunt their quarry down themselves if special Gestapo men were permitted to join in the hunt. After some hesitation the Swedes agreed, on condition that the German agents should do nothing on their own authority, but restrict themselves to helping ferret out Wollweber's hiding place.

Wollweber must have received a warning. Though he lived in the heart of Sweden, in the midst of the city of Stockholm, the Swedish police, Canaris's counterespionage men and the Gestapo were not able to arrest him.

The reason was very simple. For three months Wollweber did not leave his small apartment near the Sture Plan in Stockholm. He never issued into the street by daylight; he saw nobody besides his girl friend, Hertha, who had to continue all the work under his direction, and she came only after nightfall.

The same precaution was taken by the man who edited *Die Welt,* a Hungarian Communist. His aliases were many, but at the time his name was Arpad. Arpad was arrested in spite of his three months' recess in his apartment. The Swedish police were informed by a member of the Executive Committee of the Swedish Communist Party in the pay of the police.

Wollweber's hiding place was never betrayed because he did not trust the Executive Committee, and no Swedish Communist knew his address.

Thus Wollweber had again escaped his pursuers. The Nazis decided to put a price of $50,000 on his head, and the hunt began anew.

12. Sweden—International Spy Center

The greatest manhunt Europe had seen for decades was on. Nazi Germany and the police of the occupied Scandinavian countries had been rallied. Wollweber's picture was publicly posted all over Norway and Denmark. But the man was as elusive as ever. No Dillinger had ever had so many detectives on his trail, yet Wollweber remained one step ahead of his pursuers. Admiral Canaris's Anti-Comintern Division, the Swedish police, and the united forces of the Danish, Norwegian and Finnish police hunted him from city to city. Now and then clues were found, and then all trace of him would disappear for months.

Joseph Stalin knew the danger haunting his friend, and in Swedish Communist circles it was said the Russian Premier had insisted that Wollweber retire for a while to the safety of Moscow. But Wollweber did not want safety; he refused to leave Scandinavia until he knew he was no longer needed—that is, until his sabotage and espionage apparatus could function without him.

The failure of the Nazi espionage services to find him was a serious blow to the myth of the "total efficiency" of the Nazi Secret Service. Indeed, it is well to note that the Nazis were by no means such efficient pursuers as they would have the people of the democracies believe. Along with many successes, Nazi espionage suffered a goodly number of failures in Scandinavia.

Whether in politics or in espionage, Nazis do well only when they can employ the weapons of violence and money; where original thinking is necessary, they are sadly lacking. Here is a prize example of their intelligence: the Gestapo sent three armed storm troopers to Norway's greatest publishing house, Gyldendal, in order to extract from the publisher Maxim Gorki's present address. The publisher, who had brought out Gorki's collected works, regretted that it was impossible to give this information. For this remark he was almost arrested, for the Nazis refused to believe that Gorki was dead. The publisher showed them the date of the author's death in a Norwegian encyclopedia, but the Nazis did not understand Norwegian and remained obdurately suspicious until an auxiliary policeman of the Quisling "Hird Guards" confirmed the publisher's explanation.

Wollweber, however, was far superior even to the brainier Nazi Governor, Josef Terboven. He continued his work, undetected and undetectable, declaring that he was transforming the V campaign into an S campaign—S for sabotage. Railroad stations burned down, cables leading to the Oslo electric plant were slashed, ships exploded in the port of Bergen—and no one ever glimpsed more than Wollweber's shadow. Canaris grew impatient and demanded that his agents show some results for all their work, and Norway's new Governor, Josef Terboven, stormed, for with the situation as it was, he could not begin to wipe out the opposition in the land.

Josef Terboven is generally considered a handsome man. All his life he has made a career of his charming face. His is an interesting story, and one intimately linked with the politics of Nazidom, for only under the Nazi standard could an unemployed gigolo become the ruler of one of the most progressive nations in the world.

Josef Terboven was a Rhinelander by birth, and in his youth worked in the Ruhr industrial area. He fought in World War I, later became a bank clerk, working for Krupp and Thyssen, and joined the many unemployed in Germany in 1923, during the inflation. He did not want for money, however, for an elderly lady saw fit to "keep" him in the style to which he was accustomed. At this time Terboven joined the Nazi Party; his mistress found him even handsomer in his splendid new uniform. She decided to support the new party financially. Her money was so welcome to Hitler, who was always in need of money in those days, that he rewarded Terboven by appointing him a group leader.

His comrades in the Nazi Party never referred to Terboven by any other name than "the gigolo." Nevertheless, they prized his connections. Through his aging lady-friend, Terboven brought Hitler into touch with the Ruhr industrialist, Emil Kirdorf, who administered the "lobbying" fund of the German steel industry.

For a long time Emil Kirdorf, Fritz Thyssen and Karl Krupp had been hoping to put in power a political party that would assure them the enormous profits of war industry. Terboven told them that Hitler was no threat to German industry, in spite of his radical phrases. The slender, good-looking young man suggested that a conversation among Hitler, Krupp, Kirdorf and Thyssen might prove profitable to all parties. Kirdorf, always cautious and conservative, welcomed the suggestion; he wanted to see this man Hitler and hear him outline his plans in person. And so, in 1924, Terboven arranged the first meeting between Hitler and the Ruhr industrialists.

This meeting bore much fruit—above all for Terboven himself, whom Hitler appointed to a well-paid post on his staff. Since that time Terboven has clung to Hitler with abject loyalty.

Terboven has always had a gift for filling the purse of the Nazi Party. Perhaps this is why he was chosen chief plunderer of Norway.

It was Josef Terboven who took over the administration of the Thyssen fortune and the Thyssen factories after their owner fled from Germany, only later to fall again into the hands of the Nazis. Terboven did a good job; he incorporated the entire Thyssen concern in the Hermann Goering Werke, and himself became one of the biggest shareholders.

At present this able pickpocket resides in the Oslo Storting, the building of the Norwegian Parliament.

In the middle of the year 1940 Terboven called a joint conference of German and Norwegian police officials. He gave the men to understand that if Wollweber were not caught, he would be forced to hold them personally responsible. That same night Oslo was without lights. The blackout was not an intentional one by the authorities; Wollweber had decided to play a practical joke on the Governor and his Quislings.

Nevertheless, the insistence of Canaris and Terboven got results. Not, to be sure, the results they wanted, but interesting results all the same. They did not find Wollweber, but they found a great many other spies.

In neutral Sweden, the first who fell prey to the counterespionage hunt was a British agent named Fredrik E. Rickmann—a tall man, above fifty years old, and a loyal British patriot.

He was discovered more by accident than by intention, but the outcome was the same. He was unwittingly betrayed by the mother of his sweetheart.

Rickmann had lived in Sweden for many years, and had long been engaged to a Swedish girl. The girl's mother did not like "foreigners"; she was incensed that her daughter would not marry a Swede. She talked about this a good deal to her friends and acquaintances, mentioning incidentally that Rickmann was very rich, that he traveled by car throughout Sweden and that he spoke astoundingly good Swedish for one of the notoriously unlinguistic Britishers.

Her neighbors agreed with the mother and in their turn repeated the story, until at last it reached the sharp ears of Canaris's agents. The Nazi counterespionage set about investigating the case of Fredrik Rickmann.

The Nazis were efficient once the trail had been pointed out to them, and they learned a good deal. They turned their information over to the Swedish police, and Rickmann was arrested.

The Nazis had secretly searched the cellar of Rickmann's home and found a suitcase containing a considerable amount of dynamite. They claimed that Rickmann intended to use the explosive for sabotage in the two greatest Swedish iron ore ports, Luleå and Oxelösund.

Rickmann's trial took place behind closed doors. He was sentenced to eight years' imprisonment. Furthermore, the court decreed that the testimony was to be kept under seal for ten years.

Rickmann declared frankly that he was an officer in the army of those who were fighting against Nazism for freedom. He denied having had any sabotage plans, but admitted that he considered Sweden's shipments of iron ore to Germany a reprehensible and important contribution to the Nazi war machine.

I met Rickmann in Stockholm. He was a sober, quiet man who secretly had anti-Nazi pamphlets printed in Sweden and shipped to Germany. He worked as a commercial artist for the Cooperative League, and had also had a book published in Britain on Swedish iron ore and on the

Swedish-German ore trade. It was a work of considerable importance; Rickmann is considered England's foremost authority on Swedish iron ores.

Today, Rickmann is in a Swedish prison. The Allies must make it a point of honor not to forget this man and to obtain amnesty for him at the end of the war, for otherwise he will not be released until 1948.

But Wollweber was still at large. The Nazis could not catch up with him. Nazi counterespionage discovered more and more enemy agents, but Wollweber was never among them. They discovered, for example, that the four Czechoslovak press attachés who worked in the Czechoslovak news agency were informing their government in London about Nazi activities in Scandinavia. The unfortunate Czech agents had no loophole through diplomatic immunity, as had so many German spies in Sweden, because they represented an occupied country and a Government-in-exile.

The Stockholm Court found guilty Vladimir Vanek, former counselor of the Czech Legation. He was sentenced to two years at hard labor for "procuring military and political information and transmitting it to his employers abroad."

Paul Joseph Hodin, a brilliant Czech author, was given five months, Miloslav Dolezel three months, and Walter Taub, former correspondent of a Czech news agency and well-known anti-Nazi in the Sudeten district, two months. The Court ordered the minutes of the case impounded and sealed from the public for twenty-five years.

Stockholm had once more become an international spy center, as it had been during World War I.

The physician of the German Legation, Dr. Michel, was proved to be a spy. A network of Nazi cells called the "Brown Marine" which had been established with the Swedish Navy was discovered. Sweden's alien squad had their work cut out for them, especially since the country lived in daily fear of invasion. They had to be more than cautious in their treatment of German spies, since the Nazis constantly threatened reprisals and blackmailed Sweden with hints of imminent invasion or stoppage of coal deliveries. Whenever a Nazi spy was deported, the Nazi diplomatic corps protested.

When Pflugk-Hartung's intimate friends, the naval spies Martin Bolte and Alexander Bogs, were proved to have engaged in espionage, they were not expelled from the country; they preferred to leave voluntarily. But here the case was too patently an open-and-shut affair; the Swedish police had, after all, found Consul Bogs photographing the coastal fortifications of Ystad.

Sweden attempted to treat agents of the democracies and Nazi spies with equal severity, but Nazi pressure often forced her to commit injustices. Three internment camps were established for the many foreigners suspected of espionage, for foreigners with insufficient papers, and for foreigners who might be Communists. The internment camps serve smorgasbord; compared to camps in Poland or Germany they are idyllic. But they are nevertheless political camps; the inmates say of them that they are a "gilded cage, but still a cage."

Sweden's Minister in the United States, Vollmar Bostroem, has called these camps Sweden's Ellis Island. The analogy holds true to a certain extent, but there are significant differences. Political internees on Ellis Island include Nazis and Communists; the Swedish camps hold no Nazis. Moreover, men are sent to these camps without trial. For this reason liberal and progressive groups in Sweden oppose them as undemocratic. Swedish democracy has been compelled to make compromises in this war, precisely because the country is a listening post for all sides and swarms with spies and saboteurs. The country prays daily for peace, knowing that only an Allied victory can assure its independence.

Wollweber's headquarters in Sweden had not yet been discovered. For a time the quarry seemed almost in the bag when two Swedish Communists, Folke Bjoerk and Eric Birger Holmbaeck, were arrested for industrial espionage. These Communists, on the orders of high "functionaries," had stolen the formula for the hardness of the famous Fagersta steel. They sold this formula for 1,000 kroner ($250) to the Russian Legation in Stockholm. For this accomplishment the charming Russian Minister, Madame Alexandra Kollontay, had received them personally. The Swedish Government protested against Madame Kollontay's action, but did not demand her recall, for the lady, who had been a colleague of Lenin's, was well-liked throughout Scandinavia.

But alas for the hopes of the Nazi counterespionage forces, no connection between Wollweber and the two industrial spies could be established. By now the Nazis had been aroused to a high pitch of frustrated rage. They decided upon a desperate action.

For a long time the Communists have been very well organized in the Swedish iron ore district of Norrland and Lappland, and the Nazis suspected that the OGPU headquarters would be located in the ore port of Luleå. German agents persuaded Swedish Nazis belonging to the Fascist Party of Ex-Sergeant Olov Lindholm to join them in their plan.

They intended to bomb the Party headquarters of the Communists and the printshop of the Communist newspaper, *Norrskensflamman*. Blowing up the entire building seemed to them the best way to exterminate the OGPU agents they were positive inhabited it.

The bombing took place, but it resulted only in killing five innocent bystanders: cleaning women, delivery boys and janitors. None of Wollweber's men were in the building at the time of the bombing.

Investigation led to the discovery that three Swedish Army officers and a clerk were responsible for the actual bombing. The men were: H. Borgstroem, T. Norstroem and G. Krendel, and J. Palmquist, a clerk.

Pacifist Sweden was outraged. But the Court imposed ridiculous sentences upon the murderers. Rickmann, who had never executed his alleged plans, had been sentenced to eight years; these men, who were responsible for five deaths, were let off with sentences of ten months to two years. The land of the Middle Way, in spite of all its democratic progress, stands convicted of rank cowardice in its judicial system. This is the darkest chapter in Sweden's history in World War II. Sweden has the highest standard of living of all European nations; class struggle has been reduced to a minimum; arbitration has taken the place of the strike. But the judicial system of the country has shared little in the blessings of the Middle Way.

Although the Labor Party dominates the government and the economy, its portion has been to look on while the Swedish Ministry of Justice imprisons anti-Nazis and even highly-respected democratic professors because they have "insulted Hitler."

Elsa Moeller, the wife of the Social-Democratic Minister, went to prison because she wrote a book advocating prison reform. Among the books on the Swedish confiscation list are translations of Dorothy Thompson, Harold Nicolson, Hermann Rauschning, Otto Strasser, C. J. Hambro, and many other anti-Nazi writers, not to mention my own book on Goering, publication of which led to my arrest.

No one in the country defends this confiscation of liberal books, not even Karl Gustav Westman, the Minister of Justice himself, who orders the confiscations. But the Swedes find it necessary in order not to anger Hitler and to preserve their neutrality.

Shameful as these procedures are, we must in all fairness say that Sweden hopes for nothing better than a return to normal democratic conditions; all Swedes feel these undemocratic emergency measures are a blot on the escutcheon of Swedish democracy.

Sweden is caught in a painful quandary between England, Russia and Germany. She must compromise with the Axis to prevent invasion and to gain time for preparation. To the honor of Sweden it can be said that though she does make compromises that help Hitler, she tries to retain as much as possible of her own freedom. She is appeasing Nazi Germany as long as possible, just as every other nation in the world did for years. Sweden's statesmen can boast that they have succeeded longer with appeasement than any other country—though the last word is not yet spoken.

There is no doubt that Wollweber wanted Sweden to be a battleground—but only for a discreet battle between the spy machines. The unsuccessful attack on him at Luleå infuriated him. He had often been in Luleå, and indeed had left the town only two days before the bomb explosion, on his way to Northern Norway. He had taken over the difficult task of delivering short wave apparatus to his collaborators in Norway, so that these agents could stand sentinel on the "Road to Murmansk." Wollweber's men were to report all movements of Nazi warships and submarines toward North Cape, Petsamo and Kirkenes, for these were the U-boat bases from which British, American and Russian freighters were sunk on their way to Murmansk.

The work of these agents proved invaluable in effecting the victorious outcome of the Battle of the Arctic.

Romantic Lapland had remained romantic in spite of the war. The Lapps still migrated with their herds of reindeer from Finland to Norway and from Norway back to Finland. Their life remained the hard life of the nomad, though more and more Lapps, charmingly outlandish in their colorful costumes and pointed caps, appeared on railroad trains and in towns and villages. Wollweber's agents, who had once led an existence confined to Gothenburg beerhalls and to the stale smoke-laden air of Party headquarters, now joined the bands of Lapps and made long trips on skis along the Finnish, Swedish and Norwegian borders. They knew more than the Nazis suspected, and hidden in their handbags of reindeer hide were radio sets to send important information to Russia.

All methods were one to Wollweber. He recognized no revolutionary or conservative theory of espionage. The Lapps in the iron ore district, the Lapps in northern Finland, and the Lapps in Narvik did not understand German or Swedish; they spoke only the Lapp language and a smattering of Finnish. It would hardly occur to the emissaries of Admiral Canaris that some of these little nomads understood Russian and used Russian codes for their radio messages.

Since 1933 Wollweber had been in continual flight. His nerves had held in spite of the tension of being pursued, but from 1936 on the net began to be drawn ever more closely around him. By 1940 his sphere of activity had been even further narrowed by the war. The enemy knew all about him, had pictures of him, had his fingerprints, and had placed great prices on his head. Yet with his customary fearlessness and boldness, he had no thought of stopping.

At last the combined forces of the Scandinavian police came very close. They did not find Wollweber himself, but they wiped out his entire organization in Sweden's greatest port, Gothenburg. For three months the office manager of the Communist Party in Gothenburg had been shadowed day and night. At last the watchers learned that Sven Rydstedt, the leader of the Gothenburg Communists, had established a dynamite cache in the waterfront district. Rydstedt was Wollweber's liaison man in the port and regularly received orders through couriers instructing him where to send dynamite, on what ships to place it, and so on. He was well known in Sweden and his arrest created a considerable stir.

Wollweber, however, had never come in personal contact with Rydstedt during 1940 and 1941—he was far too clever for that.

Also arrested was a ship's stoker, Erik Gotthard Paulsson, who used to send information on Nazi shipping to a telegraph operator in the State Telegraph Bureau. The telegraph operator was caught in the act of transmitting a code report on German merchant shipping to Russia.

Wollweber's Gothenburg agents had stolen over two hundred and twenty pounds of dynamite from the Kiruna iron mines and smuggled the explosive to Norway via Narvik. Dynamite had also been placed on ore ships sailing for Germany, thus causing several mysterious fires and explosions.

Some of the dynamite had been stored in Gothenburg "for special purposes"—and it was this store that the police had discovered through Rydstedt's lack of caution.

Rydstedt was sentenced to three years and four months' imprisonment. In the course of the trial he declared that he had heard of Wollweber, but had never seen him.

Duel for the Northland

The year 1941 was a year of successes for the German counterespionage in Scandinavia. Though the main enemy had escaped, Russians, Englishmen, Czechs and other Allied spies had been tripped up. Wollweber's organization in Gothenburg had, of course, connections with other organizations throughout the country, and by following the trail the Swedish police were able to make some arrests in Stockholm. A number of operators of Wollweber's secret radio stations were located by German spies and turned over to the Swedish police.

Wollweber's work was not seriously hampered by these arrests, for he had scattered his short wave transmitters all over the country; no sooner was one of his agents arrested than his successor began work from a different locale. Often his agents sent reports to Russia from fishing boats. The German spies and the Swedish listening posts were never able to locate such stations, for they changed their positions from minute to minute. At other times Wollweber would suddenly forbid his agents to use their radios, in order to throw the enemy off the track, and all information would be sent by couriers.

One of Wollweber's couriers was a former carpenter. Wollweber fitted him out as a traveling salesman, buying him a handsome suitcase filled with ladies' garments and radio sets. The man traveled through Sweden delivering his radio sets. He also collected the information various agents gave him on German troop transports and on German merchants who, while buying up the eel catch, were trying to bribe fishermen, and so on.

Another of Wollweber's agents, Russian-born Bertil Erikson, was especially valuable. He succeeded in entering the Swedish National Guard. Most of the trained volunteers who went to Finland from Sweden to fight with the Nazis against Russia came from the National Guard. Bertil

Erikson was therefore in a position to find out a great deal about the aid given to Finland, and reported on the quantities of Swedish arms and Swedish food supplies that were sent to Finland.

The arrest of Wollweber's Stockholm assistants did serious damage to his organization. Sooner or later—and probably sooner—destiny and the spies of Admiral Canaris would catch up with Wollweber. This appeared certain. But Wollweber did not run away. He wanted first to rebuild his forces in Gothenburg and Stockholm. Before he could do so, the next blow fell, with the arrest of five leading spies and saboteurs in the iron ore district of Northern Sweden.

With these arrests, the Wollweber League appeared destroyed. Only the leader himself remained at liberty, somewhere in Sweden or Norway. He was seen one day in Oslo, some time afterward in Gothenburg, but each time the police arrived too late. At this point Stalin demanded that Wollweber return to Russia. Wollweber consented, but asked for six weeks more to complete his new network of agents.

Those six weeks were to be his undoing.

It is one of life's neatest ironies that this dauntless man, who for eight years had been the very embodiment of the OGPU, should, when he at last fell into a trap, be caught not by the dreaded Gestapo or by Canaris's master spies, but by a humble Swedish police constable. It is ironic that Europe's greatest spy and saboteur should stand not before the implacable Elite Guard judges of the Leipzig People's Court, but before the mild-mannered and slightly bewildered judges of the little "härads-rätt"—the district court of the iron ore city of Kiruna. And that he should be called upon to answer a charge not of high treason, manslaughter and arson, but of using a forged passport. Ironic, too, that in the end he should be sentenced not to be hanged by the neck until he was dead, but to serve three years in a distinctly comfortable Swedish prison.

One of the five agents who had been arrested in Northern Sweden lost his nerve and confessed to save himself. The man's name was Gustav Ceder; he turned State's witness and informed the Swedish police where Wollweber would meet his men to receive freshly-stolen explosives. And so Europe's greatest spy and saboteur was arrested by the Swedish provincial police.

The Swedes, Danes and Nazis all had accusations against him, Pflugk-Hartung had drawn up a long list of his crimes. But the Swedish Court soon found that they had no proofs to convict Wollweber on charges of espionage and sabotage. Although the master mind had always given the orders, his own hands were clean.

The Nazis were jubilant at his capture, but the Swedish authorities were not. For even as a captive Wollweber remained as much of a perplexing problem to them as he had been while still at large.

In the first place, the prisoner refused to talk. Day after day, and often night after night, the best brains of the Swedish criminal squad grilled him without result. Wollweber would reply only to such questions as he saw fit to answer, and his replies were always curt, negative and deliberately misleading.

All he would admit was that he was Chief of the International Seamen's Union. The Swedish prosecuting attorney prepared translations from Jan Valtin's book, hoping to use Valtin's information against Wollweber. But Wollweber refused to comment. He admitted that he knew Valtin; if they wished to use Valtin as a witness against him, they had the right to do so. But the Swedish police were never in a position to obtain a statement from Valtin against

Wollweber. Moreover, they wanted to keep the Wollweber case under cover; any sort of publicity might have international repercussions. They therefore decided to get along without the data Valtin had given about his former boss in *Out of the Night*.

Sweden knew that Germany and Russia would fight for this precious prisoner; the Swedes hoped to avoid international difficulties by handing down a verdict as swiftly as possible.

A few days after Wollweber's arrest a formal demand for extradition had been received from Berlin. Nothing could have been more embarrassing to the Swedes. They were fully aware that it would be contrary to international law and to Sweden's policy of neutrality if this man, whose many crimes were all of a strictly political nature, were handed over to the authorities of his Nazi homeland. The democratic Swedes had refused extradition in the case of Heinrich Stau, the Luebeck airplane engineer; they would refuse it in Wollweber's case, too—for extradition would mean certain death for him.

But the Swedes also knew that Germany had drastic means to back up any demands she considered it expedient to make. To make this cat-and-mouse game all the more tense, the following day extradition requests came from Norway's Judas Lie and from the Danish Minister of Justice, Thune Jacobsen. The Nazis were really putting on pressure. Sweden was caught in a pincers between Soviet Russia and Germany, for she had just concluded a profitable trade agreement with the Soviets, which would surely suffer from the consequences of a political scandal.

What was more, a considerable number of Swedish engineers and technicians were employed in Russia. Any one of these men might be picked to serve as a hostage for Wollweber. The practical Swedes were quite aware that Stalin grows grim when the life of a friend is at stake.

It was Wollweber himself who finally pulled a trump card on his captors. That occurred when, after another long and fruitless hearing, a police commissioner grew impatient and snapped at him:

"You had better come clean now, or else we'll send you to Germany. You know how much you are wanted there. . . ."

Wollweber, the king of saboteurs, remained stonily calm. Slowly, disdainfully he gave his answer to that threat:

"I am a Soviet citizen."

The Swedes gasped. They had thought of the man as one more of the helpless German refugees. Those you could deal with as you pleased, for they are men without a country, without status or protection. But this was different! If Wollweber were a Soviet citizen, then . . .

At the Soviet legation in Stockholm Madame Alexandra Kollontay confirmed Wollweber's claim to citizenship. The embarrassment of the Swedish police grew. They turned the matter back to the Foreign Ministry, which passed the buck to the judiciary.

The case now went before the Stockholm City Court which rejected the German, Danish and Quisling-Norwegian requests for extradition on the grounds that they had been insufficiently substantiated.

But Admiral Canaris and Dr. Werner Best, who were eager to lay hands on their victim, were not so easily put off. A few days later Best sent a new request for extradition, tricked out with more trumped-up charges against Wollweber. The matter was now ripe for the Supreme Court. For the next three weeks, the chief justices of Sweden put their heads together. They puzzled how best to reconcile the interests of justice with those of the country. Finally the court reached a decision but it was not made public. As usual in matters affecting the security of the State, the court resolved that the records of the proceedings should be kept under seal for a period of ten years.

I do not pretend to have penetrated into the secrets of that well-guarded State document. But we can surely infer that the extradition was refused, since in October 1941 Wollweber was transferred to the county jail of Kiruna in Lapland, to be arraigned on a new charge of conspiracy to commit sabotage. Here he was tried, together with his five comrades arrested in Northern Sweden.

In the company of ten Swedish citizens indicted on a variety of counts including theft of explosives, gun running, sabotage against ships, mines, power stations and so forth, Wollweber went on trial at Kiruna in November 1941. The proceedings again were held in secret, but on November 17, 1941, the *Tidningarnas Telegrambyrå* (official Swedish news agency) announced that Wollweber had been sentenced to three years in prison. The Nazis will have to wait at least that long before they can get their game, unless, of course, they should invade Sweden before then.

Wollweber, well knowing that this trial was being closely followed in Russia, imitated Dimitrov and played the role of a hero. He was the perfect model of a modern Russian Communist, turning the court into a tribunal, so that at times it was difficult to say whether he was accused or accuser.

Ceder, the witness for the Crown, felt himself terribly important and told the Court everything he knew. But the Swedish authorities soon discovered that he knew very little; he could recount petty details, but he had no idea how extensive was the activity of the Wollweber League.

In the course of the preliminary hearings, Ceder had surrendered to the police dynamite shells that the League had employed. When asked who had made them and whether he had received them from Wollweber, Ceder could give no answer, for he knew most of his League comrades only by their first names and had no idea who had manufactured or stolen the dynamite shells. He testified that dynamite had been stolen during the years from 1936 to 1941, and that it had been transmitted to Norway by men on skis. He knew also that in the code of the Wollweber League dynamite was always referred to as "reindeer meat," and orders to blow up a ship or warehouse were called "Lapp knives." Ceder also revealed that cleverly designed belts filled with dynamite had been placed on ore ships bound for Germany and on boats sailing to Fascist Spain.

Edvard Nyberg, one of the men arrested with Wollweber, had formerly been the bootleg-king of Sweden. He had smuggled huge quantities of liquor into the country, until he abandoned this type of smuggling for the more dangerous game of taking dynamite into occupied Norway. Among Nyberg's friends were men who worked in the Kirunavaara ore mines. With their help the dynamite stores of the mines were robbed and sacks of dynamite weighing fifty to a hundred pounds were stolen, packed in knapsacks and taken across the border to Norway by skiers.

The sentences were very mild. Wollweber almost certainly never expected to get off with only three years. But it was a logical sentence, since the really big acts of sabotage—such as blowing up the power plant in Porjus, which would deprive the iron mines of electricity—had never actually been carried out.

An interesting postscript to the case was a request in December 1941 from Vidkun Quisling and his Minister of Police, Jonas Lie, that they be allowed to inspect the documents of the Wollweber case, so that they could arrest his aides in Norway. Sweden replied laconically that the documents had been impounded and sealed and would not be given to the public until 1951.

We are justified in doubting whether Vidkun Quisling will still be living in 1951.

13. Axel Wenner-Gren—Agent of Death

"No compromise with Satan is possible."
                Henry A. Wallace, Vice-President
                May 8, 1942

There is one man and one man alone who really profited from the Russo-Finnish war. Finland lost more men than her birthrate can replace; Russia's soldiers are buried by the thousands and tens of thousands in the deep Arctic snows; and many Nazi soldiers will never again gaze upon their beloved Rhine or the beautiful blue Danube.

But one man pocketed the financial profits of this carnage with his right hand while with his left hand he dealt out great sums for "aid to Finland." This man is one of the best-known financiers and industrialists in the world. He is even ranked today as the richest arms merchant in the world—the true successor to Sir Basil Zaharoff.

Sweden has produced several great financiers who have played their parts in world politics. Ivar Kreuger, the match king, has become a legendary figure in Sweden; many Swedes refuse to believe that he committed suicide, and the Nazis assert that he was murdered on orders of "Jewish-American Finance." Meanwhile, Kreuger's swindles, the bank crashes he engineered which ruined large sections of the Swedish middle class, have been forgotten by many people of short memories.

Now that a new star has risen in the firmament of international finance-capital, the Swedes will have none of the newcomer. The Kreuger scandal made them sceptical of tycoons, and they prefer to give a wide berth to the richest man in the country. Axel Wenner-Gren, Sweden's cannon king, has become resigned to the fact that his name is greater in the rest of the world than in his native land. He consoles himself with the old saw concerning the status of a prophet in his own country. . . .

Axel Wenner-Gren comes from a family of farmers. He was educated both in Sweden and Germany, graduating from the Berlin *Handelsakademie* in 1902. For a time he worked in Germany in the Alfa-Laval Separator Company, and it was at this time that his interest in electrification developed. As a matter of fact, he gave evidence of considerable talent in the study of electricity. At the age of twenty-six, in 1907, he went to the United States, where he worked in a New Jersey factory for fifteen cents an hour, and was happy eventually to land a job as salesman with the Swedish Lux Company, which manufactured electric bulbs.

Wenner-Gren made most of his fortune during World War I. His first big deal was the securing of the contract to provide lamps to floodlight the Panama Canal at its opening on August 15, 1914.

Shortly afterward he returned to Sweden, for he realized that America would become involved in the First World War and he saw that his great chance for amassing a fortune lay in the war business in Europe.

During the next two decades Wenner-Gren piled fortune upon fortune. He sold everything from bulbs to vacuum cleaners, refrigerators and ball bearings. In 1917, he became head of his electric bulb firm. At this time he married Marguerite Gauntie Ligget, an opera singer and daughter of a successful Kansas City manufacturer.

In 1921 he founded the famous Electrolux Company which sold vacuum cleaners and electrical apparatus from Berlin to Tokio, from New York to Stockholm. In 1928 he paid two inventors $500,000 for patents of electrical refrigerators. It was this stroke that brought his fortune to its climax. Royalties streamed in from the United States, England, France, Germany, Scandinavia, from virtually every civilized country on the globe. With his profits he was now able to buy a large share of the Swedish armament works in Bofors, the greatest armament works in Northern Europe and the fourth greatest in Europe, outranked only by Schneider-Creuzot, Armstrong-Vickers and Krupp.

By the end of 1938, Wenner-Gren had acquired a fortune conservatively estimated at $50,000,000. He was by far the wealthiest man in Sweden and one of the richest men in the world. The total value of his enterprises was more than one hundred million dollars.

He acquired majority shares in the Nobel explosive works and proudly followed in Alfred Nobel's footsteps. He did not, to be sure, establish a peace prize, but he gave the sum of $7,500,000 to establish the Axel Wenner-Gren Foundation for Nordic Cooperation and Research.

Wenner-Gren was Europe's great man of peace. Again and again he spoke out for international understanding. He published books in Sweden, in England and the United States urging world peace. The English title of one of these was *Call to Reason*. He also traveled between Berlin and London, negotiating with Neville Chamberlain and Hermann Goering. And all during this period before the outbreak of the war, when he was advocating peace, the production figures of his Bofors works rose at a fantastic rate, and the profits poured in. The stock of Bofors rose three hundred per cent. The following table explains why.

TOTAL SALES OF ARMS
In Swedish Crowns ($1.00 = Kr. 4 1/5)

1937	51,155,432
1938	91,047,236
1939	156,208,016
1943	320,000,000 (estimated by Swedish newspapers)

And Sweden's chief pacifist acquired more and more plants. He bought a new airplane factory, bought stock in the Svenska Aeroplan Aktiebolaget, controlled the Irano-Swedish Company and the Tuolluvaara Iron Ore Mines, which send ninety per cent of their production to Hitler.

With the Swedish rearmament drive getting under way, Wenner-Gren and his Bofors concern laid the foundation for a powerful Swedish aircraft industry at Trollhättan. This plant by now has reached full productive capacity and is turning out bombers and fighters on German, Italian and American models. As managing director of the firm he installed his old crony, Sven Winquist, founder of the SKF ball bearing concern and a former director of Bofors.

Then Wenner-Gren acquired majority shares in the Svenska Cellulosa Industry, the biggest pulpwood producer in Sweden, which owned some five million acres of Scandinavian timberland.

The main offices of his Electrolux Company are still located in Berlin and Hamburg and the name of Wenner-Gren has not appeared on any German blacklist, although the Germans know that he has sold war materials to the Allies. After all, does not Japan sell rubber to Soviet Russia?

Today the Bofors works are no longer exporting to Allied countries—not because Wenner-Gren would not like to, but because transportation from Sweden is no longer available. His factories are now working for Finland, Sweden and Nazi Germany.

But through all this the pacifist merchant of death has gone on paying lip homage to progressive movements and to democracy. And Swedish refugee committees have received sizable checks from Mr. and Mrs. Wenner-Gren, although the Polish refugees know well that Bofors anti-tank guns have destroyed the tanks of the Polish Army.

Wenner-Gren enjoyed this double role of the giver and receiver; he is always outraged at the fable of himself as the mystery man who shuns the light of day and is ready to deliver weapons to all who can pay for them.

Sweden will never forget how her wealthiest citizen fled the country two days after the outbreak of the war. The newspapers and musical comedies ridiculed him, and popular songs were written about his flight. But the man in the street worried, for he felt that the financier must know what he was doing.

Wenner-Gren crammed his yacht, the *Southern Cross,* full of canned food and gasoline, which were already scarce in the country. His wife hurriedly selected fifty dresses from a Stockholm department store.

Then the two stepped aboard their yacht, and the *Southern Cross* with the Wenner-Grens and their crew of 315 men sailed gracefully out of Stockholm harbor, leaving the "dumb Swedes" to their fate and their rationing. The Swedes will not easily excuse him for the thousands of cans of food he took with him aboard his yacht.

The *Southern Cross,* sleek, white, splendidly appointed and as long as a destroyer, left Sweden for an unknown destination. The average Swede took Wenner-Gren's flight as a bad omen, and expected Hitler to invade the country at any moment. But Wenner-Gren was not at all worried. He had left his Bofors plant in safe hands—for he had seen to it that the Swedish Government took over control of the company. Several years before the war Wenner-Gren had owned Bofors jointly with Krupp. In 1934 he had the Swedish Government informed of Krupp's secret share in the company; it seems that through dummies Krupp had acquired large blocks of stock. The Swedish Government thereupon passed a law to make sure that no foreigner controlled any armament works.

Krupp was forced to sell its one-third interest in the Bofors concern to a group of Swedish industrialists, headed by Wenner-Gren, who at this time was president of the mighty Electrolux Company and principal shareholder in *Svenska Cellulosa A.B.* Shortly afterwards Wenner-Gren further expanded his interest in Bofors, becoming its principal stockholder.

Bofors had more orders than it could fill, and filled more orders for Germany than for Sweden. Shortly before the outbreak of the war the Swedish Cooperative newspaper *Hyresgaesten* was so indiscreet as to warn the inhabitants of Gothenburg that their city had virtually no anti-aircraft guns. The reason was that the Wenner-Gren-Bofors plants had been delivering all such guns to Germany for a year or more. Gothenburg, a city of predominantly wooden houses, felt none too comfortable.

After the war broke out Wenner-Gren made a clever move in order to keep himself off the British blacklist. He resigned from the board of directors of the International Electrolux Company and turned his post over to an Englishman with whom he was closely linked, Sir Harold A. Wernhem. Thus the Electrolux Company was able to go on doing business with both sides.

Rounding the northern tip of Scotland on his flight from Sweden, Wenner-Gren's yacht chanced to be near the spot where the *Athenia* was torpedoed. His crew rescued 399

Duel for the Northland

survivors, and the thousands of purloined cans were, after all, put to good use.

Then the *Southern Cross* sailed toward the Western Hemisphere.

Wenner-Gren and his wife landed in the Bahamas, where they own a spacious white mansion on Hog Island which is lovely despite its name. Significantly enough, Wenner-Gren calls this retreat Shangri-La, and it is indeed a miniature paradise, with gardens, terraces, lily ponds, rivulets and even transplanted tropical forests.

When the Duke of Windsor and his wife came to the Bahamas, the two couples struck up a close friendship. The Windsors were photographed frequently with the Wenner-Grens; they spent a good deal of their time in Shangri-La, and made their first trip to Miami on the *Southern Cross,* which Wenner-Gren lent them for the purpose.

In 1940, the Swedish cannon king left the Bahamas for Washington. Here he conferred with Finnish Minister Hjalmar Procope on the problems of shipping arms to Finland. At the same time this man, who was making millions from Finland's tragedy, made generous contributions to the American "aid to Finland" movement.

On his return to the Bahamas he received a cable from Reichsmarshall Goering requesting him to return to Sweden and use his influence to bring about a negotiated peace between Russia and Finland. The Nazis were anxious for a quick peace, for they feared Russia would conquer all of Finland in a few weeks. Failing that, they foresaw that Russia would make complete conquest as soon as spring came.

Wenner-Gren did return to Europe. Whether he played a part in the peace with Russia or whether the negotiations were handled largely by Sven Hedin, the pro-Nazi explorer, is a question that will not be cleared up until after this war. We know only that the ship on which Wenner-Gren sailed to Italy had among its passengers Undersecretary of State Sumner Welles; whether this happened by chance or design we cannot say.

It is known, however, that the correspondent who accompanied Sumner Welles had a number of heated discussions with Wenner-Gren, in the course of which the Swedish industrialist declared that Goering was "the best hope for bringing Germany into mediation negotiations."

After the Russo-Finnish armistice, Wenner-Gren returned to the Western Hemisphere. It is said that he was received by President Roosevelt and had a "long and intimate conference" with him. Interviewed in March 1941 by English newspapermen in the Bahamas, Wenner-Gren declared himself a believer in democracy. He said:

"I shall always prefer peace to war so long as there is a reasonable basis for hoping for peace, but never at a sacrifice of the principles of freedom and progressive democracy."

At this time he financed the Wenner-Gren Aeronautical Laboratory of the University of Kentucky. Its purpose was to test airplane motors; it later became a branch of the United States Army Air Corps' program of training and research.

In April 1941, he arrived once again in the United States.

In July 1941, he sailed on the *Southern Cross* for Peru, ostensibly to direct excavations at Cuzco, where he had financed the establishment of an "archeological park" under the supervision of the well-known explorer Dr. Paul Fejos. As recognition for his founding the "Wenner-Gren Archeological Park," the University of Cuzco bestowed on him the honorary title of Doctor of Philosophy, a title that the farmer's son had always longed to possess. His servants were at once given orders to call him Dr. Wenner-Gren.

From Peru Marguerite and Axel Wenner-Gren sailed on the *Southern Cross* to Mexico, arriving there in November 1942. He was given a grand reception, presented with the golden key of the city of Mexico and royally entertained by the brother of Mexico's President. To newsmen he declared he came to engage himself "in economic activities here, in collaboration with American and Mexican financiers." Informed financial sources spoke of two projects that Wenner-Gren had in mind. One was the creation of a ten-million-dollar oil trust in which American, British and Mexican capitalists would own shares. The second project was of interest to his friend Maximino Avila Camacho, the President's brother; it was the establishment of a modern highway and transportation system in Mexico.

The Nazi espionage service, however, reported to Berlin that Wenner-Gren had conferred with former New York State Senator John Ambrose Hastings and discussed plans for spending over one hundred million dollars to transform Mexico into an industrial country.

While he was in Mexico, Wenner-Gren quite casually had his *Southern Cross* transferred to Mexican registry.

But the day of reckoning was approaching. The American authorities knew very well that Wenner-Gren's firms were trading with Nazi Germany, they knew that his right hand worked in the Western Hemisphere and his left hand supported the Axis. The United States decided to blacklist him as one who traded with the enemy. Great Britain was forced to follow suit, though Wenner-Gren's friendship with the Duke of Windsor and his business dealings with England had thus far kept his name off the British blacklist. At the same time that the British placed Wenner-Gren's name on the blacklist, the Duke of Windsor was informed. So far as is known, he has not seen his old friend since.

The Bahamas Government confiscated Wenner-Gren's Nassau properties, which are valued at three million dollars. In July 1942 the General Foods Company took possession of the canning plant he had owned in the Bahamas, and was, it was said, expected to take over all the boats operated by Wenner-Gren's interests. In Mexico nothing was confiscated, for two hours before the confiscation decree was to be executed, Wenner-Gren withdrew all his funds and papers from his Mexican Bank, altogether some ten million dollars. The Swedish Government also intervened in his favor at this time.

He presented his luxurious yacht to the Mexican Government with the words, "I can't use it now, anyhow. If I took it out, people would say I was fueling submarines." And so one of the largest privately-owned yachts in the world, which had once been the property of the millionaire round-the-world flyer, Howard Hughes, by strange vicissitudes passed into the hands of the Mexican Government.

At the time of his blacklisting, one of his secretaries in Mexico declared, "It is all a terrible mistake." Wenner-Gren, however, did not think it a mistake; he reasoned that the United States had blacklisted him for fear of his competition in Latin America.

"I am a fast friend of the United States," he explained, "and I can get along with the Latins. I could have organized the production of things the United States needs. It's a shame."

Shame or not, the United States Government preferred to have no dealings with arms merchants who delivered weapons to friend and foe alike.

The American branch of the Electrolux Company, which in New York is known as the Servel Company, was not blacklisted. Wenner-Gren had, to be sure, declared as late as 1940 that he controlled the firm, but the company itself maintained that Wenner-Gren had had nothing to do with it since 1937 and that he owned no stock—at least, we may add, not under his name.

Axel Wenner-Gren is one of the last survivors of a once widespread type: the international financier, the mystery man who delivers arms to both sides in wartime and profits mightily by international tragedy. Wenner-Gren had delivered arms to Loyalist Spain during the Civil War. He often refers to this fact to prove that he is no Nazi sympathizer. But the explanation is simple enough. Franco was getting all the arms and munitions he needed from Krupp; Wenner-Gren supplied the Loyalists because they were the only available customer.

Opportunism apart, however, there seems to be little doubt that Wenner-Gren does not love the totalitarian way of life. But like some other Swedes, he is an old friend of Germany and has never dreamt of severing his economic and social ties with that country. He may not look forward to a Nazi victory, but a catastrophic defeat of the German Army would mean serious financial loss to him. For although Wenner-Gren competes with Krupp, Krupp uses Bofors patents and pays royalties on them.

An epoch of appeasement, accompanied by frenzied rearmament, meant good business for the munitions king. Destruction of the Axis and permanent peace would mean hard times for the Bofors armament works. Wenner-Gren is certainly not one who wants a total defeat of the Axis. Which is why his name was put on the blacklist, and why it belongs there.

Gunmaking is a matter of specialization. The Wenner-Gren Bofors management holds it a fixed dogma that twenty years of training are required for a really good machinist and at least four years for an ordinary workman.

Working on these principles, Bofors and Wenner-Gren have assembled an incomparable group of highly-skilled workers, natives of a region which has a long tradition of Swedish metal working.

Wenner-Gren has produced the famous 40 mm gun, a cannon whose merits place it in a class by itself. It can be swiftly transported by car or by tractor over the most difficult terrain and set up in position in less than half a minute. It sends out an uninterrupted stream of one hundred and twenty high explosive shells a minute. The barrel can be screwed off and replaced in a few seconds. It is the ideal weapon for defense of bridges, docks, factories, power stations and similar objectives to hit which the enemy plane must descend to a comparatively low altitude.

The early years of World War II have shown the efficacy of this Wenner-Gren gun, which has played a tremendous role on the battlefields of Poland, France, Africa, Soviet Russia, and indeed everywhere fighting has taken place. The gun has been used by belligerents on both sides, for Wenner-Gren sold the patents to England, Germany and Japan, and delivered the finished product to Finland. Wenner-Gren may be on the Allied blacklist, but the Allies are glad to use his 40mm cannon. England has been manufacturing it for a long time, and in the United States Chrysler has been making the gun since February 1941.

Wenner-Gren cannot, to be sure, claim any royalties now from us but there is no doubt that he will make claims after the war. When that time comes, it might be well for the United States to remember one of Wenner-Gren's few careless remarks:

"If there should happen to be a stalemate and a negotiated peace, I might be of great use. I have a good standing in Germany."

PART SIX
Dominium Maris Baltici
14. Spies and Saboteurs in the Russo-Finnish Struggle

"Together with the Finns, we stand from Narvik to the Carpathians."
                    Adolf Hitler on June 22, 1941

Wollweber was behind bars. The triumphant Germans could now work undisturbed in Scandinavia; at last the ore transports would reach their goal in safety, and the Russian submarines in the Baltic would not have full information on ship movements.

To their dismay and amazement, Sweden and the Nazis discovered that it was not enough to imprison the leader of the saboteurs, for a whole series of inexplicable acts of sabotage began.

This time it could not be Wollweber. Indeed, his League was operating without its leader with redoubled fury, taking bitter revenge for the arrest of the chief. On May 26, 1941 a munitions factory in Tostårp, in Skåne, Southern Sweden, suffered an explosion that cost six lives and many minor casualties. The Swedish press, taking a hint from high quarters, reported that it was an accident. But to Wollweber in his prison cell the news was reassuring proof that the new formation of his League could continue its work without his personal direction.

Less than two months later there took place one of the greatest railroad accidents in the history of Scandinavia. Even when Wollweber himself had held the reins, there had been few such drastic examples of sabotage.

On July 19, 1941 a devastating blast rocked the important railway junction of Krylbo, in Central Sweden, as three trains stood in line on the rails. So terrific was the explosion that station buildings were totally shattered, flames leaped two hundred feet into the air, and windows were broken half a mile away. It must be regarded as nothing short of a miracle that no one was killed by the blast and only twenty-four persons were injured. Property damage exceeded one million dollars.

Why should the Wollweber League blow up trains in neutral Sweden? Sweden was not at war with Russia. In fact, Swedish Foreign Minister Christian Guenther was at the very time bending every effort to maintain relationships of equal amity with Germany and Russia. The situation was made all the more mysterious by the statement of the Swedish news agency that rumors of sabotage were false; the train was a Swedish munitions train, the agency declared, which had blown up after an axle bearing overheated. This story of the overheated bearing seemed quite peculiar. It was revealed as utter nonsense when several days later the liberal and Communist press published long eyewitness accounts of the explosion.

The train had been a munitions train to which were attached a long line of German freight cars. Shells, of which more than four hundred unexploded specimens were picked up in the vicinity, were of German make. The newspapers published sworn statements of the witnesses that the freight cars laden with German munitions bore the inoffensive label: Food.

The Nazis had camouflaged the munitions train and labeled each freight car "Food," hoping that the Allied

Secret Services would be deceived by this transparent trick. But the OGPU had learned during the loading of the boxes in Norway that each box bore the official stamp of the German Army.

After long negotiations democratic Sweden had agreed to transship to famished Finland German food supplies from Germany and from Norway (which was certainly equally famished). These were the trainloads of food supplies which were passing through Krylbo from Norway to Finland. For months such trains had been bringing aid to the "hungry" Finns.

The publication of the sworn statements finally compelled the Swedish press authorities to inform the people of the bare unpalatable truth. It was admitted that since the occupation of Norway Germany had blackmailed Sweden with the constant threat of invasion, and had forced her to consent to the transit of soldiers from Germany to Norway and from Norway to Finland over the Swedish railroads. The Wollweber League had selected the railroad junction of Krylbo for sabotage in order to stop German supplies from reaching Finland.

Sweden is unhappy about the "Transitania," as the agreement is called there, for it constituted active assistance to the Nazis. Every Swede feels a deep sense of shame when he encounters in Swedish railroad stations the Nazi soldiers who are being sent to Norway or to pro-German Finland.

On August 24, 1941 the *Voelkischer Beobachter* stated that none other than the aged King Gustav V had given permission for this transit of German troops and munitions, and that he had done so against the will of the Social Democratic Government and the union leaders. The well-beloved king, however, had done only what everyone else in the country would have done; he had yielded to the

Nazis to avoid invasion. A significant hint of Sweden's difficulties is contained in the statement issued by the Swedish Foreign Office after the outbreak of the Russo-German War. The statement said:

"In this situation that has arisen because of the war between Germany and Russia, Sweden will steadfastly continue her efforts to maintain her liberty and independence and to remain outside all warlike conflicts. The new situation has, however, confronted us with certain specific questions. Thus both from the Finnish and the German side a demand has been made for permission to transport a force not exceeding one division from Norway to Finland. After consulting the Riksdag, the Government has agreed to this in a form compatible with Swedish sovereignty."

The Nazis had, of course, transported a good deal more than one division over the Swedish railroads to Finland.

The British Government sent a very sharp protest against such troop transportation through neutral territory. But the protest remained "a scrap of paper," while Wollweber's agents found distinctly more forceful means for interfering with the "food" trains to Finland.

Sweden must certainly have expected that her granting the Nazis transit rights to Finland would evoke Russian counter-measures. And these Russian measures were typically Russian in character. They resulted in many accidents such as that caused by the "overheated bearing" in Krylbo.

A recent example was provided on October 19, 1942 when the ferry *Deutschland,* carrying 1,000 Nazi troops from the German port of Sassnitz to the Swedish port of Trelleborg, was torpedoed in the Baltic. Seventeen Germans were killed and many more wounded. The incident also highlighted the enormously-increased activity of Russian and British submarines in the Baltic. In recent months submarines have sunk or damaged about a dozen

Swedish freighters bound for German ports with cargoes of iron ore.

The Stockholm evening paper *Aftontidningen* which is supported by the trade unions and therefore is pro-democratic and pro-Ally, commented: ". . . it would be best if the entire traffic (meaning the transit of German soldiers) could be liquidated. It has raised bad blood, and it is unfortunate that it was ever brought into existence. But if it cannot be avoided and cannot now be changed, it at least ought to be held strictly *within original limits.*"

Three weeks had passed since the Krylbo bombing. Wollweber was again questioned by the police, who hoped to extract information from him on the other members of his ring. But they soon gave up, for it was evidently impossible to make the man talk.

Even while the police were examining him, a new example of Wollweber sabotage occurred. On August 7, 1941, a tremendous fire broke out in the dockyard district of Gothenburg, consuming large stores and destroying some thirty motorboats belonging to the Swedish Navy. No trace of the incendiaries could be found—the case remained one of the many mysteries in the files of the Swedish police. Of only one thing were the police certain: that too many fires were taking place in strategic places for it to be a matter of chance. Moreover, the trials in Denmark had shown that most ship fires had been started by the Wollweber League. The Swedish police, of course, drew the natural conclusions.

The most dreadful example of the work of Wollweber's League took place on September 17, 1941 in the Haersfjaerden Naval Yard in Stockholm in the midst of Stockholm's most beautiful archipelago. Three of Sweden's best and most modern destroyers exploded and sank. Thirty-three lives were lost, a large number of people were injured, and property damage exceeded eight million dollars. It was by far the most terrible catastrophe in the history of the Swedish Fleet.

As in the case of the train explosion in Krylbo, the Swedes declared it was an accident. A boiler aboard the *Goeteborg* had exploded, setting off some 650 pounds of trotyl and sinking, along with the *Goeteborg,* the destroyers *Claes Horn* and *Claes Uggla.*

When the Swedish populace remained skeptical about the story of the exploding boiler, the Swedish news agency declared that a torpedo on the *Goeteborg* had blown up for unknown reasons.

Wollweber could count himself fortunate that he was in prison, giving him a perfect alibi, and his successors continued their work in obscurity.

The Wollweber Sabotage League had learned that Swedish warships had begun convoying ore ships to Germany; it had learned also that food supplies and deliveries of munitions from the great Swedish armament works in Bofors were being convoyed to Finland. The explosion of the three destroyers was the OGPU's reprisal for Sweden's latest aid to the Axis.

Sweden has not only lost warships in this war. In spite of her neutrality, her merchant shipping has suffered terrible losses, for both German and Russian warships attack Swedish shipping—depending on where it is bound. By the early months of 1943 almost two hundred Swedish ships had been sunk, totaling in round numbers half a million deadweight tons. And nearly fifteen hundred Swedish sailors had lost their lives.

At last, when a tremendous explosion occurred in the Bofors munitions works in November 1941, the pretense of "accidents" had to be dropped. The Swedish pro-Nazi press openly called it the work of the Wollweber League.

Duel for the Northland

There is little doubt that it was. The Bofors Munitions works belonged to Axel Wenner-Gren, of whom we had something to say in the last chapter.

The Russian Secret Service was ordered to intensify its activity in neutral Sweden, to do the utmost harm to German and Swedish aid to Finland, and to ferret out the secrets of Germany's forces in the Baltic and in Norway. Railroad trains and ships were blown up as a tactic of Russia's war against Germany and Finland. Thus much of the battle of Finland was not fought in Karelia, in the vicinity of Leningrad, but in Stockholm's archipelagoes and in the forests of Central Sweden.

Finland today is one of the most unfortunate countries on this globe. A democratic country, she has an obsessive fear of all things red and Russian. For centuries the Finns fought Russia, fought the Czars and fought their successors. The country at last won her freedom in 1918 with the help of German bayonets. The Land of the Thousand Lakes has retained a deep affection for the Germans to whom she owed her independence.

In the course of World War II, Finland tried to maintain her integrity against the encroachments of her neighbor to the East. The upshot of her efforts was occupation by Germany. Finland is nominally independent today, but she no longer can determine whether she will be at war or at peace. With 400,000 German troops stationed in the country as "allies," Finland is as much an occupied country as is Mussolini's Italy. There were socialists in the Government when the alliance with Hitler was concluded. These socialists found themselves linked with the archenemy of all their beliefs; they were coerced into this by the chauvinist sentiments of the country as a whole and by the fascist clique in the Army, which was constantly growing in strength. This fascist clique, dominated by Marshal

Mannerheim, forced Finland to link her fate with that of the German Reich.

Finland had declared her independence on December 6, 1917.

Almost immediately a bloody civil war broke out in which the "Reds" fought against the "White Guards." At the head of the White Army stood a tall middle-aged aristocrat with a chequered past, Gustav Emil Baron von Mannerheim. For thirty-five years Mannerheim had faithfully served the Russian Czars who were holding his homeland in bondage. Up to the very year of 1917, this Russian-Swedish-Finnish nobleman had not even bothered to learn the language of the country of which he was to become the revered "Pater Patriae." Even today, Mother Suomi's "greatest son" speaks Finnish haltingly and with an accent.

Born June 4, 1867, Mannerheim entered the military college of Fredrikshamn at the age of fifteen; later he joined the Czarist Guard. He became a lieutenant of the Nikolaevsky dragoons, then commanded a regiment of Uhlans in the Russo-Japanese War 1904-05. He arrived too late for the Battle of Mukden, and on the whole failed to distinguish himself at the front.

Nevertheless, the young aristocrat with his irreproachable manners and excellent connections was assured of a swift and easy career. He was promoted to Colonel in 1905 and to Major-General in 1911. During the First World War, Mannerheim, now a Lieutenant General, commanded the Twelfth Russian Cavalry Division.

Until the collapse of the Czarist regime, Mannerheim behaved more Russian than the Czar himself. It was not until he saw that his career in Russia was at an end that he remembered his Swedish-Finnish origin and from a Russian War Lord transformed himself into the "Liberator of Finland."

From his headquarters at Vaasa, Mannerheim opened his drive on the Reds in January 1918. Although directed against a numerically inferior ill-equipped and poorly trained enemy, the campaign lagged and Mannerheim was forced to beg the Kaiser for help.

In March, a German expeditionary corps under the command of General Count Ruediger von der Goltz landed at Hangö. With the aid of the Germans, whom he had faced in war only a few months before, Mannerheim at last was able to defeat the Reds. On April 5, 12,000 Reds capitulated at Tammerfors and on May 16 Mannerheim triumphantly entered the capital. The Civil War was over.

The grateful White Guards decided to erect a monument to their brothers-in-arms. It was set up at Hangö and the inscription, in German, Finnish and Swedish, read:

> German troops landed here on April 3, 1918
> to aid our country in its battle for freedom.
> Let this stone bear witness of our perpetual
> gratitude.

This inscription explains better than any amount of theorizing the deeply-rooted friendship between Finland and German militarism.

The Kaiser had already selected a Hohenzollern to be king of Finland: Prince Karl Friedrich von Hessen. Mannerheim, however, though he was grateful for German aid, preferred to keep the rule of Finland for himself.

When the Germans, disregarding Mannerheim's displeasure, contrived to get their candidate "elected" by the Finnish people, Mannerheim, in a fit of rage, left the country in disgust. But the King Elect was never crowned, for before he could ascend the throne, Germany collapsed and her soldiers returned home.

Thus in December 1918, Mannerheim was able to return to Helsinki, where he had himself proclaimed "Regent." He held this post until July 25, 1919 when the new Republican constitution came into force. Mannerheim ran for President but was defeated and Kaarlo Juho Ståhlberg, a Liberal, was elected first President of the Finnish Republic.

In the meantime, Mannerheim and his henchmen had begun a reign of terror and massacre which is without parallel in modern history before Adolf Hitler. At least 15,000 people, including 4,600 women and children, were executed or murdered in cold blood by Mannerheim's hordes. More than 90,000 were thrown into jail, and of these 15,000 died of starvation, ill treatment and lack of medical care. Of the remaining 75,000, all but 8,000 were sentenced to long terms at hard labor.

Such were the acts that won him the name of the "Bloody Baron."

During the first Russo-Finnish war Mannerheim's bloody past was forgotten and the country followed his lead for the sake of unity. But in the second Russo-Finnish war, when Mannerheim became the ally of Hitler and tied democratic Finland to the leading strings of the Axis, the Finns bitterly remembered. In spite of opposition, however, Mannerheim tightened his grip on the nation. Today he has maneuvered her into an unenviable position.

For both Russia and England are at war with Finland, and the country trembles lest the United States declare war upon her. Without America's sympathy and aid, Finland has little hope of ever regaining full independence; she would probably once more become a Russian province, as she was for centuries.

Nevertheless, the Finnish Government has rejected several urgent pleas by the United States and Great Britain to

Duel for the Northland

stop fighting against Russia. This is not only due to the influence of the Nazis; the Finnish fascist circles also wish the war to continue. The Finnish armies are no longer fighting for the recovery of their own soil. They are fighting for "living-space," for Marshal Mannerheim's dream of a Greater Finland which would include Soviet East Karelia, the Kola Peninsula and possibly even Leningrad.

During the past centuries Sweden and Finland have not always been close friends. There were times when the Swedish language was outlawed at the Helsinki university, although a third of all Finns are of Swedish extraction and speak Swedish rather than Finnish. During her wars with Russia, Finland, while gladly accepting what aid came her way from Sweden, has grumbled over Sweden's neutrality. A bitter anti-Swedish cartoon created something of a sensation in both countries. The cartoon pictured a Finn who had broken through thin ice and was crying for help. At the brink stood a fat Swede in a fur coat tossing the drowning man a hundred crown note and preparing to walk away. That is to say, in the eyes of the Finns the wealthy Swedes seemed willing to give money, but would lend no effective aid. Within Finland the Swedish minority group consists for the most part of large landowners; the cartoon was thus aimed also at the Swedish Finns.

Finland did not always fight to defend her frontiers. She has been making war beyond the old frontiers of Finland, and her leaders have justified this in pan-Finnish terms. On July 13, 1942 Marshal Mannerheim declared after an interview with Hitler:

"We promise the Karelians that our sword will not be sheathed until Karelia has been liberated. The provinces of Viena and Aunus have waited twenty-three years for the fulfilment of this promise, and since the Winter Campaign of 1939-40 Karelia has waited for the dawn of the day that is to bring her freedom. Her battalions are now marching in our ranks."

The freedom of Karelia, Marshal Mannerheim continued, "and the Greater Finland is the goal that beckons us forward in this mighty whirl of historic events. For us this war is a holy war against the enemy of our nation, and at the side of powerful Germany we are firmly determined to bring the crusade to a victorious end. . . ."

Russia had no intention of giving up her territory to Mannerheim to form a Greater Finland. Consequently, Wollweber's Sabotage League was instructed to employ the utmost ruthlessness against Finland. After Sweden's King and Government declared, "Finland's cause is ours," the Wollweber League at once included her in the ranks of Russia's enemies.

The Nazis and Finns had entrusted the territory of the Soviet Arctic to good hands. Vitalis Pantenburg of Cologne and Professor Friedrich Wilhelm Borgmann, an old friend of General Karl Haushofer, had been assigned to espionage work in this area. Their task was to prepare for the conquest and occupation of the Soviet Arctic, above all of the ice-free port of Murmansk.

Borgmann, a Finnish citizen of German descent, was the owner of a travel bureau in Helsinki. Behind this front he had guided espionage work in the Arctic regions for years, and was considered one of the foremost authorities on the Soviet Arctic and the Lapp regions of Norway and Finland. Pantenburg, who had been expelled from Norway and Sweden after his spy activities were exposed, had worked for Borgmann for many months.

Vitalis Pantenburg was one of the best Nazi spies in Europe. In his travels through Scandinavia and Lapland he acquired blueprints of all important fortifications in the

Arctic, including those of the Boden Fortress in Northern Sweden and the Fortress of Narvik.

Olaf Sundlo, the Norwegian Commander in Narvik, was a close friend of Pantenburg's. Sundlo was the commander who gave furloughs to his entire garrison when the Nazis landed in Narvik. (His treason has been splendidly portrayed in John Steinbeck's *The Moon is Down*.)

Pantenburg's and Borgmann's espionage work in the Arctic regions was to lay the foundation for the military expedition of Col. General Nikolaus von Falkenhorst and General Eduard Dietl to conquer Eastern Karelia and the Kola Peninsula. The first and principal goal of this drive was the port of Murmansk. Had they succeeded in taking it, they would have cut off one of the few routes by which fighting Russia could be supplied from the outside world. Finland had promised Nazi Germany the conquest of Murmansk, and the "crusaders" for a Greater Finland were willing to sacrifice everything to obtain the port.

The OGPU in Scandinavia had a special division that concerned itself solely with counterespionage in the Soviet Arctic and in Eastern Karelia. Kept informed by this branch of the OGPU, Russia was able to arrest and execute Finnish as well as Nazi agents who were planning to sabotage the port facilities of Murmansk.

What is this city that is so vital to Russia and to Russia's enemies?

Twenty-five years ago, when the name of Murmansk first became familiar beyond the boundaries of Russia, the place was little more than a large fishing village. After the Revolution, Murmansk counted some 2,500 to 3,000 inhabitants; in 1926 the population numbered 6,400; in 1931, 8,800; seven years later the fishing village had become a large industrial and commercial metropolis of some 100,000 inhabitants. The present population exceeds 120,000.

It was in the '30s, then, that Murmansk underwent the transformation from a small town to a large city. This metamorphosis coincided with Soviet Russia's growing "Arctic consciousness." But it is also probable that the rapid growth of this Far Northern city was motivated by Soviet Russia's constant fear of attack from without and her realization that the Arctic Ocean might one day become the last loophole in a strangling blockade.

Today, with vast docks and wharves, shipyards, repair shops, power stations and airfields, Murmansk has come to be the greatest trade, fishing and shipping center in the Arctic. It has by far outstripped its older and larger rival, the White Sea port of Archangel. In the past few years a constantly increasing share of Soviet Russia's foreign trade has been shipped from Murmansk, so much so that just before the outbreak of the war, the port had an annual turnover of 2,000,000 tons of freight.

Moreover, Murmansk is the chief Arctic base of the Soviet Navy and the headquarters of the ice-breaker fleet. It ranks with Kronstadt and Vladivostok as one of Russia's principal naval strongholds.

The spectacular development of Murmansk is due partly to nature, partly to the persistent efforts of man. The Murman coast is inhospitable in the extreme: barren, woodless, swept by furious gales and shrouded half the year in the long Arctic night. But into the Arctic waters reaches a stray current of the Gulf Stream, the same current that also brings warmth and life to the coasts of Norway and Finland in a latitude where, in the Western Hemisphere, there is nothing but ice and snow. Because of this current, a stretch of some 220 miles on the Murman coast is permanently free of ice. And even in this uniquely favored tiny segment of Russia's 18,750 miles of Arctic coastline there are no harbors or anchorages for large vessels except for some fifty miles of coastline between the Finnish border and Kola Bay.

About halfway between these two points, in a deeply-indented firth, lies Murmansk, which experts have pronounced the finest, largest and best-protected harbor in the extreme north of Europe. Even a giant liner like the *Bremen* was able to take refuge there.

The city is protected by a screen of forts at Poljarnoe, some twenty miles to the north. Because of its deep, permanently ice-free waters and its easily-defended approaches, Poljarnoe was long regarded as an ideal naval base, except for the storminess of the coastal waters.

In addition to its favored location in the only ice-free corner of the Barents Sea, Murmansk is the terminus of two great traffic arteries that cross the swamps and wastelands of Eastern Karelia to link the city with Leningrad and Moscow. These are the Murman Railroad and the Baltic-White Sea Canal.

The partly-electrified 900-mile railroad from Leningrad to Murmansk is one of the best railroads in the USSR. It was built in 1916-17 by an army of 200,000 workers, mostly German and Austrian prisoners of war. Since then it has been expanded and improved. The line proved to be surprisingly good during the Finnish-Russian war of 1939-40. In the early days of the present Russo-Finnish war the Germans and Finns succeeded several times in cutting the railroad at important points, especially near Kandalaksha, but in spite of local and temporary dislocations of traffic supplies from Britain and America have been getting through.

No less important for the development of the Soviet Arctic has been the Baltic-White Sea Canal ("Russia's Kiel Canal"), which connects Leningrad with Archangel and Murmansk by way of Lakes Ladoga and Onega and the

Svir River. The main part of it, the "Stalin Canal," which extends 141 miles from Povenetz at the north end of Lake Onega to the White Sea port of Soroka, was completed in 1933.

Through this extensive system of canals, rivers and lakes, the Soviet Admiralty is, or was, able to move submarines, torpedo boats and even light cruisers between their Baltic bases and the Arctic. However, like the White Sea, the Stalin Canal is icebound for six months of the year, and moreover has been damaged severely by repeated bombardments of locks and gates.

If Eastern Karelia is of little value, except for the traffic arteries traversing it, the same cannot be said for Murmansk's hinterland, the Kola Peninsula. Cold and inhospitable, partly covered with "tundra" (marshy, moss-grown land), partly with "taiga" (dense, marshy forest), this vast territory does not lend itself too well to human settlement, but it is a prospector's dream. Of the many minerals discovered in the peninsula, only a few have so far been exploited. In 1934 a geological chart issued by the Soviet Arctic Institute listed no fewer than 228 known deposits of copper, nickel, lead, tin, zinc, graphite and gold.

The most important of Kola's mineral resources is nickel. With the opening, three years ago, of a large factory at Montsjegorsk, the USSR became the world's second leading producer of nickel, next only to Canada. Rich deposits of apatite have also been discovered on the peninsula. Clearly, this wealth of minerals has stimulated Hitler's appetite for Murmansk and the surrounding country.

Until I visited Finland in 1940, I had scoffed at the "Greater Finland" talk. I attributed it to clever Russian propaganda, for how could little Finland hope to take territory from her great neighbor? Finland imperialistic? The idea appeared fantastic to me, a madman's fantasy.

Perhaps they were madmen. At any rate, in June 1940 some high officers of the Finnish Army declared to me:

"After Germany, we have the best army in the world. Five Finns can hold three hundred Russians. We will not lay down our arms until we have reconquered Karelia and obtained a longer coastline along the Arctic Sea. For Petsamo will never flourish so long as the Russians hold Murmansk."

The fascist army clique, who were securing ever-greater power in the country, never forgot what they owed to the Germans for helping them establish the Finnish nation. These fascists like to call themselves "the Prussians of the North." Steadily, they drove from the seats of power the moderate Social Democrats and liberals who wish an understanding with Russia and cooperation with England and America, instead of the existing mesalliance with Germany.

Before the outbreak of the second Russo-Finnish war the land was swarming with Nazi spies, and Nazi troops were secretly stationed in the country. When I reported this in the American press, the Finnish propaganda bureau in Washington and New York indignantly denied it. This bureau, I remark in passing, has since been closed down for carrying on pro-Nazi propaganda in this country.

Besides Friedrich Wilhelm Borgmann and Vitalis Pantenburg, a large number of skilled spies and observers were at work in Finland, bending every effort to swing this formerly democratic nation to the side of the Germans.

In Helsinki German Minister von Bluecher labored persistently to attain this goal. His right-hand man was a Finnish Count, Constantin Stamati, who had fought in 1918 under Mannerheim and who was not far behind his chief in bloodthirstiness. Stamati was considered an authority on the Baltic Countries; he was the naval expert for Canaris's indefatigable Intelligence Bureau on Finland, Esthonia, Latvia and Lithuania.

It was Stamati who stirred up anti-Semitic sentiment in the country, although there were scarcely 2,000 Jews in all Finland. He organized the literature campaigns of various German propaganda agencies like the *Fichtebund* and the *Weltdienst*. This Nazi literature was, for the most part, printed in Germany in the Finnish language. Stamati also sent spies to Soviet Karelia and set up the espionage group charged with guarding the Swedish iron ore district, which was so vital to German war industry.

The most active of all the spies in Finland was one of Pflugk-Hartung's tools: Albrecht Joachim Gruessner. Gruessner was a tall sturdy fellow whom the Swedish and Norwegian police had been hunting down for years. It was he who did most of the dirty work with his own hands, and it was he who was assigned the task of spying in the strategically vital Aaland Islands.

The Aaland Islands formerly belonged to Sweden, and the population is still Swedish. The people have their own Government and their own flag, and despite their connection with Finland the Islands are not considered participants in the war. Swedish is still the official language, and by special statute land can be sold only to Swedes.

Through Swedish accomplices Gruessner had bought land in the Islands and used the land as a base for his naval espionage. He sent out fishing boats to take soundings of the sea; he located potential landing fields and locations for mine fields. The Nazis went to a great deal of trouble to spy out all the secrets of the Aaland Islands. They remembered what Napoleon had written in 1809 in a letter to Alexander I of Russia:

"To take Finland without Aaland would be like appropriating a portmanteau of which someone else had got the key."

The Czar agreed—and in the Peace of Fredrikshamn took both Finland and Aaland from the Swedish Crown.

Duel for the Northland

Aaland is not as yet under formal German occupation, but Gruessner's spies are still busily at work. "Phantom flyers," as the Swedes call unidentified planes, use the Aaland Islands as a base from which to defend the territory from Northern Sweden to Leningrad.

Strategists and diplomats have long known that the Aaland Islands are potentially one of the worst danger spots in Europe. Hence, there have been many efforts in the past to neutralize them.

The archipelago was first demilitarized in 1856, after Russia had lost the Crimean War. In 1908, however, Czar Nicholas declared the provisions of the Treaty of Paris obsolete, and during World War I the Islands were heavily fortified by the Russians. In 1917 occurred an incident that never came to the knowledge of the general public. Twice in that year Kaiser Wilhelm sent a special emissary to King Gustav V of Sweden promising him the Aaland Islands if he would exert himself to the extent of taking them by force of arms. Happily, Sweden rejected this temptation, which would certainly have embroiled her in the First World War.

After the war, a powerful popular movement arose among the islanders, demanding return to the Swedish mother country. This led to a diplomatic tug-of-war between democratic Sweden and pro-German Finland, which was at last referred to and settled by the League of Nations.

The sovereignty of the new Finnish Republic over the archipelago was recognized, but Sweden was granted two important concessions. First, under the Home Rule Act of May 6, 1920, the Aalanders were allowed cultural and administrative autonomy. Secondly, the Islands were again demilitarized and neutralized under the International Convention of October 20, 1921.

The new Convention under the aegis of the League was signed by ten powers: Denmark, Esthonia, Finland,

France, Germany, Great Britain, Italy, Latvia, Poland and Sweden. In effect it restored to Aaland the status of 1856. Under Article 3 of the Convention Finland is expressly forbidden to establish military, naval or air bases of any description on the Islands.

Small wonder that the German military machine had designs on unfortified Aaland. Swedish Foreign Minister Rickard Sandler, after reading reports of German espionage activities in the Islands, resolved to block their plans in 1939. Tall, gaunt, pro-Ally Sandler suggested that Sweden and Finland jointly fortify the Islands to defend them against the Nazis. He also wanted to allow British troops transit to Finland. But the Foreign Minister stood almost alone in Sweden, and because of his militant policies his old friend, Premier Per Albin Hansson, was forced to dismiss him from the Cabinet. Nevertheless, Sandler is to this day considered one of the most capable diplomats in Sweden.

As early as 1937 Bluecher and Stamati were able to employ a Finnish cruiser, the *Vainominen,* for their own devices. Under the protection of this Finnish warship their men explored the strategic waters of the Gulf of Bothnia and the Esthonian islands of Dagoe and Oesel which stand guard at the entrance to Leningrad.

A list of Finnish military men who secretly worked for the Nazis would fill many pages, for the Finnish army officers were and are pro-German. Among Canaris's aides were Major-General Valve, the chief of the Finnish Air Force, and Lieutenant-General Rahola, Chief of Finnish Coastal Artillery.

Indeed, so powerful were the Nazi spies in Helsinki that they ventured to plan a coup d'état. Before 1929 Finland had passed through a period of fascist dictatorship, during which workmen's club buildings were burned down and concentration camps established. The regime came to an end with the overwhelming triumph of the Social Democratic Party in the next elections; the Social Democrats then proceeded to affiliate Finland with the other Scandinavian democracies. This was distasteful to the fascist military clique, to say the least, and they gladly joined with the Nazis. German and Finnish fascists made plans to seize power and install General Martin Wallenius as Finland's Hitler. Finland's President K. J. Stahlberg was kidnapped, and a march on Helsinki was organized in 1932. But the plan was nipped in the bud by the alert Russian spies, who ferreted out the entire plot and warned the Finns. An amusing detail of this story is the fact that General Wallenius had a white charger ready for his triumphal entry into the capital.

General Wallenius was dishonorably discharged from the Army, but this has not deterred Marshal Mannerheim from appointing him to one of the most important posts in the Finnish Army of today: Commander of the Finnish North Army.

In Finland the German espionage system had an easy task. It was not necessary to look for Quislings; the Finnish fascists volunteered their services. They were flesh of one flesh, kinsmen of the same blood who were fighting the same foe in the East.

The Wollweber League, conversely, found Finland a hard nut to crack. In Helsinki the Finns worked with German thoroughness; all who wished to live on peaceful terms with Russia and dared to say so were arrested. Thus it was difficult for Wollweber's men to find assistants. The Russian spies had to limit their activities to demoralizing propaganda and to infrequent sabotage in Helsinki's waterfront district. This, indeed, was part and parcel of Russian policy, for the Russians had always hoped to conquer Finland by propaganda rather than by force of arms.

Anyone who has seen the battlefields of Poland and Holland would be amazed at the bombed regions in Finland. The Russians have been merciful—not, to be sure, from love for the Finns, but because they hope to wean Finland away from Germany and out of the war.

This may be no vain hope. Many of the Finns want peace and are unwilling allies of Hitler. This is especially true of the Social Democratic Party, which is the Government Party. Ministers such as Karl August Fagerholm and Vaino Tanner are forthright anti-Nazis. But there was nothing they could do against the pressure of the fascist clique; their only choice would have been to resign. The courageous editor of the Social Democratic *Arbetarbladet,* Arto Wirtanen, took this course.

Wirtanen's last letter to his readers was read in 1942 over the Russian radio and distributed throughout the land in thousands of illegal pamphlets. It is a moving letter that voices the spirit of democratic Finland, of the Finland that belongs to the Scandinavian bloc.

"Today," Wirtanen wrote, "we meet once more, but only to say farewell. It is some time now since I have spoken out in these columns, but the reason is easy to explain. Freedom of the press has dwindled steadily. It is not easy to be a journalist under such circumstances—that I am sure you realize all too well. It is the sad truth that, when the weapons of war speak, the voice of the law must remain silent, as must the voice of common sense. Until the very last we have believed in the healthy motive of self-preservation, but instinct has the last word, and when instinct is rampant, reason must sleep. We have experienced the most unbelievable things. Unfortunately, I cannot write about them here, but the time will come when they will be told. Until the day when Freedom shall once more awaken in Finland—as it will; let us never doubt this—all we can do is endure and try to maintain our newspaper. Though we may not be able to do anything positive, we may, perhaps, keep the damage as small as possible. The hour has arrived when we must sacrifice or lose all that is dear to us, but there is one thing we must never sacrifice or lose: the ideals and liberties for which our Social Democracy has fought for the last fifty years."

In another passage, evidently pointed at the members of his Party, including Tanner, who had given their approval to the Government war policy, Wirtanen wrote: "We must not condemn those who have weakened and who have disappointed us in this historic crisis, for who knows how he himself would have stood the test? Only cynical double-crossing must not be forgiven. Nemesis never forgets. We will all see one another again, perhaps soon, perhaps after a long interval. But the day of freedom will not fail us."

Wirtanen was diplomatic, but his friends were not. Five of his friends in the Finnish Parliament were arrested for calling for peace and refusing to fight with Hitler. The left wing—a group of moderate radicals—emigrated to Sweden and there printed an underground newspaper urging the Finnish people to struggle for peace.

The OGPU, of course, spent hundreds of thousands of dollars in its underground campaign to destroy Finnish morale. But as long as Nazi troops are stationed in Finland, a peace movement is simply not possible. Were any such movement to emerge, Hitler would instantly set up a puppet Finnish Government, employing for this purpose the Finnish fascist officers who want to fight for a Greater Finland.

On February 15, 1943 elections were held in Finland. The incumbent President of the Republic was reelected. The elections were not the kind of popular election by which Presidents of the United States are chosen; three hundred electors chose the President of Finland, who has the power to decide upon war or peace.

A few hours after pro-German President Risto Ryti was reelected, the Moscow radio remarked that the 300 electors—who were themselves elected seven years ago—no longer had a legal right to office; their terms had expired. The Soviet press declared—and the statement is wholly objective: "Finnish ruling circles made a comedy of the Presidential elections. All the roles were distributed beforehand, and the election results were known beforehand."

Ryti was elected by the votes of Finnish fascists and Finnish socialists. It is hard to conceive of a more confused state of affairs. Marshal Mannerheim was also a candidate for the Presidency, although he had no chance for victory, since the strong Socialist Party did not support him. When it became apparent that he could not win the election, he made it known that he had been nominated against his will.

The new Presidential election convinced the Russians that the rumors and portents that Finland would make a separate peace in the near future were so much dishwater. The Russian Telegraph Agency, Tass, laconically reported that Finland would continue to fight for Germany, to act as a base for German submarines and aircraft operating against American and British ships, and that "Finland has turned Finnish diplomatic missions into *German espionage centers."*

The OGPU, of course, was never a mere propaganda agency. Words were silver, but sabotage was golden. And so the Russian Secret Service determined to cut off Swedish aid to Finland. Wollweber's men planned to blow up the bridge connecting the two border towns of Haparanda in Sweden and Torneå in Finland.

Either the Finnish Secret Service got wind of this plan, or it had cleverly anticipated just such an attempt. In any case, an OGPU agent was discovered at the moment he was about to light the fuse that would have blown up the bridge, and was shot down. His name was never learned, for he carried no identifying papers. His features appeared to be Finnish.

The German-controlled National Tidende in Copenhagen reported that three other Finnish Communists were found with the type of short wave apparatus used by Wollweber's agents. They, too, were shot.

The struggle to stop deliveries of food and war materials to Finland cost the Russian Secret Service terrible losses. Wollweber, of course, could not be replaced, and what with numerous arrests of less important agents, the OGPU again and again had to start its activities from scratch.

In peacetime, Russian espionage had been dangerous enough, but that was a bed of roses compared to the perilous situation of wartime. Comrade Ceder was not the only one to give confessions to the Swedish authorities on the activities of the Wollweber League. One day an unknown Swede appeared at police headquarters in Stockholm and announced that he was a member of the new Wollweber League. He stated that he had received dynamite to store away for eventual use against railroad trains carrying German troops through Sweden, or transporting war materials in Finland.

The man related that the head of the new sabotage group was Fritz Nikolai Rohm, whom Wollweber had appointed. He was an Esthonian, about thirty years old, an experienced OGPU worker whose territory had been the Franco-German border in Alsace. Rohm was traced and arrested. His arrest produced a bit of a sensation, for with him the police arrested one Erika Moeller, a beautiful young dancer who had entered the dangerous profession of espionage out of love for Rohm.

Erika Moeller was born in Riga, Latvia, but she had acquired Swedish citizenship through marriage. She had come to Sweden at eighteen, and was a dancer in a traveling circus. After falling in love with Rohm, she used the tours with the circus as a chance to spy out locations for sabotage work.

Two other men and one woman were also arrested at this time. And for some time thereafter agent after agent was captured. But the OGPU always had others to replace them.

On August 17, 1942 the German and Swedish Secret Services learned that Russian-born, fifty-three-year-old Michael Katz, a Swedish citizen, had kept Russia informed about ship movements in the Baltic. A secret radio transmitter was found in the Katz home, over which his eighteen-year-old son, Lennart, had transmitted the information in code.

On August 12, five days earlier, the Gothenburg police had arrested three Swedes who were charged with espionage and preparation for sabotage against ships and trains. Those arrested were Ivan Blackman, G. S. Lindstroem and Bertil Austrinsky. The police accused them of possessing incendiary bombs and time fuses, and receiving 6,000 kronor (about $1,500) from a foreigner who had left the country. Two of the men were captured when they broke into a storehouse near Källared, taking more than twenty pounds of dynamite and detonators.

And yet, despite all these arrests, there is no doubt that the majority of the spies and saboteurs in the Baltic regions are as yet uncaught.

Espionage of the sea lanes was of vital importance to Russia's war effort. General Haushofer may have considered

Duel for the Northland 239

the Baltic a German Sea, but the Russians had other ideas about it. If railroad trains could be blown up, ships delivering food, arms and Swedish volunteers to Finland could also be torpedoed. Iron ore shipments need never reach Germany if the Russian Baltic Fleet knew when and whence the boats were sailing.

The three destroyers that exploded in Stockholm were only the first fruits of Russian espionage work. Other achievements were to follow. Thus, the Red Fleet was informed that the *Ada Gorthon,* a ship of 3,950 deadweight tons, would pass Oeland Island with a cargo of iron ore. She was sunk by a Russian torpedo. A large number of other sinkings, such as the destruction of the *Galeon, Luleå, Margareta* and *Liljevalch,* may be attributed to the activity of the OGPU.

The *Liljevalch* was sunk in August 1942. She was en route to Germany with a valuable cargo of iron ore, and was leading a convoy of ships under various flags; for the most part they were Finnish and Danish vessels. The convoy was escorted by several Swedish destroyers. The fate of the convoy's twenty-one vessels is not known, since the German Admiralty issued no statements, but the Russians also claimed the sinking of several Finnish boats. The Swedish Foreign Ministry protested vigorously against the torpedoing of Swedish ships. In reply came polite denials, accompanied by a tactfully-worded inquiry as to why a neutral country was shipping war materials to Germany and Finland.

During the years 1942 and 1943 the Russian and British Secret Services found it advantageous to cooperate in the Battle of the Baltic. This collaboration represented a great stride forward for the United Nations. The combined Intelligence Services were able to direct the activity of both Russian and British submarines in the Baltic. By now British and Russian submarine warfare in the Baltic has grown so formidable that the only safe passenger link between Nazi Germany and Sweden is the long rail and water route via Flensburg, in Danish Jutland, and Copenhagen. The length of the voyage has increased from three hours to some four days.

At Sassnitz (the harbor facing Swedish Trelleborg) the Nazis have massed numerous destroyers and submarine chasers. The German Intelligence Service is convinced that British submarines enter the Baltic by way of North Russian waters, through the Stalin Canal into Lake Ladoga and the Gulf of Finland—the same Stalin Canal that has been "destroyed" many times over in German and Finnish communiques.

The Nazis maintain that the Russian OGPU is now guiding the British submarines; Sweden, they cry angrily, is "tolerating" this espionage.

The combined efforts of the Russian and British Intelligence Services have greatly hampered the regular shipments of iron ore from Sweden to Germany. And iron-ore shipments from Norway's Narvik are under the constant surveillance of the British and Norwegian Intelligence Services, which inform the Navies of Britain and Norway about every boat leaving the port of Narvik.

On April 9, 1940, the day of the invasion of Scandinavia, Hitler swaggered forth as possessor of *Dominium Maris Baltici,* but 1942 and 1943 have pricked the bubble of his pride. British and Russian submarines are dealing with the Nazis as the Germans dealt with the United Nations in the Battle of the Atlantic—with but one difference: the Battle of the Atlantic was won by the United Nations, and the Battle of the "German Sea" will not be won by Germany and Finland.

15. Sweden in the Pincers

In the life of Gustav V, the liberal King of Sweden, fate has several times knocked on his door in the guise of a German.

We have seen how Kaiser Wilhelm advised him to take the Aaland Islands. Adolf Hitler, characteristically more grandiose than the former ruler of Germany, offered King Gustav the crown of occupied Norway. Gustav was to be declared King Haakon's successor and the two lands were to be united once more in a personal union, as they had been until 1905.

King Gustav was wise enough to withstand this temptation; he refused the opportunity to stab his Norwegian brothers in the back, and preferred to keep his Sweden a smaller but happier country. However, his choice was not dictated by mere political sagacity, but by honest abhorrence of such an act of treachery. The quality of the King's character forbade it.

Gustav of Sweden is descended from the House of Bernadotte, from the General Jean Bernadotte whom Napoleon sent to rule Sweden. The Bernadottes brought with them into aristocratic Sweden the spirit of democracy and libertarianism, and this infusion of the spirit of the French Revolution prevails today. The King leaves the business of state in the hands of Parliament and the Cabinet.

King Gustav attends the Stockholm opera in the clothes of an ordinary citizen; he has all-night bridge sessions with the former Foreign Minister Rickard Sandler; and he is, of course, internationally famous for his tennis. Nevertheless, he is a responsible statesman and knows very well what goes on inside and outside his country.

On a visit to Germany the King had lunch with Hitler and Goering and presented the Field Marshal with the Swedish Vasa Medal to add to his collection. A social visit, to be sure, but before he rose from the table he had secured amnesty for two Swedish sailors who had been arrested in Germany, accused of smuggling Wollweber's propaganda into the Reich.

Into this democratic idyll, this land of wild natural beauties, came the mailed might of the Nazi war machine and its mass army of spies.

The enemy agents came long before the outbreak of the war. Professor Torgny Segerstedt, Sweden's most distinguished liberal newspaper editor, wrote in his *Göteborg's Handels och Sjöfartstidning* that the Swedish Foreign Office possessed proofs that Hitler had spoken of the possible necessity of invading Sweden. Before a meeting of the Nordic Society of Luebeck, Segerstedt declared, Hitler had announced that should invasion prove necessary, he would need help from his Swedish and German friends in the country.

Hitler's wishes are commands. The Nordic Society thenceforth became the chief espionage organization in Sweden. Hundreds of Nazi spies swarmed into the country. And many native Swedes were enlisted in the Nazi espionage service.

The sister of Karin Goering, Countess Fanny von Willamowitz-Moellendorf, is among the most fanatic adherents of her brother-in-law, Hermann Goering, and advances the Nazi cause in Sweden with every means at her command.

The leader of the Nazi Party in Sweden is Ex-Sergeant Sven Olof Lindholm, who was recently discharged from the Swedish Army and had the impudence to go directly to King Gustav to complain—in vain—to him.

The most important fascist in the country is Sven Hedin, the famous explorer of Tibet and other strange lands, author of a biography of Chiang Kai-shek and the book *From Pole to Pole.* Although he himself is one-eighth Jewish, the stocky, black-haired Swede is one of the most fervent of the Swedish Hitler-friends. Hedin is a member of almost every German-Swedish organization; he calls constantly for "greater understanding of Hitler Germany," and openly expresses his hope that Germany will win the war. This is no new sentiment with him; in 1914-18 he was an equally enthusiastic adherent of Kaiser Wilhelm.

Swedish political gossip maintains that Hitler asked Sven Hedin to arrange peace between Finland and Russia in 1940.

Hedin receives a large pension from the Swedish Government, on which to live and continue his scientific research. Nevertheless, Hedin has stated on several occasions that he is heart and soul with Germany in her struggle and will always be loyal to her. He had a great regard for the Prussian Empire of Kaiser Wilhelm, and he is grateful for the friendship of Adolf Hitler. Hedin's greatest ambition is to do some indispensable service for the Nazis.

It must be understood, however, that Hedin is one of the intellectual leaders of Fascism in Sweden; he is not one of the enemy agents who do the dirty work of espionage and sabotage.

Active shipping espionage was handled by such men as Carl Johan Torin, a Cuban-born Swede, who lived in

Gothenburg. Torin was an employee of a great Swedish shipping firm; as such he had many opportunities to gather data on ship movements. It was Torin who informed the Nazi Naval Intelligence of the escape of the Norwegian ships blockaded in the port of Gothenburg, the information resulting in the torpedoing of several Norwegian boats.

The chief of the Nazi agents in Sweden was the notorious Friedrich Stengel; he was the salesman for *Electroscandia* who possessed the plans of all the airports in Sweden because his firm had installed the signaling apparatus. In 1940 the Swedish police sent a report 150 pages long to the Ministry of Justice and asked permission to arrest the Nazi "gauleiter." They were too late; a few days before Stengel had been appointed an official of the German Legation, thereby acquiring diplomatic immunity.

He is still at large.

The three naval spies who worked under Pflugk-Hartung have already been mentioned: Alexander Bogs, Consul at Malmö; Hermann Bolte, Pflugk-Hartung's personal friend from by-gone days when Pflugk-Hartung himself had lived in Sweden; and Hermann Wildfeuer, the chief of the German sailors' organization.

Consul Bogs, who left Sweden in the course of the war, was the most obnoxious of the enemy agents in the country. With suave arrogance, he behaved as though Sweden were a country that would be taken over by the Fuhrer at any moment. As we have noted, he was eventually caught photographing Swedish military installations. But long before this, the Chief of the Malmö Fire Department had come to fisticuffs with him in a public street after Bogs impudently refused to move his car to make room for "the Swede." Bogs' first encounter with the Swedes ended in a black eye; his second in a hasty and undignified departure from the country.

The Nazis were never able to make much progress in Malmö. The city was a stronghold of the Social Democrats, and their idea of the middle way held sway in all branches of civic life. Malmö was a thriving port, receiving the traffic of Germany, Denmark and Norway. Its people were not sequestered from the outer world, and yet never abandoned their own simple mode of life.

The inhabitants of Malmö spied on Bogs more attentively than he spied on the Swedish coast. It was through such "unofficial" counterespionage that they learned that the doorman of the German Legation rented a six room apartment below the Legation which was chockful of telescopes and radio apparatus.

The German Minister in Stockholm, Prince zu Wied, had always been considered little more than an illiterate who owed his job to Goering's gratitude; before 1933 he had often given the Nazi leader financial assistance. His wife, Princess zu Wied, was a trashy amateur painter who did paintings of brown storm troops marching, with the ghosts of martyred Nazis hovering above their heads.

Early in 1943 Prince zu Wied was recalled, for the situation in the north had become too complicated for his distinctly limited abilities, and the Nazis had now to reckon on a possible Allied invasion of Norway. He was succeeded by Hans Thomsen, former chargé d'affaires in Washington.

One of the best Nazi agents is a Swedish deputy, small obese Consul Otto Wallen. Wallen is a member of the Peasants' Party. He owns large properties in Berlin, having made his fortune in the last war by selling Swedish food to the Baltic countries—though Sweden herself was suffering from severe food shortages. Wallen has made several speeches before Swedish Nazis in which he has declared himself a wholehearted supporter of their cause. This man's office, unfortunately, gives him the right to attend every secret session of the Swedish parliament.

The best Nazi propagandist in Sweden is the wealthy newspaper publisher, Torsten Kreuger, brother of the ill-fated match king. Out of the wreckage of his brother's fortune Torsten Kreuger salvaged the two largest newspapers in the country. Stockholm's *Tidningen* and *Aftonbladet.*

Both newspapers openly support Hitler, preach appeasement, and incite feeling against the Swedish Jews and against the refugees from Czechoslovakia, Germany and Norway. Both newspapers have been publicly condemned by the Swedish press organization as a blot upon the profession.

Hitler's enemy agents systematically tried to undermine Sweden and win the Swedes over to the "new order." The Swedish Government had repeatedly declared that it wanted no part of the "new order," and disavowed the compromising articles that appeared in Torsten Kreuger's newspapers. Nor did the Swedes feel sympathy for the "Nordic" ideals of Alfred Rosenberg, the prime mover behind the Nordic Society of Luebeck.

To combat these healthy democratic instincts, the Nazi agents commenced a flood of subversive propaganda.

Twenty-five thousand of Stockholm's municipal employees and business men received copies of a little pamphlet known as Mr. Chamberlain's dagger-umbrella. The handle of that celebrated ornament comes out of its paper sheath and discloses a knife remarkably like that worn by the S.S. The addresses of the municipal employees are secret, and can only have been copied by a Swede "in the know," presumably a National-Socialist.

One hundred thousand copies per issue of Dr. Ley's publication, *Freude und Arbeit,* published in Swedish and German, are sent free to individual Swedes.

Four thousand Swedish libraries receive free copies of Swedish translations of the speeches of Hitler and other

Nazi leaders, distributed by the Swedish publishing house Svea Rike.

Thousands of young Swedes interested in sport were sent an anti-British Press bulletin from Berlin which prints sport news along with political comments. Twenty-two German newspapers and periodicals were sent to the Stockholm library throughout the year. Hotels were supplied free with German papers. Stockholm doctors were sent three or four German papers free every day.

This list is by no means complete. Every day carloads of fresh German propaganda enter the country.

Sweden had much sympathy for Germany after World War I. She felt that Germany had been harshly treated at Versailles and as harshly at Geneva. But sympathy is not proof against economic reality. It was a fact that Germany had been defeated and impoverished; and therefore the great markets to exploit, the goods to buy, were British and American.

This transference of Swedish interest (and of Danish also) is expressed in the Swedish educational system. On the whole people learned languages in order to do business, and, a language once learned, they absorb the ideas to which it gives currency. German used to be the first foreign language in the Swedish and Danish schools before World War I; subsequently it was displaced by English.

The old pro-German feeling of the Swedish upper classes, who before the First World War ruled the country, lingered on; even today the great landlords in Skane, in spite of the utter disregard of the Nazis for conservative ideas, retain an affection for Germany.

But the Quisling reign of terror in Norway made a profound impression upon the Swedes; they have no desire to see the same experiments carried out in their own country. The Nazi agents in the country deplore Sweden's total incomprehension of the National Socialist idea and blame it on the unions and the successfully operating cooperatives.

The only feasible line the Nazis could take was to convince the Swedes that they could maintain their neutrality only by aligning themselves with a "German Europe," since the blockade had cut them off from England and America.

With German money the Lindholm Nazi Party was organized. Support for this Party was found in the circles around the former diplomat, Rutger Essen, a Swedish "geopolitician." For the rest they depended mainly on the German colony, which was organized after the manner that Pflugk-Hartung had organized the Germans in Denmark.

Sweden's resident Germans are by far the largest foreign colony. They number 5,973, of whom 2,481 are in Stockholm alone. These Germans are corralled into fourteen organizations which act as propaganda cells for the Nazi Party. These are:—the colony, the Winterhilfe, the Ortsgruppe of the National Socialist Party, the Arbeitsfront, Bund Deutscher Frauen, Deutscher Kulturbund, German Club, German Sport Club, A. D. V. Frohsinn, Reichsdeutsche Jugend, Hitlerjugend, Svensk-Tyska Foereningen, German-Swedish Chamber of Commerce, Riksfoereningen Sverige-Tyskland.

German citizens are required to fill in forms at their Legation or Consulates. They must report on their knowledge of modern languages and their *fuehrerschein,* or "special qualifications."

The Nazis tried to apply all forms of propaganda.

In the field of radio they began by pressing the Swedish Broadcasting Company, Radiotjänst, to accept propaganda records in Swedish. When this kind offer was rejected, the German station at Konigsberg started its own broadcasts in Swedish. Similarly, the *Svensk-Filmindustri* was invited to put ready-made propaganda films and newsreels into circulation, and when it refused to do so the German Travel Bureau decided to start a cinema of its own for this purpose. The Swedish authorities, however, decided otherwise.

The German Travel Bureau has also had its wings clipped once again. In Sweden foreigners are required to give a written pledge not to engage in propaganda. In spite of this, the show window of the German Travel Bureau began to be filled with anti-Ally posters and photographs from the moment the war started. In the end the Stockholm police confiscated the window displays and, for the time being at any rate, the German Travel Bureau is obliged to behave itself.

Where the Nazis could not seize complete control of a police department, they sent spies into the department. Thus Dr. Fritz Rose, a language teacher in Sweden, spent two years gradually winning the friendship of Gothenburg Chief of Police Fontell. Finally Fontell hired him as teacher of German to the members of the Gothenburg police force.

Fortunately, democratic counterespionage agents were on the alert. Suspecting Rose, they employed a young girl to strike up an acquaintance with him. It was an ancient trick, but it worked. One evening she persuaded Dr. Rose to take her to the theater. While Rose was safely at the theater, they searched his apartment and found some remarkable documents. There was an extensive correspondence with the "German Academy of Munich"; in one letter the Academy congratulated Rose for having secured a position as teacher in the police force, in spite of his German citizenship. As a reward for this success, the Academy informed him, his salary as an agent was to be increased. There were also letters from Gestapo headquarters instructing Rose how to ingratiate himself with the police and win their confidence. He was requested to send to Berlin the names of police officers who were anti-democratic, anti-labor and anti-Semitic; these officers would then be invited to Germany for their summer vacation, with all expenses paid. The Gestapo would then do the rest; that is, would convert these men into effective Nazi spies.

Chief of Police Fontell was completely innocent, the victim of his own easy-going, unsuspicious temperament.

Democratic counterespionage agents published the letters in the Swedish press. They created quite a stir. It was particularly infuriating to the Swedes to read, in the Gestapo's instructions to Rose, that he must "ply the Swedes with food, drink and dancing; they are most easily won over by such things." Theaters, concerts and such cultural activities did not really interest the Swedish people, the instructions commented. The scandal grew in proportions when it was learned that Rose had direct contact with the Adviser of German Instruction in the Swedish Ministry of Education, Dr. Kappner.

Dr. Rose was, of course, expelled from Sweden. The Nazis, as a matter of fact, had consistent difficulties in placing men with the Swedish police, for the major part of the police force consisted of patriotic Swedes who were not at all pro-German.

Robberies—Pflugk-Hartung fashion—were also arranged in Sweden by the enemy agents. One night the Youth group of the Nazi Lindholm Party broke into the office of the radical student organization, *Clarté*. They stole all the money and the entire membership list of the organization, demolished the files and furniture, and forthwith boasted that now they had possession of the "future death list" for National Socialist Sweden.

The boys involved in this robbery were young hotheads, to be sure. But the Court proceedings proved conclusively that the robbery itself had been "made in Germany," so to speak. The leader was August Clementson, a young man who had recently been sent from Germany by the Nordic Society. He had received money from the Cologne branch office of this society and used it to finance espionage activities. It was revealed that his group had planned robberies of the Communist "Red Aid" and of the Stockholm synagogue.

It should have surprised no one that the Nordic Society of Luebeck, and particularly its branch in Cologne, should have been engaged in espionage work. For the chief of the Cologne branch was none other than the man who had photographed the fortifications of Narvik in Norway and of various Swedish forts: Vitalis Pantenburg, the master-spy in Finland.

The Nordic Society had existed before Hitler's time as a purely cultural organization. In 1933 it had only 8,000 members in toto. By 1938 it had become the largest international organization in Germany, possessing over thirty-five branch offices and a membership of 150,000. It is without question one of the most extensive of the German espionage organizations, and to it the Nazis in large part owe their successful invasion of Scandinavia.

The German and Swedish Nazis were trained for their espionage tasks in Stockholm itself. The Canaris Office had sent a special instructor named Heinz Knoerck, who taught his future spies the elements of Nazi ideology and Nazi technique.

However, the Swedish police were on the alert. But as in the case of Wollweber and the OGPU they had discovered that agents were replaced as soon as they were caught; the supply of Nazi spies was equally inexhaustible.

There was, for example, Hans Queling, a well-known writer of juveniles, who in Germany had written excellent children's books on India. He came to Sweden as a tourist, fell in love with a little dressmaker, and persuaded her to rent a small summer cottage in the Archipelago of Stockholm, so that they could spend their "honeymoon" there. When the police at last caught up with him, the dressmaker learned that he had been spying on the Fort of Waxholm and sending his reports—with Prussian thoroughness—in septuplicate to Germany.

Among Queling's possessions the Swedish police found a long list of Swedes whom the agent considered "likely prospects." He had recommended that the Nordic Society invite these Swedes to Germany—with all expenses paid. They would, of course, return fully equipped to spy for Canaris. Queling left Sweden voluntarily to avoid deportation. One of the most impudent acts of the Nazi agents was their establishment of a secret recruiting office for Swedish volunteers to fight in Finland. In order to avoid the legal complications involved in a foreign state's recruiting soldiers, the office was set up in the German Legation. The recruits were incorporated into the "Waffen S.S."

The Swedish police soon discovered this illegal traffic and the Swedish Foreign Ministry sent a sharp protest to Berlin, demanding that it be stopped. The Nazis replied with a formal apology—and found other ways to continue recruiting volunteers for Finland.

Exactly how many Swedish "volunteers" are fighting in Russia no one knows for certain. Swedish spokesmen put it as low as one thousand (1,060 according to Maurice Feldmann in *The Nation*).

Financially, however, Sweden supplies enormous assistance to Finland. Without Swedish food and money—and without the arms from the Bofors armament works—Finland would scarcely be able to fight on. If Swedish aid were withdrawn, she would be more inclined to make a separate peace with Russia.

Certainly, fighting Finland has received from her neutral neighbor more assistance than did Norway in her struggle against invasion. Nevertheless, Finland today has lost at least half the Swedish good will she enjoyed during the first Russo-Finnish war. Swedish Social Democratic Youth has denounced aid to Finland with the slogan: "Finland's cause is not ours."

The aims of German espionage and counterespionage in Sweden may be divided into the following categories:
 1) Naval espionage along the entire coastline.
 2) Counterespionage against Russia and Britain.
 3) Anti-sabotage work against Wollweber.
 4) Anti-Allied propaganda.
 5) Continuation of aid to Finland.
 6) Espionage and counterespionage to protect iron ore shipments.

The last category—the struggle for Swedish iron ore—remains the chief task of the Nazi Intelligence Service.

Although the Gällivare ore deposits have been known since 1704, and mined since 1800, it remained until the turn of this century for the Lapland mines to be exploited on a really large scale. The decisive date in the history of mining in that district was the year 1902, when the "Malmbanan" or Iron Ore Railroad Line was completed. It connected Kiruna and Gällivare with the two export harbors of Narvik, Norway, and Luleå, Sweden. Then Sweden's first great ore boom began.

Sweden's immense mineral resources lying north of the Arctic Circle place her among the first in the world's iron ore market. There, in Northern Lapland, is a mining district which is estimated to possess more than two billion tons of ore, or over nine-tenths of the total high-grade iron ore in Europe. The value of these mines is the greater for the reason that Lapland ore consists of sixty to seventy per cent pure iron, while the average content in the United States is fifty per cent, in Spain forty-six to forty-nine per cent, in France thirty-three to thirty-six per cent, in Great Britain thirty to thirty-one per cent. The percentage in German ore is even lower. Stored in Lapland is enough such high-grade ore to last another 200 years, even at the present wild pace of mining.

Sweden is the world's biggest exporter of iron ore. True, three other countries—France, Russia and the United States—produce more ore, but these consume a much greater portion of their output than does Sweden. Sweden, although priding herself on one of the finest steel industries in the world, cannot utilize at home more than a tiny fraction of her vast mineral wealth. The reason is that Sweden lacks coal. Sweden's steel industry depends principally on charcoal, and from its inception specialized in high-quality products, leaving it to the countries with ample coal resources to develop a large-scale output of standard goods. At present, less than one-tenth of Sweden's iron ore is used at home; nine-tenths of it is directly shipped to foreign mills.

The Lapland mining area falls into two distinct centers, with a distance of some fifty miles between them. One center is the small town of Kiruna, around which are grouped the ore deposits of Kirunavaara, Luossavaara and Tuollavaara. The other center, situated near Gällivare, includes the famous "Malmberget" or Ore Mountain.

Sweden possesses other important deposits of iron ore, which do not, however, compare with the Lapland fields, either in size or quality. Foremost among these secondary deposits are the Bergslagen mines in Central Sweden which have been exploited ever since the Middle Ages, when Sweden already was world-renowned for her iron and copper. The ore mined in the Bergslagen district is different in character and quality; it is less rich in iron than the Lapland ore (52 to 55 per cent as against 60-70 per cent), but has the advantage of greater purity.

This purer ore, unexcelled for the manufacture of steel, is reserved for home consumption. Hence the high quality of steel made by the Swedish manufacturers. All the impurer ores are exported, especially to Germany where the basic Bessemer process is in wide use.

The total amount of ore available in the Bergslagen district is estimated to be 200 million tons. Three-quarters of it is owned by the Grängesberg Ore Trust, while the remainder belongs to several private companies, many of them affiliated with the German steel industry.

The Swedish police guard the iron ore districts with extraordinary vigilance. The German and Russian spies in this region have been arrested almost to the last man, for the police make it a practice to simply arrest everyone who has no apparent business in the region.

The ore mines are a sight worth seeing. One feels oneself in the heart of an American industrial center rather than in bleak Lapland. For here, beyond the Arctic Circle, we find electrified railroads and one of the most advanced loading systems in the world. Kiruna is counted among the world's most modern industrial cities. The mine workers are the highest-paid workers in the land. It is said that the Swedish railroads make greater profits from ore transport than from all other freight and passenger traffic in the country.

The story is told that the original owner of the mines, upon selling them to an international trust in 1900, asked for a royalty of 10 öre (two and a half cents) on each ton of ore sold. The trust happily accepted this modest demand. It did not suspect that by 1943 it would be selling eleven million tons of ore and paying 1,100,000 kronor in royalties to the fortunate former owner.

For half a century now, Swedish iron ore mines and German steel mills have been closely and almost inextricably associated. This connection was first established in the 'eighties when the German Possehl concern of Luebeck ventured to introduce the highly phosphoric Lapland ores into the German market. First to utilize them on a large scale was Thyssen.

During World War I, Swedish iron ore which had now become an essential raw material for Krupp and the rest of the armament industry, was a factor which saved Germany from an early defeat. Both German and Swedish experts have testified that the Reich, without these supplies, would have been unable to hold out for more than two years at the utmost.

Between four and five million tons of iron ore, nine-tenths of Sweden's total shipments, was Germany's annual share in the period 1914-1918, but later the Allies enforced a more just distribution of supplies between themselves and the Reich.

In the post-war years, Sweden shipped an average of three-fourths of her total exports of iron ore to Germany, the rest being divided between Great Britain, Czechoslovakia, Belgium and the United States. Proportionately, Germany's share of the ore exports shows slight declines, since Britain's demand increased. But since the mining is much heavier, Germany's share in absolute figures has been rising steadily. The following table will illustrate the evolution:

GERMAN IMPORTS OF SWEDISH IRON ORE
1932   1,521,000 tons
1933   2,253,000 tons

1934	5,158,000 tons
1935	5,561,000 tons
1936	8,131,000 tons
1937	9,326,000 tons
1938	8,994,000 tons
1939	11,292,000 tons
1940	9,285,000 tons
1941	9,477,000 tons

These official Swedish export figures show that Sweden for the three years from 1939 to 1941 has been providing in round numbers ten million tons of high-grade iron ore a year for the German war effort. The German-Swedish trade treaty that was concluded on October 20, 1942 gives little cause to hope that Nazi Germany will receive any less iron ore in the future.

While Sweden is still sending Germany all the raw materials she demands, the Reich has completely failed to fulfil its commercial commitments toward Sweden. In the first nine months of 1942 Germany shipped to Sweden less than 2,400,000 tons of coal and coke, though she had promised to deliver 5,700,000 tons for the entire year.

Germany, besides being traditionally the supreme customer of the Swedish Ore Trust, also controls, directly or through figureheads, many of the smaller ore deposits, especially in the Bergslagen district. These belong to various private companies which are linked up with the German Hoesch concern. Inasmuch as aliens are forbidden by law to hold real estate in Sweden, the Hoesch interests are represented by a Swedish dummy company, the "Gruv A. B. Lekomberg." Of late years this company has displayed a marked tendency toward expansion. It has bought up mines that have been lying idle ever since 1818, refurbished them and put them to work again. The same fate has overtaken many ancient mines throughout Central and

Southern Sweden, which had long ago been abandoned as unprofitable, but are now being revived. British and German prospectors—especially the latter—are swarming over the country, intent on restoring every rusty, half-forgotten mine which no Swede with any business sense would dare to touch. But profit or loss is no object for the Great Powers whose ore famine is such that they will spare neither pain nor expense to open up new supplies for their arms industry. As a result, mining operations have recently been started or resumed even in such fourth-rate districts at Småland (Taberg and Ulvö) and Skåne (Ystad).

Compared with the huge output of the Lapland mines, the ore produced by the German-owned mines in Central Sweden may seem of petty value; its importance, however, lies in the fact that Germany in this war can count on constant and secure deliveries.

It is only in the light of this background that we can understand fully the significance of Wollweber's ambitious espionage and sabotage league. Wollweber knew that cutting off the ore transports would mean the severing of one of Hitler's main life lines. A. F. Rickmann, England's iron ore expert, also understood this.

Sweden delivers the iron ore to Germany for hard cash, making prodigious profits. The well-paid iron ore workers would be the last to strike, or to boycott the shipments to Germany, for they know that their livelihood depends on these shipments. Every attempt to propagandize among these workers has utterly failed.

Nevertheless, these workers prize the independence of Sweden. They are conscious that stoppage of iron ore shipments is the only threat they can employ as a weapon against Germany. One of Sweden's leading union leaders declared to me in 1940:

"Germany knows very well that should she invade us as she did Norway and Denmark, we would blow up all our iron ore transportation facilities. The Nazis would never again get a ton of ore out of our mines."

The German spies have learned—without too much difficulty, for the Swedish Government wishes them to know it—that all the transport facilities of the ore regions have been mined, and can be wrecked at a moment's notice.

The iron ore mines have so far shielded Sweden's independence. Nazi Germany will not attack the country unless she is forced to by a desperate situation, such as the opening of a new front in Norway or in Finland. If such a situation should arrive, there is no doubt in Sweden that the land of the middle way will find herself fighting on the side of the United Nations.

16. Labor Traitors

The Nazi espionage service was keen enough to deposit its agents within every organization that could possibly be of aid when war began. Thus agents were sent into peace organizations that agitated for appeasement. There were Nazi agents in literary clubs, in diplomatic circles, in industry, among the munitions workers, in high society, and finally in the labor movement. They cried loudly, "Keep out of war," reasoning that "the workers die and the capitalists profit," calling this war a "capitalist war."

Until the day Soviet Russia was attacked, the Nazi agents within the Communist movement agitated for the maintenance of peace, and many of the agents were highly successful in their dangerous game. In America, the National Maritime Union was victimized by unscrupulous Nazi seamen, who on the one hand called for peace and on the other hand transmitted information on ship movements to German espionage headquarters—with the consequence that many of their fellows were drowned at sea.

Sweden and Norway provide us with two perfect examples of labor traitors. It was difficult for the Nazis to gain a direct foothold in these countries, ruled as they were by a moderate labor movement. It was therefore necessary for them in Scandinavia to find men like the Jacques Doriot type in France—former Communists who had a following in the labor movement and who would serve the Nazi cause in the name of "peace."

The labor traitors in Scandinavia are black examples of that sad phenomenon in the history of the labor movement: the conversion of talented and ambitious labor leaders to fascism. What was formerly their deadliest foe became their new friend. Men who began as idealists became the readiest and cheapest tools of Nazi espionage and of the entire Nazi system.

One of the most interesting figures to emerge from the Swedish Communist movement was Nils Flyg. His rise within the Party was rapid, due to his twofold talents for writing and organization. He entered the Swedish youth movement at the age of seventeen. After the First World War, he was one of the founders of the Swedish Communist Youth Movement. Later he became a Communist deputy. He occupied the distinguished position of chief of the Fram Förlag, the Communist publishing house. He wrote dozens of serious books and hundreds of impassioned pamphlets and was one of Sweden's most popular speakers. He composed propaganda lyrics which enjoyed the widest favor.

But the day came when the Communist International ordered the party in Sweden to destroy the Social-Democratic labor unions and set up Communist unions in their place. Flyg refused to obey. The issue provoked a tremendous upheaval, and when the smoke of battle faded, the Communist Party of Sweden had practically ceased to exist. In its place the Socialist Party, led by Nils Flyg and his close friend and comrade, Karl Kilbom, made its debut before Swedish labor with a strongly anti-Comintern and anti-Russian manifesto.

The new party grew by leaps and bounds. Flyg and Kilbom managed to get possession of the party building and the former party organ, the *Folkets Dagblad,* as well as the party publishing house and the entire printing plant. Thus equipped, the new party prospered. It elected representatives to both houses of Parliament. Ture Nerman, Sweden's great labor writer, and other men of note joined its ranks.

But no party can live on indefinitely with a negative program. Fighting the Social Democrats on the one hand and the Communists on the other was not enough. A group arose calling for a more realistic approach to the problems of the labor movement; Flyg's associate, Karl Kilbom, put himself at the head of this wing. When Kilbom approached Prime Minister Hansson of the Social Democratic Party with offers of unity, the question was immediately proposed to the membership of both Parties. The unity resolution evoked enthusiastic majority support from the Social Democrats and the Socialists. Flyg and the survivors of his once great party were left holding the bag.

Without an organization, without money, without political power this fair-weather friend of Swedish labor was forced to look for a new field of endeavor. After many false starts, he finally ingratiated himself with Torsten Kreuger, whose pro-fascist sympathies were already well-known, and coaxed from him an initial loan of 20,000 kronor. Through Kreuger he also met Colonel Gyllenkrok, one of Pflugk-Hartung's friends, who had been dismissed from the Swedish army for his Nazi leanings.

His next step was to visit France for the express purpose of seeing the ex-Communist Jacques Doriot, who had already enrolled himself among Hitler's and Laval's staunch supporters. With him went Hakon Meyer, former ultra-radical of the Norwegian Labor Party and an inveterate egotist.

Hakon Meyer had always aspired to become the editor of *Arbeiderbladet,* the world-famous Socialist government organ in Oslo. He achieved that high state, but only after the Germans invaded Norway when he immediately sought to aid Vidkun Quisling, General Nikolaus von Falkenhorst and Josef Terboven, the new Governor, to create a new totalitarian labor organization. The ruse did not work. *Arbeiderbladet* was finally suspended, and the Germans having learned that more direct methods were needed, shot the union leaders or threw them into concentration camps. Hakon Meyer was consoled with the post of Commissioner for the Railroad, Telegraph and Telephone Workers' unions. Flyg and Hakon Meyer had fought with Doriot against the Communist International when the latter still called himself a Communist. At that time he had only just begun to climb the ladder of fame as Mayor of St. Denis, the noted Red suburb of Paris. Like Flyg and Hakon Meyer, Doriot was a brilliant propagandist and writer, and like them, he was inordinately vain and ambitious. Doriot had a strong personal following, part of which he maintained in the form of a military bodyguard after the pattern of Hitler's early Storm Troop organization. Like his Scandinavian colleagues, Doriot had turned to the fascists of his country for support in creating his "Partie Populaire," the "new dynamic party of the French working class." With fascist funds he was able to buy control of *La Liberté*, an important French afternoon newspaper of reactionary, royalist tone. Like Hakon Meyer he had been for a brief period Trotsky's personal friend and champion after the Red Army leader was sent into exile.

   It is particularly interesting that all three of these renegades capitulated so completely to the Nazi ideology that they aped even the anti-Semitism of the Führer. Hakon Meyer had been the friend and admirer of Leon Trotsky, and Nils Flyg had once appealed to the radical Jewish banker, Olav Aschberg, to finance his party. In one short year they became as bitterly anti-Semitic as Jacques Doriot, who today urges the "total destruction of the

Jewish-Masonic system which has paralyzed the French nation," and demands complete elimination of the Jews from public life.

Today Jacques Doriot is one of the big men of France. But his two colleagues, who came suing for his support, which they received in the form of a hearty recommendation to the German Führer, have become ineffectual and insignificant cogs in the Nazi machine.

Nils Flyg is now an acknowledged Nazi working with Rutger Essen, Patrick Ossbahr and the Nazis around Lindholm for a Nazi Sweden which will probably never come. He was the man through whose devices the Nazis hoped to ensnare the workers of Sweden. But he no longer has the workers behind him. Ernst Friedrich Wollweber had a great deal to do with his failure.

One of the "big guns" in Flyg's Socialist Party was Herbert Timm, the Party's specialist for Russian affairs. Timm had come to Flyg out of a clear sky. One day he made his appearance in Flyg's office at 52 Luntmakaregatan in Stockholm and insisted on seeing Nils Flyg. Flyg came out to see what he wanted and recognized one of his former associates in the Communist Party, a comrade who had been an EX.R. (Executive Committee Representative of the Comintern).

Though Flyg was not at all pleased to have a Communist in his office, Herbert Timm pressed him to hear his story out. He had been deported from Russia for Trotskyist sympathies and opposition to the party line, he said. At first, the Russians had refused to let him leave the country, but he had enlisted the aid of the Nazi consulate in Moscow, pretending sympathy, and the Germans had helped him get out of the USSR. Instead of going to Germany, however, Timm had escaped to Esthonia and thence to Sweden. His luggage was still at the pier and the steamship company was holding his wife on board till he paid what he owed. Would Flyg advance him a little money to release his wife and get food and lodging?

This Herbert Timm became one of the most widely-read contributors to Flyg's anti-Communist newspaper. Knowing Russian conditions, he could write intelligently about Russian industrial, political and cultural problems and he turned out articles, pamphlets and books in large numbers. Sweden's largest publisher, Albert Bonnier, put out his book on the weakness of the Red Army, and the conservative *Svenska Dagbladet* printed his anti-Communist articles. Within two years, Herbert Timm was attending every meeting of the Executive Committee of Flyg's and Kilbom's Socialist Party. He was considered one of the most brilliant and capable members of the Party. Not until then did he start his real work. His articles about Russia became more and more fantastic. His statements were so palpably untrue that not only he, but the party for which he wrote, was increasingly discredited in the eyes of the intelligent public. When Flyg went to Doriot, Timm was so indiscreet as to spread the story of this secret visit. He also clumsily exposed Flyg's relations with Torsten Kreuger. His final *faux pas* was to confess that Flyg's closest adviser was a man who had had to flee Germany for complicity in a dynamiting. He did not mention that this person was Timm himself.

Too late Flyg realized that the viper he had been nursing in his bosom had been sent to him by the Communist OGPU chief, Ernst Friedrich Wollweber.

Karl Kilbom took Timm's revelations in another sense. He insisted on an immediate clean-up in the party and an alliance of the honest elements within it with the Social Democrats.

The OGPU had used Herbert Timm to destroy the Kilbom-Flyg party. The method they used is a commonplace espionage tactic. It was used by the Nazis before Pearl

Harbor, when they instructed their agents to support John L. Lewis and his strikes in order to cut down American production.

Timm left Sweden shortly afterward, allegedly for Mexico. His wife, for whom the plot had evidently become too thick, returned to her mother in Germany.

The *Folkets Dagblad,* created by Zeth Hoeglund and Fredrik Stroem to serve as an opposition organ against autocracy, came to a dishonorable end; the relics of the proud and powerful Socialist Party have been strangely transformed under the whip of Friedrich Stengel and his Hitlerite friends.

The young enthusiast who had written labor songs of freedom still hopes that he may become the Quisling of Sweden. But he has fallen so low that not even the Nazis can find a use for him.

Herbert Timm had masterfully carried out his assigned task of destroying the anti-Communist "Socialistiska Partiet"; Russia's enemies in Sweden were, except for the Nazis, disorganized. Consequently, the dissolution of his Party compelled Flyg to turn more and more to the Nazis. Flyg turned his coat completely; instead of the "Internationale" he now sings the "Horst Wessel Lied."

Sweden's Nazi book stores distribute Flyg's writings; the Nazi newspapers print his articles; and he himself runs articles by leading Nazis in his own newspaper. But Flyg today is almost completely isolated; his former followers stepped off the train when he went into the Nazi camp. At the last election he lost his seat in Parliament; his political future now depends solely on German bayonets.

Hakon Meyer, his morbidly ambitious Norwegian friend, paid a visit to Berlin on Dr. Ley's invitation. In the German capital the former Marxist received instructions concerning the German conception of a labor movement. He visited German armament plants, studied the Nazi compulsory labor unions, and at last returned to Oslo to report on the wonders that Hitler Germany has done for labor. Then he made a trip to Finland. But the Finnish Labor unions, though they find themselves unwilling allies of Hitler in this war, refused to receive this traitor to the Norwegian working class.

Hakon Meyer and Nils Flyg are lost creatures. Their careers failed to meet the demands of their vaulting ambition. They wove theories of world revolution, were ready to supply the solutions for all economic and social problems—but they had no idea how to solve their own personal problems. Today they are clay in the potter's hand, and like Vidkun Quisling they have discovered that Potter Hitler despises them more than do their enemies.

In November 1942 Hakon Meyer reported to Quisling and Terboven on his observations in Sweden and Finland. He told the two Nazi leaders that close cooperation with the Swedish Nazis would be the best means for furthering the interests of Nazified Norway in that country. But, he added, the Nazi parties in Sweden had no chance to take power, even if Sweden should become involved in the war. He mentioned that he had had a number of conferences with his old friend, Nils Flyg, and suggested that the best line for Sweden would be a "Doriot" policy, such as had been applied in France.

While he was in Sweden, Hakon Meyer organized an espionage branch charged with the task of spying on the thousands of Norwegian refugees in Sweden. This espionage unit also spies on the Norwegian aid organizations.

This action marked the lowest point in the degradation of Hakon Meyer. The revolutionist who used to visit Trotsky almost daily while the former Soviet leader was in Norway had now become no more than a tool in the Quisling espionage service. His "love for the oppressed" had become a determination to exterminate them.

Some years ago, when I met Hakon Meyer, he told me that his entire life was devoted to the welfare of the proletariat, and that he considered Hitler a pestilence like the Black Death. But this same man today finds it quite convenient to help the spread of the "Black Death."

Nils Flyg is an accomplished demagogue who enjoyed the role of idealist—and found it very profitable. In reality he worked for himself alone. His followers were useful to pay the rent of the Party headquarters, and to supply funds for his newspapers and his own living. His followers were idealists; Flyg extorted from their idealism the money he needed. Once upon a time he must have believed in his principles, but that was long, long ago.

Herbert Timm, who by destroying the Socialist Party drove Flyg into the arms of the Nazis, was an unprepossessing man. A small man, he always walked the streets wearing an enormous black felt hat. He loved the German game of "Skat," and he loved whiskey.

He was a man of Wollweber's type. His very presence made people uncomfortable, for he was always nervously alert—never at rest. People sensed that he was capable of anything, and most of his comrades in the Party avoided him, even during the days when his anti-Russian articles were most popular. Timm was a sharp politician and psychologist; he knew how to incite the members of Flyg's Party against one another, and to incite the country as a whole against the Party. By destroying Flyg and his Party he eliminated one of Russia's most dangerous enemies in the labor movement.

Timm's name was not, of course, Timm. But the Swedish police never did find out his real name.

17. Agents in Arms

To properly appreciate the Quisling intermezzo in Norway, one must have a well-developed sense of humor. Quisling's accomplishment has been, essentially, to set up villages *à la* Potemkin not in the steppes of Russia, but upon the ice of Norway. This spectacle was built not for Catherine the Great, but for Adolf Schicklgruber, and all the Nazis in Norway have donned their ballet costumes to play in the comedy.

Quisling, with scarcely five thousand adherents in the country, assured Hitler that the entire people were behind him. Josef Terboven, the gigolo Governor, discovered the deception after a year's time, but he became a party to it because he did not have the courage to confess the truth to his führer.

Thus Quisling was permitted to continue his farce, and each succeeding scene grew more absurd.

On January 13, 1941 Führer Quisling issued a proclamation to his people. He called upon all young men between the ages of seventeen and twenty-five to join the colors to form a "Regiment Nordland," which would fight side by side with Norway's Aryan German brothers.

Four weeks later, when Untersturmführer Heinz Kaehler visited Oslo to inspect the gallant volunteers, he found that fifty men had enlisted—among them Police Chief Judas Lie and Minister of "Justice" Sverre Riisnaes. The Nazi inspector was shocked by this miserable showing, and reported Quisling's failure to his chief, Heinrich Himmler. Himmler gave Quisling four weeks to muster the regiment, and declared he would then come to Oslo to see for himself. Hitler had still not yet been informed, for Himmler, too, did not dare to break the unpleasant news.

Quisling set to work frantically to find volunteers for the Nordland Regiment. First the age limit was raised from twenty-five to forty years. Families were promised financial support while their wage-earners were at the front. Both college and high school students were told they would receive their degrees without examinations if they volunteered. Revealing the desperate need for volunteers, nine criminals from the Trondheim District Prison were pardoned on the condition that they join the regiment.

When Heinrich Himmler arrived in Oslo, the regiment numbered a grand total of three hundred men. Himmler ordered Quisling to discontinue the recruiting drive; the situation was becoming too embarrassing. At the dedication ceremony, Himmler scornfully informed the Norwegians that the Germans were willing to give them back the "honor of bearing arms." Three hundred men did not make a regiment. Nevertheless, he did not dismiss them. They were placed under German command; the regimental language was German, and every man was forced to learn German in a hurry. The Nordland Regiment was given six weeks of training in Germany, then sent into the Balkan campaign, Judas Lie fighting with them for several weeks.

One month afterward seventy-five men were left of the three hundred volunteers; the rest were dead or wounded. This was the inglorious end of the Nordland Regiment.

Judas Lie returned to Oslo and resumed his duties as Minister of Police and Norwegian espionage chief. He was accompanied by several deserters from the regiment. Once in Oslo these men were promptly clapped into jail. They were given the alternative of remaining in prison or volunteering to serve on the Russian front.

This, however, was not the end of the farce. For Hitler began to wonder why he heard no reports of the heroic deeds of the Norwegian Legion—composed, after all, of fellow-nordic supermen. He repeatedly asked where the Norwegian Legion was serving. Consequently, Quisling received new orders from Berlin to muster up a legion.

This time the recruiting of volunteers was to be so arranged as not to permit another fiasco.

Quisling suggested to Governor Terboven a simple conscription program. Terboven, however, had had too much experience with sabotage in Norway; he did not dare to place arms in the hands of the Norwegians. The recruits would have to be volunteers.

And so Oslo witnessed a magnificent historical comedy, a spectacle without parallel.

Military bands in Quisling "Hird" uniforms marched through the streets of Oslo playing Norwegian marches and bearing placards urging enlistment. When the Norwegians called out to them, however, they remained stolidly silent. They could not speak a word of Norwegian. Quisling had not been able to raise enough Norwegian Nazis, and had been compelled to use German musicians.

This recruiting office was in the Karl Johanns Gaten, Oslo's Fifth Avenue. It was located at first in one of the city's most modern buildings, but the office remained pathetically deserted, and Quisling at last decided to move it to a less-frequented side-street, in order to avoid further unpleasant publicity. The former office was taken over by the German Travel Bureau.

After a month of campaigning, some 200 men were enlisted. Every means of propaganda was employed to attract men for the "crusade against Bolshevism." Ninety-year-old Christian Sinding, the famous Norwegian composer, was decked out with a legionnaire's uniform. A dozen medals were pinned upon him, and the old man, who could scarcely walk, was trotted out at meetings designed to attract recruits. Sinding did not know what it was all about, and died after several weeks' service, in consequence of the unusual physical strain.

Another old man, eighty-three-year-old Knut Hamsun, who had been an ardent Nazi since 1933, personally tried to raise recruits for Quisling's army. But Hamsun found he had lost his former strong hold on the minds of Norway's youth; the great writer's appeals met with stony indifference, and the quantity of volunteers remained wretched.

Thereupon Quisling mobilized twenty-seven pastors, who published a proclamation in all newspapers imploring Norwegian youth to answer the call to the colors of the Norwegian Legion. The public soon found out who these twenty-seven were—out of 1,200 Norwegian pastors. Most of them had been men of God only a short time. It seemed that Quisling had established special short courses for men of the proper convictions. A man could become a pastor after three months' study, provided he was willing to preach the word of Quisling rather than the Word of God.

Norway laughed at Quisling's fledgling preachers, and no more soldiers joined the Legion.

Quisling's Propaganda Minister, Gulbrand Lunde, decided to apply modern advertising technique. Advertisements were published containing coupons which were to be filled in by those wishing to enlist.

This proved an enormous success. Thousands of letters poured into the recruiting office; a dozen additional secretaries had to be hired to open the letters. Then it was discovered that all the coupons had been filled out with names that were not those of the senders. Coupons bore

Duel for the Northland 275

data such as: Vidkun Quisling—profession: traitor; Judas Lie—profession: hangman; Josef Terboven—profession: prostitute; Adolf Hitler—profession: murderer.

On July 4, 1941 Quisling organized a monster mass meeting at Oslo University. Thousands of Germans and Norwegian Nazis were to march in parades and drum up volunteers.

The Nazis were the only ones who attended. The people of Oslo arranged a demonstration of their own to celebrate America's Independence Day and their hope of Norwegian freedom. In great crowds they went to the Frogner Park and laid wreaths on the Lincoln Memorial that stands in this park. With heads held high the people of Oslo marched silently past the benignant figure of the Great Emancipator.

The Quislings heard of this unofficial demonstration, and the meeting on the university grounds was hastily disbanded. The storm troopers swarmed to Frogner Park, and a violent brawl ensued between the Nazis and the Norwegians. Since great numbers of sturdy, broad-shouldered Norwegians had come to pay tribute to Lincoln, the Nazis soon were driven off.

Despite this new fiasco, the Quislings at the university meeting formally proclaimed the establishment of a new "Norwegian Legion." True, there were few soldiers to fill the ranks, but two commanders of the Legion had already been appointed.

Two regiments were formed this time—on paper, of course. One was known as the "Viking Regiment," the other as the "Viken Regiment." The commanders were Major Jörgen Bakke and Major Kjellstrup. Both had been lieutenants until recently; Bakke was one of those officers who had sent his soldiers home on April 9, 1940, instead of leading them into the fight against the invaders.

Since the two regiments now existed, it was obviously mandatory to find soldiers for them. From the Orje Institute for Alcoholics every inmate who could possibly stand erect was impressed into the Legion. Criminals in Norwegian prisons serving terms of less than two and a half years were released on condition that they volunteer. Psychiatric institutions sent their less severe cases to the recruiting authorities.

Some criminals refused. One master safecracker who had spent half his life in European prisons was named repeatedly on the coupons the people sent in to the recruiting office. When the criminal heard of it, he commented, "I haven't yet sunk so low that I'll fight for Quisling."

Quisling promised more and more money, but nothing helped.

When Himmler paid another visit to Oslo, he found 800 men under Quisling's flag. Most of them were criminals, alcoholics, psychotics or Norwegian Nazis who had been forced to join. To ease the situation, the Oslo radio declared that there was no military urgency for a Norwegian Legion; Hitler had enough soldiers. The Legion was intended as a symbol of the international crusade against Bolshevism. The symbol was, after all, damning: the great Führer found his Norwegian Legion composed of the scum of Norway.

The 800 men were sent to Hannover, Germany. Only a third of them had had previous military training.

Before their departure Quisling had these men take the following oath:

"I swear before Almighty God that I will fight in full faith against Bolshevism, that I will be a brave soldier, and that at any time I will gladly give my life for Adolf Hitler, my salvation for Vidkun Quisling."

Regimental Commander Jorgen Bakke then spoke and expressed his gratitude for the honor of fighting at the side of Adolf Hitler. He was followed by a member of the

Norwegian colony in Berlin, which had contributed sixty-two men to the Legion. These sixty-two men had simply been conscripted by the Nazi authorities.

The Norwegian Legionnaires were sent first to Finland, to fight on the Murmansk front. Quisling impressed on his faithful 800 men that they must conquer the Kola Peninsula, for this peninsula had been promised to Norway. It had, incidentally, also been promised to Marshal Mannerheim. And, incidentally, the Russians have never shown any inclination to give it up.

In December 1941 the people of Norway heard news of their legion for the first time. The *Oslo Illustrated* published a letter from a young Quisling Party member, Per Kjoelner, who had fought first on the Murmansk front and later been sent to the Ukraine. He wrote:

"The enemy fights to the last drop of blood—and then goes on fighting. He attacks incessantly. The Russians are big, strong young men who are driven on by devils in human form—the political commissars. I do not like it here in Russia; there is something uncanny about everything. There are rumors that the Norwegian Legion will not be sent home this winter. I am prepared to remain here, even though I do not like it."

The morale of Quisling's warriors was consistent with their equivocal pasts.

In September 1942 the Norwegian Embassy in Washington received the report of a deserter from the Norwegian Legion who had escaped to the safety of a neutral country. This deserter said that the seventy-five survivors of the original Nordland Regiment had been assigned to the Legion, so that it numbered about 900 men. By July 1942 only 340 were left. The remaining men are desperate, for the Nazis employ these foreign legions for the most dangerous missions, as suicide squads. The Norwegians were granted no furloughs, because all furloughed legionnaires deserted.

At first, fallen legionnaires were buried with great ceremony; afterward they were tossed like animals into mass graves. The Norwegian chaplain, a graduate of Quisling's special course, was habitually drunk at the burials. The Norwegians, however, preferred his drunken babbling to his patriotic speeches when sober.

Because of the terrifying casualties among the legionnaires, Quisling found it necessary to raise new recruits. The only course was to force Nazi Party members and workers in the Labor Service to enlist. But all these men, despite their convictions, trembled at the prospect of going to the front, for they had the appalling example of the Legion before them. The losses could not be concealed; obituaries of fallen legionnaires appeared daily in the Norwegian newspapers.

Members of the Quisling "Nasjonal Samling" who refused to enter the Legion were disgraced by being compelled to sign a declaration of cowardice that read:

"Despite my oath to the Führer, and although I understand clearly that the Führer's position in Norway depends upon my cooperation, and although I know that my own safety depends on the judgment of the military authorities, I hereby declare that I am too cowardly to do my duty and join the Legion."

Quisling's heroes preferred to fill out this pleasant little declaration rather than be sent to the Russian front.

In 1942 Heinrich Himmler again visited Oslo, to see for himself the active and passive resistance of the Norwegian people and to confirm in his own mind the utter incompetence and cravenness of Quisling and his followers. On this visit he met the courageous Archbishop of Norway, Eyvind Berggrav. He took occasion to ask the Protestant bishop why the Norwegian people were so opposed to the Germans and how they, the Germans, could find out what the people really thought. The Archbishop replied:

"If you wish to find out what the Norwegians think, give the Norwegian press three days of freedom."

A few days later Archbishop Berggrav was arrested.

According to reports received in February 1943 at the Norwegian Embassy in Washington, D.C., the Norwegian Legion which had been fighting on the Leningrad front, has now been dissolved. The Legion suffered heavy casualties during recent battles, and several times the spirit of the men bordered on mutiny chiefly because the Nazis have not kept their promises of granting furloughs as stipulated in original contracts. The suspension of furloughs is believed to have been due to the large number of desertions among men who have been given leave and have returned to Norway during the past six months. The remaining members of the Legion are being transferred to German divisions where they will be kept under more strict control.

On Independence Day, 1941, when Quisling proclaimed the establishment of the Norwegian Legion, "Fat Fritz" Clausen, the Danish Quisling, issued a similar proclamation in his newspaper, *Faedrelandet*. A Danish Free Corps was to be established; the youth of Denmark were called upon to join up.

The Danish Foreign Legion was somewhat more successful than its Norwegian counterpart—chiefly because German-born Danes from Schleswig-Holstein were conscripted into it. Nevertheless, the Free Corps at no time numbered more than 3,000 men, and fifty per cent of these were Germans.

The first contingent of Danish troops were sent to the Finnish-Russian front during the fall of 1941. They received their baptism of fire at Lake Ilmen. Their leader was a Danish officer on active duty, Lieutenant Colonel P. C. Kryssing. Kryssing was evidently unsatisfactory, for in the spring of 1942 he was recalled to Berlin and removed from his post. He has not been heard from since. His seventeen-year-old son fell at Lake Ilmen.

His successor as commander of the Danish Legion was a nobleman, Count Christian von Schalburg, a lieutenant-captain in the Danish Royal Guard. Count Schalburg went to the Russian front wearing the green uniform of the Royal Guard, although King Christian himself protested against this effrontery. The rest of the legionnaires wore the

uniforms of the German Elite Guard, with the additional insignia: "Freicorps Dänemark."

The fate of the Danish Free Corps was as tragic as that of the Norwegian one. Schalburg, the new leader, fell shortly after his arrival at the front, on June 2, 1942. Fritz Clausen and the Danish Nazis wept publicly for him, declaring him one of Denmark's great heroes and a martyr for freedom; he was built up as the Danish Horst Wessel who had given his blood in the struggle against Bolshevism.

The rites for the fallen Free Corps commander resembled a German state funeral. German Minister Cecil von Renthe Finck (the predecessor of Dr. Best) attended, together with General Kurt Luedtke, the commander of the German forces in Denmark, and the then Foreign Minister, Erik Scavenius, who shortly afterward became the quisling Prime Minister of Denmark. Scavenius, although his government had given him no authorization, declared at the grave:

"In the name of the Danish Government, I lay this wreath on the grave of a brave man."

Duel for the Northland

From then on Scavenius became the unofficial protector of the Danish Legion. Scavenius is a diplomat of the old school, a man who is far more clever and dangerous than Quisling. Because he is a conservative rather than a Nazi, he wields immeasurably greater influence among his countrymen than does the Norwegian traitor. Scavenius undoubtedly has brains. Owner of the large newspaper, *Politiken,* he first became Foreign Minister in 1909, and held this office again from 1913 to 1920. During World War I he showed strong pro-German sympathies.

When the present National Coalition Government was formed after the Nazi occupation, Erik Scavenius once more became Foreign Minister. He celebrated his return to office with a statement promising that Denmark would cooperate with the German New Order. Without the knowledge or consent of his colleagues, he began negotiations for a customs and monetary union with the Reich. Fortunately, his fellow ministers learned of the plan, and Scavenius was forced to drop it.

In 1941 Scavenius was so high-handed as to sign personally the Anti-Comintern Pact in Berlin.

Despite his support of the Free Corps, however, recruits were slow in coming. The Corps seemed to have been born under an unlucky star. The new commander, Major Lettow-Vorbeck, was also killed on the Russian front a few weeks after his appointment. He was succeeded by a military unknown named Martinsen.

By the middle of 1942 only 800 of the original 3,000 Danish legionnaires were left. Early in September these men were furloughed home in a body.

Fritz Clausen and the occupation authorities arranged a splendid reception at the Copenhagen Central Railroad Station. Clausen's Nazis appeared in full uniform, and girls in white dresses threw flowers at the returning heroes. The station was surrounded by the police to make sure that the reception took place "without incident." The wife of the late Count Schalburg came, accompanied by her small son, who wore a diminutive Nazi uniform. The German Minister was present. Indeed, all the bigwigs of officialdom put in an appearance. Only the Copenhagen populace was missing.

Clausen's newspaper the following day deplored that none of the people had welcomed the heroes home; no flowers had been thrown from the windows of the city. Copenhagen had slighted the nation's best sons.

At the reception Clausen had made several enthusiastic speeches of welcome, thanking Heinrich Himmler for "having given our comrades the opportunity and the permission to fight together with the youth of other European countries." He offered special thanks to "Europe's far-sighted and self-sacrificing liberator, Adolf Hitler, who has averted the Communist menace and permitted the members of the Free Corps to fight under the Dannebrog (the Danish Flag)."

Martinsen, the new commander, was crowned with a wreath of oak leaves, and the weary eight hundred marched all day long through the streets of Copenhagen.

In the "Ströget," a very narrow central thoroughfare in Copenhagen, a boy on a bicycle was pressed hard against the curb by some of the legionnaires. When he remonstrated by saying, "We don't act like that in Denmark," he was stabbed through his chest with a bayonet.

A woman attendant of a large department store who made a grimace of disgust at the sight of the Free Corps, was wounded.

The recall of the legion was prompted by grimmer motives than the people of Copenhagen suspected. Clausen's Nazis and the legionnaires were to terrorize the city, for the native Nazis were on the point of a coup d'état. They

Duel for the Northland

hoped to make Clausen Premier and then incorporate Denmark into Germany, as a province of the Greater Reich.

The Danish Government, which still retains some independence, prevented this coup d'état at the last moment. The police were sent out; there were street battles, with one man killed and twelve wounded.

The Folketing, the Danish Parliament, was convoked to an emergency session. The parliament and King Christian sent a joint message to the Nazi Minister informing him that any change in the form of government would be followed by King Christian's abdication. The Germans were aware that the King's abdication would produce uprisings throughout the country. They had no inclination to see the conditions in Norway repeated in Denmark.

Nevertheless, the Nazis could not make a complete retreat, chiefly for reasons of prestige. They therefore attempted to force King Christian to introduce the Nuremberg Jewish laws into Denmark. To this proposal King Christian replied sarcastically: "Since we have never felt inferior to the Jews, we have no Jewish question in my country."

The Danish Legion was hastily ordered back to the front. It was an enormous economic burden upon Germany. Official statistics indicate that the Nazis spent six million kroner in 1942 for the maintenance of the Free Corps-—despite the fact that the Corps never consisted of more than 3,000 men.

This sum was paid by Dr. Werner Best from the funds of the Nazi Legation. Best had a considerable "bribery fund" at his disposal; Free Danish sources estimate it to be around ten million kroner (two and a half million dollars) a year.

The German Legation provided the Nazi organizations and the Nazi press, which alone recruited for the Free

Corps, with large subsidies. Free Danish circles have secured a list of these subsidies, which were paid to the newspapers and organizations listed below:

Nazi newspaper *Faedrelandet*	per month Kr.	50,000
Danish Nazi Party	" "	80,000
Nazi Labor Service	" "	70,000
Nazi Labor Unions	" "	30,000
Nazi newspaper *Kamptegnet*	" "	8,000

After the Danish Legion returned to the front from its furlough, it fought in the battle of Veliki Luki, losing 100 dead and wounded. In the same battle 1,400 Norwegians, Finns and Swedes died or were wounded. The Nordic Legions had been virtually wiped out.

According to the latest estimates, at most 550 of the men are still alive. Denmark does not mourn for them.

EPILOGUE
Portents that Scandinavia Will Resist and Live Again

General Nikolaus von Falkenhorst in the early summer of 1940 was the absolute master of Norway. His troops had wholly conquered the land of vast fjords and precipices.

Two German officers brought before him the commander-in-chief of the Norwegian forces, General Otto Ruge. Ruge's gaunt, wrinkled face was immobile. They had disarmed him; he was a prisoner of war of the German Reich.

Falkenhorst enjoyed his triumph to the full. For sixty-two days this son of the Vikings had resisted the mighty German war machine. Now that resistance had been broken. So he thought.

General von Falkenhorst offered his defeated enemy a chair. The Norwegian preferred to stand. Falkenhorst then said that he had come to save Norway. All Germans, he declared, felt the deepest love for their "nordic brothers" in Scandinavia.

The Norwegian general replied in words that every Norwegian remembers and takes grim pleasure in repeating:

"What you say about Germany's love for Norway may well be, my dear General von Falkenhorst. But rape is after all one form of love—the German form."

Falkenhorst chose to overlook the insult and offered the Norwegian commander another chance for reconciliation. He asked the general and all his troops to take an oath never again to bear arms against Germany. If Ruge and his soldiers would agree to this, they would be released immediately and sent home.

But the Norwegians could not be cajoled. General Otto Ruge had deliberately refused to accompany his government into exile in England. He wished to share the fate of his troops, even in defeat. During the two months of fighting in Norway General Ruge had proved himself a brilliant strategist, organizer and leader. But he showed his real stature in the surrender, or rather, in the brief address he delivered to his troops shortly after the British and French troops evacuated Northern Norway. The day was typical of the Norwegian spring, cool and sunny, when, at Saetermoen military camp, Ruge bade his soldiers farewell. He said:

"I have taken part in this war from the day the first shots were fired until today. I have seen soldiers fall, women killed, school children pursued along the highway by machine guns. I have seen towns bombed, farmsteads wiped out. I have seen all the miseries of war. Nevertheless, these two months have been the richest of my life. In them I have become warmer of soul and warmer of heart, and I have seen others become the same.

"There is no shame in being beaten, vanquished, defeated, if one has done all that lies within one's power. That is much better for a nation than to have given in without a struggle . . .

"I look forward to the day when we shall be free again. I am sure that day is coming. But no nation can rise again merely by waiting vacantly for something to happen, for some help to come from the outside. You must be ready to help yourselves when the time is ripe. It may be a long while, or it may come sooner than anyone now believes. But wait, keep faith and be ready. Whether I am living or dead, I shall be in your midst on that day. Until then, farewell, and thank you for this hour."

The soldiers stood stiffly, tears in their eyes. And the General, scarcely able to master his emotion, went to each in turn and shook hands.

Falkenhorst soon realized that he could expect no help from General Ruge. He suspected, moreover, that Ruge knew where the Norwegians had concealed their arms, and demanded that Ruge inform him of the location of the caches. Ruge coolly countered with a question: would General Falkenhorst, if he were a prisoner, turn traitor and reveal such information?

At this Falkenhorst, ordinarily a rigid, controlled, calculating man, sprang to his feet and shouted to the guards to take this thick-headed Norwegian away. Shortly afterward General Ruge was taken to Germany and imprisoned in the fortress of Königstein near Dresden.

General Ruge comes from a distinguished family. His father was related to the British Chamberlains. He himself was born in Oslo—at that time still Christiania— on January 19, 1882. He was graduated from Oslo University, completed his course at the Norwegian Military College summa cum laude, and later served as Military Instructor at various Norwegian military schools. When the invasion struck, he was faced with the difficult task of transforming within a few hours a pacifist country into a land mobilized for war. His successful two-months' delaying action postponed for a time the invasion of Holland and Belgium.

Three years have passed since Ruge's heroic struggle. The Norwegian general is still a prisoner of war; the concealed weapons have not yet been found by the Nazis; and Germany now stands in dread of an Allied invasion of Scandinavia.

Russia has given Hitler a bitter taste of Napoleon's tragedy, and who may say how close Hitler already is to his Waterloo?

In Denmark Admiral Canaris's Secret Service has set up a new office concerned solely with countermeasures against expected invasion. A new secret police force has been established, and in August 1942 Minister of Justice Thune Jacobsen, at the request of the Germans, appointed Commissioner Eivind F. H. Larsen to direct this work. Clearly, the Nazis are preparing for civil war in Denmark.

Quisling and Jonas Lie set up a similar organization in Norway. The general work of these anti-invasion divisions was defined in a conference held in Copenhagen. Some of the highest Nazi police officials were present at this conference, among them Police General Becker of Hamburg, Lieutenant-Colonel Heischmann, Major Brosicker, Commander Schoeneberg, Major Macek Stenzel, and Count Helldorff.

General Falkenhorst and his staff have demonstrated considerable nervousness ever since the first commando raid on the Lofoten Islands. The Germans are expecting a full-scale invasion. Meanwhile, they are frantically fortifying the coast—and the army of occupation is growing constantly more nervous.

On March 4, 1941 the first combined British-Norwegian commando raid took place. The attack on Svolvaer in the Lofoten Islands took the Nazis completely by surprise.

The object of the raid was to destroy the fish oil factories on the Lofoten Islands, which were manufacturing glycerine for the German munitions plants. Within ten minutes the commandos had taken over the telegraph and telephone stations and the police headquarters, and had launched their attack on the fish oil factories. The factories were destroyed; holes were bored in two gasoline tanks so that all the gasoline ran out; a third tank was set afire; and the German airport was seized. Seventeen Nazi pilots were captured. Altogether, two hundred and fifteen Nazi soldiers were taken prisoner, one Norwegian and nine German merchant ships were sunk, and an armed German coast guard vessel was also sent to the bottom. There were no losses among the Norwegians or the British, but one German officer and six crewmen went down with the coast guard cutter.

The inhabitants of the islands greeted the British and Norwegians with wild rejoicings. The Allied soldiers distributed chocolate, fruit and other foods among them, as well as yarn and cloth. Three hundred young Norwegians returned as volunteers to England. All the Quislings on the island—ten of them—were also taken aboard the warships to stand trial in England before Norwegian courts.

The expedition had left Norway on a Tuesday. It returned to England on Thursday. The Norwegian women wept when they saw the vessels departing from their Islands; they cried after the British and Norwegians to return soon—and to stay.

The Nazis took ferocious revenge. The houses of the families whose sons had gone to England were burned down. Terboven himself came to Svolvaer, arrested hundreds of Norwegians, imposed impossible fines on single villages, such as the fine of 100,000 kroner upon the village of Austvaagoy, and took a number of hostages.

These cruel reprisals did not prevent fresh commando raids, nor were the people deterred from once more lending aid to the friendly invaders. The Nazis were by no means reassured when the Royal Norwegian Government in London stated that the Lofoten raid had only been a trial, and that more and bigger raids would follow.

A month later, on the night of April 11-12, 1941, the Norwegian Navy once more paid a visit to Norway. The destination of the raiders was Oeksfjord, near Hammerfest, in Norway's Far North. The Norwegian crew of a destroyer landed and blew up another fish oil factory; it then returned on board without any losses. The destroyer was one of the fifty over-age craft that the United States had given to Great Britain. Four of these vessels had been turned over to the Norwegian Navy.

On both the Lofoten Islands and in Oeksfjord, the raiders carried off the files of the police and the Gestapo. These secret documents proved of immense value to the Allied Intelligence Services; they supplied a splendid insight into German espionage and German instructions to the occupation authorities.

There were several more commando raids upon Norway. The Lofoten Islands were again visited; early in 1943 the commandos suddenly appeared at the Sola Airport near Stavanger. All the Quislings in Norway are terrified that they may be "taken along" by the next group of raiders. At night Quislings are frightened out of their beds by telephone calls; in sepulchral voices Norwegian patriots inform them, "The British have landed."

The Nazis have a justified anxiety about an invasion, since certain military groups consider it quite possible to apply the Schlieffen Plan in reverse. If the invasion of England could be accomplished by using Norway and Denmark as bases, Germany, they reason, can be assaulted from the same bases. When and whether the Allies will attempt such an invasion is, at the present writing, a military secret. But the intensified training of American ski troops in Iceland, the commando raids that are increasing in scale and frequency, and the many pronouncements of Allied leaders that an invasion of Europe is coming—all these things have combined to throw the Nazis into a fit of terror.

Panic-stricken, they have begun to fortify the entire West Coast of Norway. At Bergen these preparations have become very extensive. At first the Germans merely dug trenches in the street and set up machine-gun emplacements at intersections and in parks. Early in 1943 these preparations began to take on a more permanent character. Streets leading down to piers have been blocked off by huge tank traps built of concrete. At all traffic junctions solid bunkers with massive concrete walls have been erected. Many buildings, including some historic ones, have been used for camouflaging these bunkers.

Similar fortifications have been built in Oslo, Trondheim and Narvik. At first the Norwegians thought these were preparations for civil war, for a rebellion of the Norwegian people. But by now it is clear that the measures are being taken against the possibility of invasion from without. Only German workers are employed on these fortifications, for the Nazis, with good reason, do not trust the Norwegians.

There are many intimations that the United Nations will one day make a surprise landing in Norway. The lifeline to Murmansk through the Arctic Ocean must be maintained, and an invasion of Norway would be the surest means of preserving it. Moreover, a position in Northern Norway would enable Allied troops to unite with their Russian allies for the decisive battle for *Dominium Maris Baltici.*

ABOUT THE AUTHOR

Kurt Singer (1911-2005) was born Kurt Deutsch in Vienna, Austria (taking his mother's maiden name after WW2). He attended the University of Zurich, starting an anti-Nazi underground newspaper in 1933. This soon meant he was forced to flee to Sweden, where he attended the Labor College in Stockholm and started writing books. He co-authored a biography on German anti-Nazi activist Carl von Ossietzky who won the Nobel Peace Prize in 1935. Singer's biography of Goering infuriated Nazi Germany, and the dangerous political situation led to his move to the United States. He had been involved in counterespionage while in Europe, and continued his work for the remainder of the War. His continued writings reflected his interest in the subject, both practically and historically. He married three times (once divorced, once widowed), had two children, and went on to write, publish, and anthologize a wide range of titles.

Also Available
Coachwhip Publications
CoachwhipBooks.com

Also Available
Coachwhip Publications
CoachwhipBooks.com

Also Available
Coachwhip Publications
CoachwhipBooks.com

Also Available
Coachwhip Publications
CoachwhipBooks.com

Also Available
Coachwhip Publications
CoachwhipBooks.com

HOW TO CODE AND DECODE

Secret Writing

An Introduction to Cryptograms, Ciphers and Codes

•

by HENRY LYSING

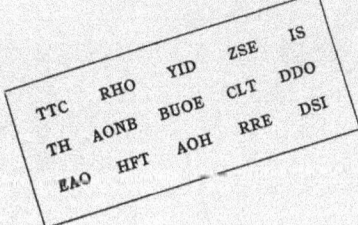

Also Available
Coachwhip Publications
CoachwhipBooks.com

BASTOGNE

The Story of the First Eight Days
In Which the 101st Airborne Division Was
Closed Within the Ring of German Forces

COLONEL S. L. A. MARSHALL

Also Available
Coachwhip Publications
CoachwhipBooks.com

Also Available
Coachwhip Publications
CoachwhipBooks.com

www.ingramcontent.com/pod-product-compliance
Lightning Source LLC
Chambersburg PA
CBHW031559110426

42742CB00036B/253